The Foxfire Book of Appalachian Cookery

The Foxfire Book of
APPALACHIAN
COOKERY

Edited by Linda Garland Page & Eliot Wigginton

The University of North Carolina Press • Chapel Hill & London

First published by the University of North Carolina Press in 1992

Originally published by E. P. Dutton, Inc.
© 1984 by The Foxfire Fund, Inc.
All rights reserved.

The paper in this book meets the guidelines for permanence and durability
of the Committee on Production Guidelines for Book Longevity of the
Council on Library Resources.

Manufactured in the United States of America
99 98 97 96   7 6 5 4

Library of Congress Cataloging-in-Publication Data

The Foxfire book of Appalachian cookery / edited by Linda Garland Page
   and Eliot Wigginton.
      p.   cm.
   Originally published: New York: Dutton, c1984.
   Includes index.
   ISBN 0-8078-4395-4 (pbk. : alk. paper)
   1. Cookery—Appalachian Region, Southern. 2. Appalachian Region,
Southern—Social life and customs. I. Page, Linda Garland.
II. Wigginton, Eliot.
TX715.F826   1992
641.5975—dc20   92-53627
                                                       CIP

Contents

Acknowledgments

This book is the result of a project that was started in 1980 by Margie Bennett (a *Foxfire Magazine* advisor) and three students: Rosanne Chastain, Kim Hamilton, and Dana Holcomb. What started out as a summer project evolved into a much larger task, yet a more challenging one for both the students and the organization.

The material collected by these students was compiled as a special issue of the *Foxfire Magazine* for our magazine subscribers. Realizing the amount of unpublished information about Appalachian cooking still in our files, in addition to the quantity of available unrecorded information in this area, we continued the research for a larger publication—the second Foxfire Press book—about the foods and the people who prepare the food in our part of the country. Each day we were amazed and excited about the vast amount of information we continued to find but, because we already had enough material for two cookbooks, we had to stop the search and start putting together a manuscript. Maybe someday the material left out of this book will appear in another volume.

So many people tend to get involved with this sort of project and there are always those who should receive some special recognition.

As always, Foxfire is indebted to the numerous students who were involved with the interviews and the taking of photographs, but I want to especially acknowledge Chet

Welch, Allan Ramey (who also took the cover photographs), and Tammy Ledford for their enthusiastic and dedicated energy during the final production of this book. Without them this book would never have been finished on time.

To all our friends who welcomed us into their homes with such warmth and enthusiasm to share with us again their knowledge of something we knew so little about; and to those very special folks like Nora Garland, Ruby Frady, Mary Pitts, Retti Webb, and Albert and Ethel Greenwood, among many others, who refused to let us leave without eating a meal with them or at least sampling their foods, I express my gratitude. Without all these people this book would not exist.

Special thanks to Ruth Cabe and Judy McCracken for their advice and dedicated time testing recipes despite one of the hottest summers ever to hit this part of the country. I also recognize all the students, parents, friends, faculty, and staff who assisted in finding and testing recipes. And for Susan Davis, who always answered the plea for help at the eleventh hour, I give thanks.

Appreciation is extended to the Atlanta Historical Society for its encouragement and support in initiating this project.

Some of the interviews and photographs in this book were conducted in collaboration with the Georgia Education Television Network.

Funding for the first year's operation of the Foxfire Press was provided by the Georgia Council for the Arts. This book was under development during that year.

LINDA GARLAND PAGE

Introduction

Though I enjoy eating, I dislike cooking in the same way I dislike washing clothes or dishes; and cook books are not really my thing. Having said that, I must also say that I am the first to affirm and celebrate the existence of those who love the task. If Effie Lord, whom you will meet in this book, were in danger of losing her unique café, I would gladly lay aside all other obligations to help lead the fight for her survival, for she represents the rare antithesis of the impersonal fast-food restaurant experience that has swept the landscape. Effie is a grandmother who cooks for her patrons as though they were guests in her home, with pride and joy in her ability, as well as love for, and a sense of obligation to, her visitors. Her food is not fancy, but the service is at least as fast as McDonald's, since guests simply walk into her café kitchen and help themselves to the meats and fresh vegetables scattered about in pans and pots over her huge stove. At just over two dollars per loaded plate, the price is certainly competitive with the fast-food chain, but with an important difference—the hostess here is a concerned grandmother who will let you settle up later if you're on the short end of a paycheck.

In many ways, Effie is a symbol for this book. Aside from the fact that she is one of my favorite people, with her spattered apron and her determined, no-nonsense air, she stands for the mountain food tradition—unpretentious, solid, and fulfilling. You'll find no slivered sautéed mushrooms in these pages, or stir-fried bean sprouts or soft-shell crabs or delicate pastries or casseroles with enough exotic ingredients to fill a shopping bag. You'll just find normal food rooted in, and infused by, an age when what was consumed was what one raised; when the only techniques of preservation were drying, pickling, and salting; when nothing was wasted ("We kill a pig and we eat everything but the squeal"); and when, in the absence of grocery stores and a cash economy, one's own winter store of food was so important that usually the only buildings locked on a typical farm were those that held the "rations."

That's not to say that affairs of the stomach were stark or desperate. Plenty of food was raised and plenty was served. The noonday "dinner" for a houseful of working folks was a woman's glory, albeit a chore—several different meats, five or six vegetables, gravy, biscuits, pickles, preserves, pies or custards, coffee, and milk—and there was variety enough, as you will soon see, except in the toughest of times, to satisfy almost everyone.

But neither is it appropriate to get unnecessarily romantic about such meals. A sense of balance is in order. Killing and scalding and plucking one's own chickens and cooking them for hours over a fireplace or wood stove is not the stuff of which many dreams are

Addie Norton's infectious smile endears her to all her friends—and everyone that she meets is a friend.

Aunt Addie and her wood stove. She told us, "I fire it three times a day—oh, sometimes just twice. I sometimes get lazy and don't fire it up at dinner time."

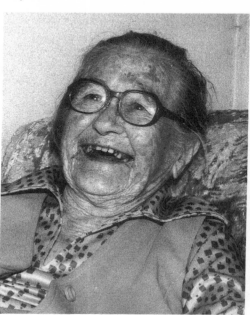

made, and the recent "set yourself free" commercials for Stouffer's products certainly strike a responsive chord in me. In other words, I can get wistful for home-cooked meals —as long as I don't have to be the cook. As ninety-two-year-old Aunt Addie Norton, one of many women interviewed for this book, said, "I have moods, honey. Sometimes I'd rather somebody take a hickory and whip me from the top of my head to the bottom of my feet as to say for me to get a meal."

There is, though, something about the foodways of the mountains—another dimension that resonates in these recipes—that is undeniably compelling, even graceful. Perhaps it has to do with the power of the experience, for older mountain women, of first having learned to cook and then of the act as a rite of passage in their lives, through which one of their more important roles, right or wrong, was legitimized and certified. Aunt Addie again:

> Just about the first thing I learned to cook, you know, is regular everyday food. You know what I mean. I made lots of [mistakes]. I lived with my daddy, and he'd be gone of a day. I wanted to know how to cook, but I didn't know nothing. I did know how to put

Aunt Addie, standing beside her mud-chinked chimney, holds vegetables from the garden she still tends.

on a cake of corn bread and I'd cooked some Irish potatoes and beans for one of my aunts, but that was about all I knowed. I didn't know much about cooking and I had to learn the hard way. So I'd look me up a recipe in the paper or something and I'd try it out. Just something like a cake, you know, and I wouldn't get enough of something in it and it would fall. If it didn't do just right I'd put it in the slop bucket and feed it to the hogs. If my daddy would've found that out, he would have whupped the hound out of me! Yeah, when it didn't look to suit my notion or taste good, I'd just put it in the slop bucket and Daddy never knew it. I guess he thought the sugar got out awful quick! I really wanted to learn. I made a lot of mistakes before I learned how to cook. I sure did; I made a many a one. I put in hours of piddling. Anyone else would have to do just like I done, come up by myself and nobody to tell me how to do nothing. But I tell you one thing, if you learn it by yourself, if you have to get down and dig for it, it never gets out of you. It stays there as long as you live because you had to dig it out of the mud before you knowed what it was. All I knowed about cooking I done myself. Mostly I'm a self-made cook.

But I had all that to learn. If you're interested, you can learn. If you don't care nothing about it, you can't learn. I loved to cook pretty good then. I thought I was doing something. You know, I thought I was doing something that was pretty up and up: I was *cooking,* a little young'un a-cooking. And I thought I was doing something wonderful. Come to find out it was just another old drudgery [laughter]!

But I enjoyed cooking for my children, them and for Lester. It was a joy for me to cook for them, to cook up something they all liked, you know, and watch them enjoy it. You know, I enjoyed that kind of cooking for children, and sometimes I have friends I enjoy cooking for, used to, but I don't have anybody who comes much and stays for meals now. They think I'm not able to get it, but I could if they would just let me [laughter].

Perhaps that compelling quality has something to do with the fact that food, for those who made the dishes described in these pages, became somehow a metaphor for the generosity and interdependence of life here that transcended the food itself. How else to interpret the argument I heard between two Rabun County people when one, who felt he had been wronged, said to the other, "I thought I could trust you. You were my friend. You ate at my table!" Or the time I myself had a serious dispute with a friend here who became drunk enough and angry enough to try to hurt me. After what must have been an hour of arguing outside his home, he made me come inside, and I did so on his oath that, "No one has ever been hurt by me sitting with his feet under my table." I believed him, he was true to his word, and we ended the discussion late that night over biscuits and coffee.

Or perhaps part of what makes the foodways compelling has to do with the fact that though overall they are rather plain and functional, like good warm quilts, there are, as with quilts, those moments of planned design and exuberance that decorate our lives—

times when a meal, like a friendship quilt, is designed to mark an event in some memorable way. These grace notes were made all the more savory years ago because of the tremendous difficulty of obtaining any foods other than staples.

Or perhaps it has something to do with the fact that, for many residents of the area, the preparation of food—Brunswick stew, for example—or the canning of it, was traditionally a means of engaging everyone's energies around a common task, passing time productively, and cementing friendships permanently. At Aunt Arie Carpenter's, cooking became an *event,* as opposed to a utilitarian task. Of the scores of visits my students and I made to the log cabin home where she lived alone, there was not a single instance when she did not ask us, with more than a little apprehension, hope, and anticipation in her voice, "Now will you'uns stay and eat with me?" Our love for each other was cast for all time during those hours when the act of cooking over her wood stove brought us all together around the tasks of drawing water from the well outside, peeling potatoes, slicing cabbage, frying sausage, making bread—and talking and laughing quietly as the food hissed over the fire and wonderful smells filled the room. The food was fine, but the activities and the conversation that preceded and followed its consumption were the main events.

In any event, here is a book the contents for which we have been collecting intermittently for eighteen years. The recipes within each section are arranged in roughly chronological order from times of cooking on a fireplace with the most basic of ingredients; through the growing availability of ingredients like sugar, vanilla, and coconut in general stores and the presence of wood cook stoves; to present times, with more modern kitchen appliances. A generous sampling of human conversation accompanies the recipes in our attempt to wed a human dimension to the foods we so often encounter here in our Southern mountains. Though most of the recipes cannot be said to have actually originated here—many having been brought intact or combined with foodways known to the immigrants who peopled our area in the 1800s from Scotland, Ireland, England, Africa, and Germany—all will be familiar to local residents, and all are gladly shared by them with you in the same spirit of mountain generosity with which they would welcome you at their tables.

—ELIOT WIGGINTON

Prologue

The most appropriate way to set these recipes, instructions, and stories in their proper context is to begin with part of an interview we conducted with Ada Kelly, who died at the age of ninety-five, two weeks before the manuscript for this book was delivered to the publisher.

ADA KELLY

A former school teacher, Ada lived on a large farm in Rabun County. By the time *Foxfire* was started in 1966, she was a grandmother many times over, and students visited her frequently to get her to teach them how to make items like bonnets made of cornshucks (*Foxfire 3*, pp. 461–64) that she remembered from her largely self-sufficient childhood. Well into her later years, she pursued the creative outlets that gave her so much pleasure —drawnwork, knitting, crocheting, making rugs and quilts, and creating beautiful compositions of wildflowers and leaves pressed between velvet and glass in wooden frames. She remembered her youth with much clarity, and she had such perspective on life in the mountains in general, that she was consulted more than once by the scriptwriters for the

Broadway play *Foxfire* to ensure its accuracy and authenticity. She was one of our favorite people.

The year before I was born, my father built a four-room log cabin with two rooms downstairs and two up. We moved into the building just before I was born, and I lived there until I was eighteen. We had a very comfortable house and a large fireplace with a hearth that came way out [into the room]. There was eight children in our family, and we all pitched in and helped with the work on the farm and was really a close-knit family. We had good parents. They were strict with us and expected us to do what was right, and that has always stuck with us. We kept a lot of cattle and some horses and some hogs and raised practically everything we used. We had sheep, and my mother and father would shear the wool. We washed, carded, and spun the wool, and my mother wove it into material. She made practically all our clothing by hand. It was customary for the children to work with the parents in most everything they did, and it was a matter of survival for everybody to do their part.

In the summertime we'd get up about daylight, and my father was usually in the fields with his crop just after daylight. We all had our job to do, and we all went on and did it and didn't ever think about not doing it. It was just a part of life. I wonder sometimes when I hear children say these days, "I don't want to." We never did say that. Just whatever there was to do, we all pitched in.

It was our job as children to shell corn and feed and look after the sheep and help do the milking as we got large enough. I remember shelling corn at night by hand to take to the mill the next day. We'd sit by the fire and shell a bushel of corn by hand. They didn't have much wheat bread then—most of it was corn bread. And we raised rye, so we had a lot of rye bread then.

I look back on my childhood, and I think I was as happy as any child that ever grew up. My father and mother were very hard workers. My father was a general farmer, and he always had a lot of animals and grew our pork, beef, and vegetables. He hauled produce in a wagon—apples and chestnuts. He'd go from here in a wagon down as far as Washington, Georgia, and Royston and all down in there to sell it. He'd probably be gone two weeks, and he'd always bring us something special, things I looked forward to. We'd always be glad for him to come home.

He also did a good bit of carpentry work, and he tanned leather. He'd bring it in, and that's one thing he did at night. He'd just work with that leather, rub it and scrape it and get it pliable so he could make it into shoes, harness, and all those kinds of things.

Mother did the cooking and helped with the milking and gardening and looking after the family in general. She visited the sick a lot and did a lot of knitting. She made all our clothes by hand till I was about ten years old. She cooked on the fireplace, too. They had a wire hung down in the chimney, and it had a hook on it. They'd hang their pot on that hook, and food would cook a long time there. They also had a big iron pot that they put vegetables in, and they'd stack one pan on top of another in that pot. You could cook vegetables and meat and anything that you had to boil in there. Or they had two or three great big iron [Dutch] ovens with lids, and they'd bake a chicken pie in one, potatoes in one, and bread in the other one. With a big family it took lots to eat.

And that's the best food you've ever eat—cakes, egg custards, chicken pies, and boiled vegetables. When they'd have quiltings, they'd cook all kinds of things for a day or two on the fireplace. The women'd gather and bring their little children. The children would play outside, and everybody'd have the best time in the world. We always had a good dinner on Sundays, too. We had lots of wild strawberries, and we'd have strawberry pies, and we'd have cabbage and turnips and pork and homemade sausage and rye bread.

I wouldn't want to go back to cooking on the fireplace, though. Sometimes I bake potatoes on my fireplace in the wintertime out of curiosity, I guess, mostly. But they are good. Well, some things are *better* cooked on the fireplace—corn bread and big old fat biscuits cooked on the fireplace was just out of this world! I don't think any stove has cooked them as good; I really don't. I remember very well when we got our first cookstove. I was about eleven years old, and my father had built a new dining room and kitchen onto the house. I remember how proud I was we had a stove. It had a great big oven. We'd cook pones of corn bread in there and bake sweet potatoes and Irish potatoes. And we'd fry meat in a frying pan.

My father wasn't a hunter, but everybody had hogs and cows and grew their own pork and beef. We'd kill and dress a beef occasionally and quarter it up and sell three quarters to some of the neighbors—a quarter apiece. One [family] would sell to the others, and another time another one would kill a beef and do the same thing. And he'd hang the hind quarter we kept up in the smokehouse where the air circulated and dried it. So we ate well. I don't guess you've ever eat any of that kind of meat, but that was the best beef you've ever eat. It was just as *tender.* We've done that since I've lived here, but that was a good many years ago. And he'd salt-cure the pork, pack it down in a wooden box that he'd made, and, after it got cool, he'd put a layer of salt and spread it all out till it'd cure. Then when we'd need meat we'd go and cut off what we needed. We never was out of ham and fatback and bacon, and most of the people, unless they was just extremely poor, would've had their own meat. You just spread it out and salted it down about the next day after you killed it. They let it cool, and then they just covered it with salt. That was the best meat you've ever eat—some of the best hams and ham gravy.

We used to have plenty of vegetables and fruits all winter, and they were delicious. We got lots of wild berries—huckleberries, blueberries, blackberries—and we always did a lot of canning. We filled all our jars and sealed them with beeswax and cloth rags. Take a clean rag cloth, dip it in hot beeswax and put three or four layers of that over a stone jar. And believe it or not, it kept just as good as anything keeps now. We dried blackberries and huckleberries, too.

Now, on roasting ears being dried—they just cut the kernels off and spread them out on cloth until they dried, and then they stored them in a jar or container of some kind. Then you could cook them when you got ready. And pumpkins, they cut them in round strips and hung them on strings up in their kitchen. They'd dry. You'd just cook them like you would a fresh pumpkin.

They also did what they called bleaching apples. They'd cut up a tub full of apples and put a little sulfur in a saucer and strike a match to it and set it in there and cover the tub and it'd burn. Nearly everybody made a tub of that, and we had those bleached apples for the winter.

Everybody grew cabbage in that country [Scaly, North Carolina], too. If you ever go up there now, the whole country's in cabbage. They've always grown some, and they'd cut the cabbage up by the tubs full and make big barrels of kraut. They'd just put layers of chopped cabbage and layers of salt, weight them down with a smooth plank with a cloth under it and over it, and just let it set there till it got sour. It'd keep all winter long. You'd just go to that tub and dip out the kraut and fry it a little. That was it except to eat it.

And they stored a lot of food whole. They'd bury cabbage and potatoes and turnips and apples in the ground. They'd dig a rather deep hole and put their hay or straw in the bottom of the pit so the food wouldn't come in contact with the dirt and fill that hole full of whatever vegetable or fruit they wanted to save there. Then they'd put some more straw on top of it and cover it with a deep layer of soil, and when they wanted some of it to use they'd dig a hole into that, get them out some, and cover it back up. And that food'd keep just as perfect there, or more so, than it would in any cellar you'd ever see.

So we didn't suffer for something to eat. Very few people did unless they was somebody that was sick, and then the neighbors would take care of them. So it was a good life after all.

The Foxfire Book of
Appalachian Cookery

1

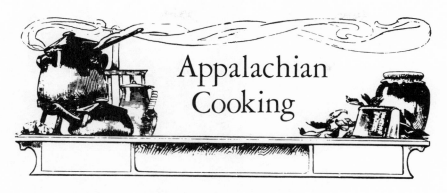

Appalachian Cooking

"As far as the <u>good</u> part of it,
I don't know if cooking today is any better."

Today most people have fireplaces in their homes as an amenity rather than a necessity. Once, however, the fireplace was at the very center of home life, used not only for warmth but also for cooking.

FIREPLACE COOKING

Cooking over a fireplace may sound simple, but in fact it requires a great deal more time and effort than using a stove. As Nora Garland told us, "Cooking over a fireplace was hotter than cooking over a wood stove. After all, you were right down over the fire. And there was a lot of extra bending and stretching, but people didn't think nothing about it then. They was used to it."

For cooking, there must be a hot bed of coals—a process that takes several hours for a new fire to produce. Hickory and other hardwoods were especially popular for sustained heat. Aunt Nora stressed the importance of keeping the wood in a shed. She said, "We didn't want no wet wood, and when it started in to rain, we'd all go running to bring in wood and stack it on the porch."

Many fireplaces had a fixed, horizontal iron bar running from side to side about three feet above the fireplace floor. Others had a bar, or "crane," that was hinged to the side

*Aunt Arie Carpenter tends
potatoes cooked in a Dutch oven.
Necessary fireplace implements—
shovel and poker—stand beyond
the oven.*

wall of the fireplace so it could be swung in and out. On these bars, pots and kettles that had a handle ("bale") would be hung with S-shaped hooks.

People used these pots suspended over the fire for heating soups and stews and large quantities of water and for boiling meat and vegetables. On a horizontal bar there was room for pots of stewed meat, leather breeches, and boiled cabbage hung side by side for a complete meal. If the fire got too hot, or if something only needed to be kept warm, the pot could be slid along the bar to the side, or swung partly out of the fireplace.

The Dutch oven—a heavy, round iron pot with a handle and an iron lid that has a half-inch lip all the way around the edge—was one of the most common cooking utensils. Dutch ovens were usually used for baking bread and biscuits, but they could also be used for baking cakes and potatoes, roasting meats, and heating soups and stews. Some of the older Dutch ovens and skillets had rounded bottoms and three little legs. One variation looks like a large frying pan with four small legs and is often called an "old-timey oven" or an "old bread oven."

While the Dutch oven was sometimes used out of doors, like most cast-iron cookware it was usually used inside by the fireplace, placed on hot coals raked directly onto the hearth. Both lid and oven were preheated before using, the oven being preheated on the coals themselves and the lid directly on the fire. When the oven and lid were hot enough, the bread dough—or whatever was to be baked—was poured into the oven and the lid set on top with pothooks. Coals would then be piled on top of the lid for additional heat, the lip around its edge keeping them from rolling off. You had to be careful that the coals under the oven were not too hot or the food would burn. The lid could be much hotter than the bottom, as it was not directly touching what was being baked.

Aunt Fay checks the progress of her bread by carefully wielding a poker. Note the pothooks at her feet and the pot of bear meat suspended from a crane in the fireplace.

Fay Long stoops to pour corn bread batter in her preheated Dutch oven.

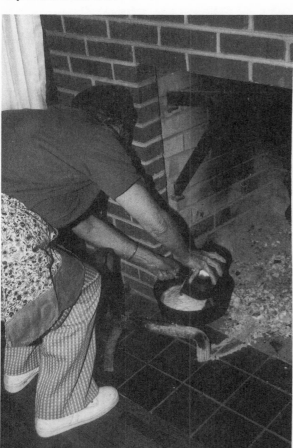

Here's how to bake corn bread in a Dutch oven:

Carefully grease the whole inside of the oven with a piece of pork rind. Then preheat the oven and the lid on the coals. Mix up the batter by combining 2 cups of cornmeal, 1 cup of flour, 1 cup of buttermilk, and a spoonful each of salt and soda. Sprinkle a handful of cornmeal on the sides and bottom inside the oven so the bread won't stick, and then pour the batter in, making sure the oven is level so the bread will be the same thickness all around. Using some tongs, place the lid on the oven and cover it with hot coals. The bread will be ready in 15 to 20 minutes, depending on how hot the coals are. It can be cut right in the oven and taken out with a fork or large spoon.

Marinda Brown found out for herself how deceptively easy this method of cooking corn bread can be: "We used to cook in iron pots. We had iron teakettles and Dutch ovens with the little legs and the lid you put your coals on. A little while back I thought I had

Having turned her pothooks into a handle or "bale," Aunt Fay lifts the finished bread from the ashes. The S-shaped hook from which pots are hung may be seen at right.

A three-legged variation of the Dutch oven

found a recipe to make corn pone like my mother used to make in a Dutch oven, and I went ahead and made up the batter and built a fire. I put on a lot of coals, and I was going to have some good corn pone. I got it too hot, though, and burned it up. I never have tried it any more."

For frying, coals were raked out onto the hearth and the frying pan set directly on them. When boiling a small amount of water or making coffee, people would set the kettle on a few coals right up against the fire. An even quicker method was to place the kettle right on top of the burning wood.

Meat was broiled simply by holding it over a bed of hot coals on the end of a long sturdy fork with a wooden handle. Popcorn was popped ("parched") by putting the shelled kernels in a covered metal box that had small holes punched in it. The box was attached to a long wooden handle and shaken directly over the fire.

Foods such as potatoes, corn, onions, and nuts—still in their protective coverings of skins, shucks, and shells—could be roasted by burying them in hot ashes for insulation and then placing live coals on top of the ashes. Ash cakes were baked by wrapping the dough in cloth, placing them in a cleaned-out corner of the fireplace, and covering them with ashes and coals. They were supposed to have a delicious flavor when baked this way, but it was difficult to control the heat and keep the bread clean. Sometimes small cakes were cooked directly on the fireplace shovel, which was hand held or propped over the firedogs while the cakes cooked.

The more common use for the shovel, however, was in the habitual task of cleaning out the fireplace. As Nora Garland said: "Mother always put the ashes on the beans she was growing in the garden. We'd put out the fire, move the firedogs, shovel out the ashes, and scour the fireplace out, too. We only did that about once a month because that was a *job*. You'd have to get down on your hands and knees with a rag and scrub."

Fruits, vegetables, and meats were often dried by the fire for several days to preserve them. The food would be placed on the hearth away from the direct heat or strung and suspended from the mantel. And Aunt Nora supplied us with another down-to-earth way to take advantage of fireplace heat: "We used to sit chairs around the fireplace and hang clothes over them to dry. We had to. We don't have winters now like we used to. Back then snow would lay on the ground six inches deep for weeks. So we *had* to dry our clothes by the fire."

During the winter, fires were kept going all day. At night, ashes were heaped over the coals to keep them hot until morning. A fire would start up again "just like you poured kerosene oil on it" when fresh wood was added. In the warmer months, the fire would be started up only when it was time to cook, and ashes would be raked over the coals to save them when no fire was needed. Homes were once constructed with dogtrots (covered breezeways) separating kitchen from living quarters mainly because the extra heat generated by fires continually maintained there made the room uncomfortable in warm weather.

Arie Meaders' account of her mother's cooking on a fireplace is one of the most vivid we collected:

My mother had a large [Dutch] oven, and I've got it here if none of them's not carried it off. It's got three legs, but it don't have any handle. She used pot hooks to go in the eyes that was in the oven. She'd set the oven on the fire and get it hot, and then she'd pull some coals out and set the oven on that. She'd put the lid in the fireplace and get it good and hot, and then she'd put coals on it [on top of the oven]. She'd make her bread up this way [making rolling and patting motion with two hands] into three pones that went around in that big oven. She'd put her bread in, put the lid on, and get that oven hot enough to cook that bread.

When she went to make a pie, it was the same way. If she was gonna make a tart pie, she had little tart pie pans that she used to make pies from fresh apples in. She'd make her pies and set them in that big oven. She'd have it ready to cook them pies done by the time she'd get another batch of pies made up. And when that one was done, she'd take it out and put another one in. She cooked a lot that way, but I wouldn't get but just one or two cooked!

She had a big pot to cook soup beans or green beans or turnips in, or boil backbones and spareribs in, or anything you was gonna have like that. I've seen pots that hang over the fire. They're cranes—our uncle had one—but we didn't have anything like that. Everything went out on the hearth. The beans would sit right in front of the fire and just

*Arie Meaders proudly holds one of
her son's famous face jugs
{see Lanier Meaders, Foxfire 8}.*

cook on one side. She'd put coals around it to keep it cooking all around, and she'd turn it around every once in a while and let the other side cook.

Then we had a great big old fry pan with a big long handle, and that's what she fried her meat in. She'd pull coals out on the hearth and set that pan right on them, and the meat would just cook. It was good. She'd pull the coals out and put her coffee pot on there, too. She'd always have a kettle that she "het" her water in—or she "heated" her water in. People laugh at me for say "het" [laughing]! She'd have her water hot, and she'd pour it in there on her ground coffee. It wasn't but a few minutes till the coffee would boil, being as the water was already hot and the coals was under it.

Right before dinner you'd have three or four different things going at the same time in the coals. You had to stay right there with it [laughs]! My mother liked fireplace cooking better than her wood stove. She was raised to it, and she'd manage it pretty good! Of course, when she went to make her cobbler pies, she'd use her stove because she couldn't get her cobbler pan in the oven and she *could* get it in the stove.

Law, I remember them blackberry pies she used to make! When she'd make one they'd be so many flies they'd nearly eat you up! It took two to mind the flies off the pie so the rest could eat. We had no screens nor nothing like that, but, oh, we *had* flies then —my, my. It was terrible. We'd use a brush from the shade tree a lot of times to keep them from the table. And we had a cane about that long [indicating three feet] we got off the creek bank, and we'd roll so many layers of paper on part of it and then split the paper with scissors. That made a pretty good fly brush. Somebody had to stand over the table while everybody else was eating. It had to be done, or they'd eat a fly! Us biggest children was always the ones that done it. Sometimes we'd sit at the table with our hand propped on the table scaring flies. I don't see how in the world people lived. It wasn't no wonder they had lots of typhoid fever back then.

Exie Dills is another contact who, as she says, "cooked on a fireplace right smart": "I'd always do baked bread or potatoes in an oven in front of the fire. You've got to have a whole lot of live coals, and you put you out some on the hearth and put your oven down on them. If you wanted to you could lay strips of meat on top of your potatoes to bake them, and if you didn't you could just rub grease on the potatoes. Bake them with the jacket on, put your lid on, and cover that lid with coals. It wouldn't take sweet or Irish potatoes either one but about forty-five minutes to bake. And I have baked bread in that oven time and again, even sweet bread. We called it gingerbread back then. We'd make it with syrup. You sift three, four, or five cups of flour and put in your salt and your soda. Then take a cup and a half to two cups of homemade cane syrup and one egg and pour in there. Lay the ginger to it *heavy* [laughing]. Work your dough pretty stiff—don't leave it soft—and pat it in that greased oven. Make two cakes, leave the open space in the middle, and just put one cake on each side of your oven. That would make it cook in the middle better, you see. It would run together a little but not like if it was put in whole. Just cover your lid with coals and bake it."

We found that many women had a soft spot for the old ways of fireplace cooking, and on occasion, a few still practice it:

LOLA CANNON: "In winter it was very nice to put a skillet on the hearth in front of a good fire and rake the coals from the fire under the skillet and bake corn bread and potatoes. The oldsters still think that the food had a better flavor then than it does now, but that may just be our idea."

As she supervises five different pots of food, Ruth Cabe demonstrates Arie Meaders' assertion that "you had to stay right there with" meals cooked on a fireplace. Behind her, a crane is moved back out of the way.

LETTIE CHASTAIN: "My grandma used to make the best corn bread I ever had in her Dutch oven. She'd bake cakes and everything. And she'd hang a little black pot over the fire and cook peas. You know dried peas will stay through the winter, and we had to have the fire in the fireplace anyways, so that's how she cooked them."

ICIE RICKMAN: "We have a fireplace in yonder and a fireplace upstairs. My husband's mother cooked in yonder on that big one. She had a skillet with legs and a lid on it. She cooked bread and the best cakes in it. It sure is good that way. His mama and daddy had a wood stove, but they just loved to cook on those old fireplaces. You ought to eat some of their good beans they cooked. The old folks did things the hard way, didn't they?"

BESSIE BOLT: "I still cook here on the fireplace with a black pot. It's about the best cooking there is, I think. I prefer it. I could own all these modern kind, but I don't care for them. I use my old wood fireplace and wood heater—just myself here and the Lord."

WOOD STOVE COOKING

For most of the people that we interviewed, cooking on a fireplace was a memory from childhood, soon superseded by a series of wood stoves. As Addie Norton reminisced:

I can remember the first stove that we ever had. Daddy took off some stuff to market. You know, we used to take things off of the farm and journey into Georgia and swap it for things we needed at home. I think now, honey, I believe that he paid for it with potatoes or turnips or corn or something or other he had raised on the farm.

Now, that's been many years, but I can remember it just like it was yesterday. He found a little number seven stove. It's a little bitty thing. And we put that thing up and some of them said, "You'll set the house afire when you put a fire in that thing." I said, "It won't do no such thing." Daddy said it wouldn't either, but everybody that came in was afraid of that stove [laughter]. We put a fire in it and we cooked on it for a long time. I thought it was the most wonderful thing to have a stove to cook on and not have to cook on a fireplace. Finally we got a number eight, I think. It was bigger than a number seven. But I remember that little number seven stove, honey. I can just see it sitting over there in the corner. It set on legs, up, oh, about that far from the floor to keep it from catching afire down below. But I can just see that sitting over there on one side of that

The classic Home Comfort wood stove, owned by Mr. and Mrs.
Andy Webb {See Foxfire Book, *pp. 349–352}*

chimney. I just imagine now the first meal cooked on it was for breakfast, and I just guess it was bacon and eggs and maybe corn bread. I don't know, maybe biscuits. Whatever we had, that's what we had for breakfast. And syrup, butter, milk and things like that. 'Course we always had plenty of that.

Back when I bought my wood cookstove, my son said, "Mother, why didn't you put on a few more dollars and get an electric stove?" At that time the electric stove wouldn't have cost much more than that one did—around toward a hundred dollars then. I told him, I said, "For the simple reason, son, I don't want one." I never had cooked with electricity or anything. I had always used wood or coal, and I'm not afraid of it, honey, and I *am* afraid of gas and electricity at my age. You know, you've not got the mind to remember things that you had when you was young. And I was afraid at that time to have one—afraid I'd forget something and leave it turned on. If there had been electric stoves when I was back young, I would have wanted one. But you see, if I put a fire in that wood stove and go out of the house, it's not gonna get hotter. It's gonna get *cooler.* That wood's gonna burn up and it's not gonna hurt nothing. If I go out and leave the electric stove on, I'm liable to catch the house on fire or something like that. I'm afraid to risk my own judgment about things like that. And I really and truly love the heat from a wood stove or a coal stove better that all your electric or anything else you can get. Yes, ma'am. I love my own heat and I absolutely freeze to death when I go to the boys'. Some of them's got electricity and some of them's got this and some of them's got the other, but I still love my old stove right there. I get awfully black and nasty with it, but I still love the heat. I reckon it's because I was raised on it and I don't know anything [else]. I don't like an electric stove. I'd burn up everything I tried to cook, or I'd do something to it that wasn't right.

Often a first cookstove was, for newlyweds, one of the bare essentials for setting up housekeeping. Billy and Annie Long recalled with some regret the fate of their first stove. Billy said, "The first stove we had was one of those big blue ranges with a warming closet over the top and a hot water heater on the side by the firebox. When the house burned up it went to pot, and we never did try to cook on it no more. The roof fell in and broke it.

Yeah, I'd went to [the town of] Clayton. Neal and a fellow was cleaning out the chicken house, for we was fixing to put in some more chickens. They all come in and eat dinner, and after they got through they went on back to work. Neal had been spraying the chicken house, and he'd just went out the back door and started up to the chicken house when he heard something. He looked around, and the house was afire where the flue come out. We had a little old hose pipe and a standpipe right there in the yard. He hooked all that up, but that thing was burning so big by then he couldn't do no good. So they run in here and begun to carry stuff out of the front rooms while the kitchen was burning.

Sometimes cast iron kettles were the only things salvaged from a house fire.

Annie continued: "We picked the kettle up that went with the stove and run out with it. It's all we got out of the kitchen."

In *Foxfire 3* (pp. 470–71), Aunt Nora Garland related the story of her first acquaintance with a wood-burning cookstove:

The first [cook-] stove I ever saw in my life was a Wilson Patent Stove. My mother had been to her Aunt Jane's, right here in town, and found out that she had a stove. Well, she wanted one; so she came back home and wanted Daddy to know about it. He told us to go back to Aunt Jane's [and find out where she ordered it]. It finally came, and they put it up and built a fire in it. We got the wood, thinking that it was the awfullest thing in this world—people still cooking on a fireplace. We hadn't had a stove and this one— with two little eyes at the top—was the first one that came out.

The neighbors came in to see it, and it began to smoke. Well, Mama watered the fire out of it and walked to Aunt Jane's to see what was the matter with it. Aunt Jane said, "Honey, the newness is burning off it. The polish will soon burn off, and it will be all right."

We were so happy with that stove. We baked a batch of bread on it. We had had to bake that in the fireplace, but we didn't have to after we got the stove. And people came in to see what was happening, and from then on nearly everybody tried to get three dollars to get them a stove.

This must have been about 1906. I'm eighty-two now, but I must've been five or six. I remember that stove so well. We even made a poem about it:

So well do I remember
The Wilson Patent Stove
That Father bought and paid for
With cloth the girls had wove.

All the neighbors wondered
When we got the thing to go
They said it would burst and kill us all
Some twenty year ago.

But twenty year ago,
Just twenty year ago
They said it would burst and kill us all
Just twenty year ago.

It never did burst. It was a stove like any other stove, but we hadn't never saw one before.

Split wood and logs were kept near the stove in any handy receptacle.

Jake Waldroup splitting wood

Whatever the risks, wood stoves were considered to be an improvement over fireplaces for cooking, but they obviously still required a lot of attention. Dry kindling and wood had to be cut to fit the firebox and kept on hand. When Annie Long said that she liked to cook on a wood stove, her husband retorted with a laugh, "Getting wood was the biggest thing she didn't like, I think." Blanche Harkins said, "I wouldn't want to have to cook on a wood stove now" because "that wood is messy."

Stove wood should be stacked in a woodshed or on the back porch where it will be protected from the weather. The drier the wood is, the faster a fire will become hot enough to cook on. Wet or green wood must dry first in the fire before it can burn and tends to smoke more than dry wood. Green wood also causes creosote buildup inside cookstoves.

We asked for some general instructions on where to install a wood-burning cookstove. If there is not a brick or rock wall for the stove to stand against, we were told that the back of the stove should be at least 36 inches from the wall, allowing room for the stovepipe. The sides should be no closer than 24 inches from a wall as most wood-burning stoves are not insulated.

An early cookstove with a variety of cookware; cloths have been placed under the front legs to level the stove.

Stove pipe inserted into chimney

Stoves are often installed with bricks under the legs to lift them higher off the floor. This would help prevent the floor from being overheated and the iron legs from making impressions or holes in the floor.

The stovepipe should be installed according to the manufacturer's instructions. A general list of recommendations and precautions follows:

○ Stove must be eighteen inches from *any* wall.
○ Flue pipe should be put together with metal screws only.
○ Chimney caps are not recommended.
○ Don't place flammable objects on or near heater when you have a fire.
○ Never use wet or green wood because of creosote buildup.

○ Have your chimney checked every other year and cleaned to prevent chimney fires.
○ Before hooking a stove or heater up to a used chimney, be sure to check for cracks in the flue and for buildup in pipes.
○ Ashes should be emptied when the ashbox is half full to keep grate from warping.
○ Before dumping, make sure ashes contain no live coals. A slight breeze is all it takes to fan them to life and start a fire where they are dumped.

The ritual of building a fire and the time-consuming process of watching it so it didn't go out or get too hot were also part of the daily routine. Anyone who has always been dependent on a fireplace for heat or a wood cookstove for cooking takes for granted the steps involved in building a good fire—one that will maintain a hot bed of coals and provide them with a heated room or a steady temperature in a cookstove. In fact, a fire—like a good friendship—needs to be built carefully and tended with patience and love. You can't rush a fire: split wood must be added cautiously after the kindling has ignited so as not to smother the young flames. Only then can the dry bolts with which the temperature is maintained be added.

In a wood cookstove, the fire was built in the firebox located on the left-hand side of the stove, right under the cooking surface. To save time, people used to take coals right from the fireplace to start a fire. To start a fire "from scratch" in your firebox, however, first shake the ashes from the previous fire down into the ashbox and open the dampers

Hands still floury from rolling out dumplings, Fay Long opens her firebox to add wood.

Corncobs were excellent kindling—especially if presoaked in kerosene.

(see diagram of stove parts). You may want to line the bottom of the firebox with a sheet of newspaper to prevent new coals and small kindling from falling down into the ashbox.

Kindling is used to start the fire. Corncobs, chips from the wood pile, broomstraw, paper, and small pieces of pine wood—"pine knots" and "light" or "fat" wood—are excellent as kindling. While these pieces of pine light quickly, they "outsmoke anything" and may be preferred to start non-food-related fires only. Some people pour a small amount of kerosene into a container and stand some corncobs up in it. These kerosene-soaked corncobs make very good kindling for starting a fast fire. A box of firewood and one of kindling should be kept in the kitchen, readily available near the stove.

CAUTION: Pouring kerosene or any other flammable liquid directly onto hot coals or into a fire is very dangerous and should never be done. As Gladys Nichols said, "I wouldn't advise nobody to do that. You're liable to explode yourself." We were also cautioned by our contacts to maintain the area around the stove or range, keeping it free of combustible materials—flammable liquids, dust, lint, paper. You should never use or store gasoline or cleaning fluids in the area where the range is located. Additional cautions include the fact that frozen wood with ice or snow on it may smother the fire or even crack the casting of the stove, and wood that has been saturated with salt water will cause corrosion of the metal and should not be used at all.

Lay a few pieces of crushed paper on the grate, cover them with kindling, and light the paper with a match. When the fire begins burning well, turn the damper on the stovepipe until it is almost closed. This holds the heat in the stove instead of letting it go up the chimney. However, if the fire begins to die out or smoke excessively, open the damper again for a few minutes, allowing more air into the stove, and the fire will blaze up again.

Add a few more small pieces of wood, and then start adding large pieces of stovewood as a bed of coals is built up. As Addie Norton explained to us: "After you get your fire burning, you get wood that's cut down and split up. It takes about two sticks to a fire and keeps fire so much longer than little ones. You don't have to be putting wood in the stove so often. If it burns up quick, you got to keep it going. The biggest trouble with a wood stove is you have to keep feeding wood to it. If you want it about the same heat, you get it as hot as you want it, and then just put in a stick or two at a time—enough to keep it the same way—and you can keep it that way all day by putting in one or two sticks at a time."

Any kind of dry wood may be used for the fire in a wood cookstove. Oak, hickory, poplar, pine, and sassafras were mentioned most often by people we interviewed here in northeastern Georgia. Oak and hickory are hardwoods, making the hottest fire and burning longer. They were overwhelmingly favored for heaters, but we were cautioned that "oak'll burn up your firebox" in a cookstove. Pine, poplar, sourwood, and sassafras are

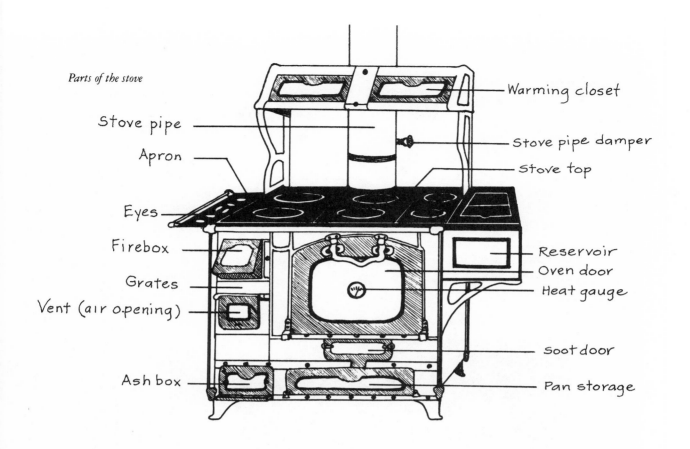

Parts of the stove

Stove pipe
Apron
Eyes
Firebox
Grates
Vent (air opening)
Ash box

Warming closet
Stove pipe damper
Stove top
Reservoir
Oven door
Heat gauge
Soot door
Pan storage

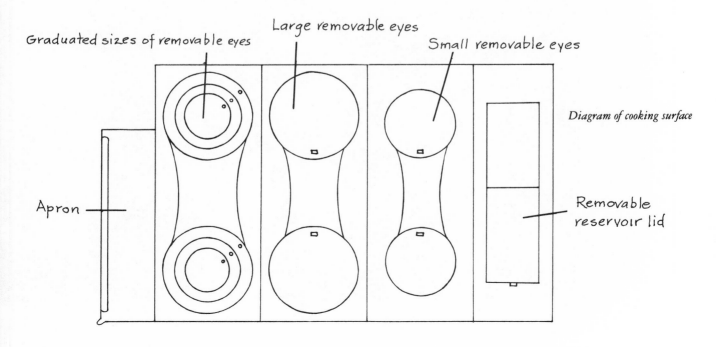

Graduated sizes of removable eyes

Large removable eyes

Small removable eyes

Diagram of cooking surface

Apron

Removable reservoir lid

softwoods and burn more quickly. They are good when starting a fire and may be followed by sticks of hardwood, if desired. Once the fire is established, the temperature in the stove can be maintained by adding one or two sticks of wood at twenty- to thirty-minute intervals. Fireboxes are usually large enough to take firewood sixteen to eighteen inches long and two to three inches in diameter.

The wood may be added to the fire through the firebox door or through one of the eyes over the firebox. The better way, we were told, is through the eye, because when the firebox door is opened there is a risk of hot coals falling out on the floor. Food being cooked on this eye may be moved to the apron on the left while this process takes place.

The floor of the firebox is a metal grate. The ashes from the cookstove's fire fall through to the ashbox, a drawer directly beneath the firebox. Some women told us that each evening, after they finish washing the dishes, they empty the ashbox, putting the ashes on the garden, as they make a good fertilizer. There is a rod that can be attached to the

Most wood cookstoves have a large cooking surface and can accommodate numerous "cookers."

grate and turned to empty the firebox of any ashes that haven't fallen through. The eye lifter is used to move this rod.

The cooking surface of a wood stove usually has six eyes. Sometimes they are all the same size, sometimes of varying sizes. The left side of the stove, directly over the firebox, is the hottest place on the top of the stove. The heat under the eyes cannot be regulated individually, so pots have to be moved from one to the other according to how much heat is required. To get the most heat, the eye over the firebox can be lifted off and a pot or pan can sit directly over the flames of the fire. Daisy Justus said, "You could take the eye off, and the pot would fit down right over the fire. If you wanted to simmer anything, you could push it back over the cooler part of the stove." Cast-iron kettles and pots were the only ones recommended for placing immediately over the flames, probably because of their weight and the fact that they are black. The eyes on the left side of some stoves have graduated sizes so that no matter what diameter a pan is it will fit snugly over the flames.

Grate

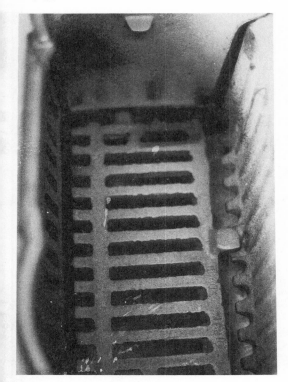

Ash box

Most stoves have basically the same four- or six-eye cooking surface, although one larger range that we saw even had a flat griddle on top for frying things like pancakes, eggs, and bacon.

The oven is usually located on the right-hand side of the stove and is heated from the left and top by the circulation of heat from the firebox. The heat flows from the firebox through a four-inch-high air space directly under the cooking surface to the reservoir on the other side.

Leftovers or food ready to serve may be kept in the warming closet until mealtime. This is a metal compartment about six inches deep located above the cooking surface at about eye level, with either enamel or iron doors to protect the food. There is enough heat in the warming closet to keep food warm for several hours.

Firebox (top) and ash box (bottom) doors stand open. Rod attached to grate is in the center under the firebox.

The eye lifter is shown turning the rod attached to the grates. Here firebox and ash box doors are closed.

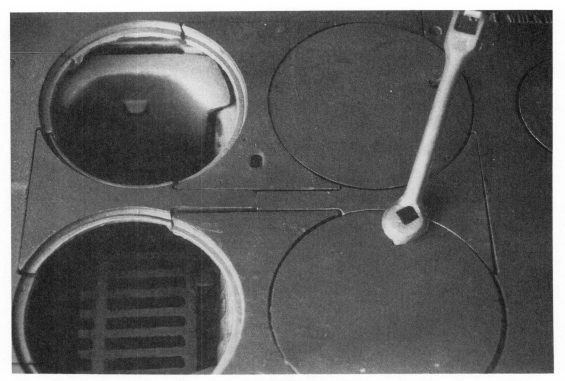

All the eyes on the stove can be taken off with the "lifter," a tool that comes with a wood-burning cookstove. Two types of lifters are shown in action.

The reservoir is a copper, steel, or iron box. If iron, the reservoir has an enameled lining that is easily cleaned. The first reservoirs sat on top of the right-hand eyes and could be moved when the eyes were needed for cooking. The more modern reservoir is usually located on and attached to the right end of the stove. On many newer wood cookstoves it holds about six to eight gallons of water, the water taken out with a dipper or pot. Reservoirs will rust out eventually if the enamel gets chipped or cracked, but they are made to be easily replaced.

Most women we interviewed said that they kept the reservoir filled with water warming for dishwashing and baths. As bread crumbs or other food might fall into the water in the reservoir, a kettle of fresh water was always kept on the stove for coffee or tea or for adding to food that was cooking.

Daisy Justus told us: "We used the water in the reservoir to wash dishes. We washed anything we had—black kettles, too. If you wanted something to get to boiling real quick, like cooked beans, you added hot water from the reservoir."

The air vents, or dampers, are very important parts of the wood-burning stove because they control the fire and the amount of heat in the stove. On most of the cookstoves we were shown there were three dampers: one beside the firebox (the vents slide to permit

A warming closet ready to be filled with food

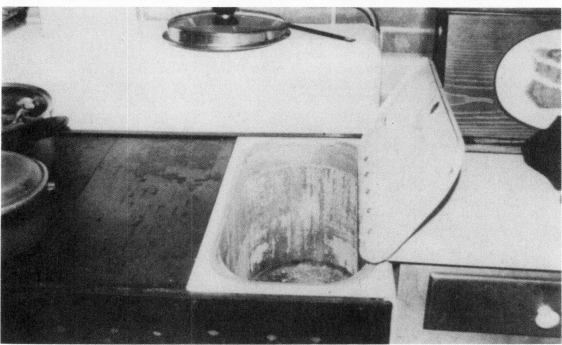

An enamel-lined reservoir, two views

The firebox damper with vents open

air and can be closed completely or partially); a second on the stovepipe above the stove (a handle twists to open or close it); and a third inside the stove, usually located directly beneath the eyes on the extreme right side (for this one, there is a small handle that extends beyond the edge of the stove on the right side, and the cook can turn this "up," to open the damper and let air draw the heat up the stove pipe, or "down," to close the damper and hold the heat inside the stove and around the oven).

Once the fire is burning steadily, and you want to keep a maximum temperature in the stove for cooking on top and for using the oven, the dampers should all be completely open. To lower the temperature, close the air vent to the left of the firebox. More heat may be directed to the oven and the front of the stove by turning the damper on the stovepipe down.

Some people "hold" a fire in their stoves from one meal to the next by adding a large piece of wood at the end of their cooking and then closing the damper on the stovepipe. This way, very little air gets to the fire, and the wood burns slowly. When ready to begin preparing the food for the next meal, the damper is opened, more wood is added to the

Soot rake lying across cooking surface

firebox, and the fire will usually begin to flame up as soon as the air reaches it. When the stove is not in use the dampers are kept closed because air will sometimes circulate down through the chimney and blow ashes and soot into the house.

Maintenance of a wood cookstove includes disposing of ashes and soot routinely. Every two to three days, the soot should be raked off the oven top and from the rest of the inside of the stove using a soot rake. The ashes can be pushed through into the firebox or raked to the soot door, which is usually located under the oven or on the bottom right side of the stove beside the oven and under the reservoir. From here the soot can be raked into a pan or onto paper and thrown out. If soot is not cleaned out frequently but allowed to build up inside the stove, the fire will not heat the stovetop as well. Bread will not cook inside the oven as quickly if soot builds up on the oven's top. Soot can also accumulate inside the stove pipe. To clean it, tap along the pipe. Since, as one contact told us, "Gravity worked back then, too," the soot will fall through and under the oven where it may be taken out the soot door.

Addie Norton described the cleaning process she goes through: "I used to clean the

Mary Cabe tests the heat in her oven.

ashes out of my stove about every three or four days when the ashbox would get full. But now, since I don't cook as much, about once a week and sometimes not that often. The ashbox holds about a half bushel of ashes. I got a little old rake that I clean it out with. Stick that little rake down in there and rake it all out of there. Then it heats better in the bottom, but I don't want it to heat too much in the bottom of it, so I don't clean it out underneath as much as I could.''

While many people may dispose of their ashes in their gardens and flower beds, there are those who find other uses for them, as Addie does: "Oh, I throw mine, usually, out there in the road. It gets bad, and I take them coals out there and put them in the trenches in the road and it keeps my road filled up [laughter]. That's where I put mine this winter, most of them.''

A large fire is not needed for cooking as told by many of our sources.

It is possible to begin cooking some foods on top of the stove within 5 or 10 minutes after a fire has been started. However, it usually takes 30 minutes or more before the oven is hot enough to begin baking, especially in a larger stove. Aunt Lola Cannon told us that her mother would put a piece of white paper in the oven, and she could tell by the way the paper browned if the stove was ready to bake cakes and bread. It should turn a golden brown in 5 minutes. An indicator for some was to have a pot of coffee on top of the stove, and when the fire was hot enough to boil the coffee, the oven was hot enough to begin baking.

Learning to adjust the temperature in the oven of a wood stove takes some trial and error. There are thermometer gauges on the oven doors of most later models, but these act as warning signals rather than as regulators. Besides, old-time stoves rarely had them, and many of the people we interviewed first learned to cook without the convenience of a thermometer. Gladys Nichols' statement, "If you cook regular like I did for all my years, you can just guess at it and tell when it's what it ought to be," was repeated by several of the older women we interviewed.

A fairly constant temperature can be maintained in the oven by adding one or two sticks of dry wood as you notice the thermometer dropping a little below the desired heat. To cool down the oven while baking, the oven door may be opened a few minutes or the damper (on the stovepipe) adjusted by closing it down, to bring in less air, making the fire burn more slowly.

The temperature gauge on the oven door should read between 300 and 350 degrees Fahrenheit for baking cakes, and they are usually placed on the middle rack of the oven. The wood cookstoves owned by most of the women we interviewed had only one rack in their ovens, although some did mention adjustable racks with two or three positions. Some of them told us that they place a pan of water on the top rack and their cake on a rack below the water. Heat in the oven is concentrated at the top, where it enters from the firebox, there being no means of fan-forcing or otherwise circulating the heat around the oven. Thus when the pan is placed *between* the cake and the hottest area of the oven,

Temperature gauges at work and rest

Most ovens only had one rack.

the water absorbs much of the heat and prevents the top of the cake from getting too brown before it is completely cooked inside.

We were warned to keep a closer watch on anything we were baking in the oven of a wood stove than we ordinarily do when using a modern gas or electric oven because of the fluctuations in temperature if wood is not added as needed. The fire might burn out and the temperature drop while a cake is baking. For something that takes an hour to bake, the fire may need to be tended three or four times to maintain the temperature. However, when baking bread or a cake for that long, vibrations from tending the fire —such as slamming the door—can jar the food and cause it to fall. In addition, if something tends to cook more on one side than the other, it has to be turned around at regular intervals.

Addie Norton explained what had to be done if you didn't have a thermometer: "You would just have to judge it by the way you was baking. You don't want to bake a cake too fast. You don't want to brown it on top before it begins to get done in the bottom. They's a lot of ways you can tell about your cookstove if you've had on as much as I have and cooked on one all your life, you know. You know exactly how to handle it. I can keep that one cool just the way I want it or I can get it too hot. You can tell very easy when your oven's too hot. The heat outside tells you. You just have to wait till it cools down. You just have to take your biscuits or whatever you got in there out and let it cool down. You can't take the wood out.''

Aunt Arie skillfully manages an array of pots and pans as she cooks dinner.

For some of the women that we interviewed, this constant vigilance and the time required before the stove was ready for baking—both of which slowed down the cooking process—were the major drawbacks to wood-stove cooking. That, and the constant battle with wood. As Margie Hedford said, "I didn't like cooking on a wood stove. It was too much hard work. You've got to keep poking those coals and putting wood in it to keep it hot, especially if you're going to can. That's hard, because you've got to keep the pressure up and you've got to keep the same temperature. I don't have to do that any more. Just like milking a cow—I don't have to do that any more, either. People say that that was back in the good old days, but they weren't that good. Of course, used to you had time, but you *had* to have time to cook and carry your wood in and keep your stove going. But now you don't have time. Besides, it was a lot harder work, and that's not my cup of tea! Electric stoves are easier, especially when you get to feeling like you don't want to wrestle a load of wood every little while."

In general, however, our contacts' preference for a wood stove was very widespread. Exie Dills liked a wood stove better for safety:

I always cooked on a wood stove up till we moved down here. About ten year ago I cooked my first meal on an electric stove. I never will get used to that thing. I have to watch whenever I start to turn a knob because sometimes instead of turning it off I turn it up. I get it hotter all the time in place of cooler. A wood stove won't cook maybe as quick, but on my old stove out yonder I'd cook bread or biscuits above electric on it any day.

I've burned my fingers a few times [on wood stoves], but nothing bad—not like the other day on an electric. I burned my hand the other morning on steam the worst I was ever burned in my life over a cookstove. I went to turn the blooming thing off, and the water for coffee was setting there on the electric stove boiling. I just reached up and turned it off, and I never noticed that steam coming right up under there. My land alive, how that did hurt! I never was burned that way by a kettle, coffee pot, or nothing else on a wood stove.

Marinda Brown also dislikes, at times, the quick, constant heat of the electric or oil stove: "I don't believe that I've burned up as much food with a wood stove as I have with an electric stove. With an electric stove, I turn on my burners and turn around to do something else and forget. It gets hotter quicker, and so it takes more moisture to cook on the electric stove than on the wood stove. And we used to cook in ironware a lot. The water didn't evaporate as fast in that as it does in the newer methods of cooking."

And women like Stella Burrell simply preferred the taste of food cooked on a wood

Cast iron and aluminum pots and pans are equally at home on the wood stove.

stove. As she stated, "I think maybe the slow process of cooking on a wood stove makes the flavor really good, especially in green beans and things like that. I had a skillet that had the iron lid over it, and you could put about three chickens in it to fry. You would brown your chicken real quick, put it all back in the pan and put it on the back of the stove. Put just a little water in it, and let it sit there and steam. It would be soft. It wouldn't be crisp unless you left it a long time, but it would cook slow, and it would be cooked all the way to the bone. It just had a *delicious* taste."

Even women who disliked cooking with wood retained an affection for their old stoves. Belle Ledford, for example, admitted, "I've heard a lot of people say that food tastes better cooked on a wood stove, but to me it doesn't and I didn't like cooking that way better, but I almost cried when we sold our wood stove. I certainly got attached to it, and if I had had the room I would have kept it. I would not have gotten rid of it."

Cast aluminum kettles

Wash pots often held hominy, lard or stew
instead of laundry.

A WORD ON COOKING UTENSILS

Many people attribute the superior taste of wood-stove–cooked food to the pots in which it was cooked rather than to the stove itself. While most pots and pans used on electric and gas stoves work just as well on wood cookstoves, skillets, Dutch ovens, kettles and pots made of cast iron were long the first—and perhaps only—choice of people in this area.

When we asked Addie Norton what kind of pots and pans she used to use, she answered, "Oh, iron ones, just like I do now. I used to have some old big pots, you know, iron pots. They've never been a mess of beans or anything cooked that's as good as they are in that old black pot, and what makes the difference I don't know. They make the best old beans you ever tasted [laughter]. I never have liked beans as good since I quit cooking in that old iron pot.

Gladys Nichols agreed, saying, "Today's way of cooking is better, but I believe I'd rather have beans with a piece of fatback meat in them cooked about three hours in an old iron pot. And if you fry your meat, a cast-iron frying pan is the best cooker there is. It's a little heavy and ugly looking, but it cooks better."

Cast-iron pots and skillets must be treated or "seasoned" to prevent foods from sticking and to keep them from rusting after being washed. To season, when they are new or have to be cleaned as described above, grease well with lard or vegetable shortening. Preheat the oven to a hot temperature, place the pan inside, and turn off the oven or let the fire gradually die down while the pan seasons for 30 minutes.

Soot, of course, will build up on cast-iron cookware when placed directly over the flames, and it needs to be cleaned off with sand or some type of rough scouring pad. Dishrag [luffa] gourds used to be one choice, as many homemakers grew these in their yards for just such use.

If a cast-iron pot or kettle becomes rusty from disuse, scour it with ashes or white sand to remove the rust. After washing it out thoroughly, fill it with cold water and heat for 15 or more minutes, after which the pot should be thoroughly dried to prevent further rust. It should then be good as new and ready to heat water or cook in once more.

Many cooks even believe the iron cookware to be healthier. Daisy Justus, for example, disputes the sales pitch of the stainless-steel and copper-bottomed pot peddlers: "All these pots and pans that the salesman talks about and how nasty that old iron cooking was. I believe it was in a nurse's book or something said the iron gave you iron out of that cooking —I mean like it was *good* for you."

We're not going to dispute that. One thing we can affirm with confidence, however, is that whether because of health, taste, aesthetics, or whatever, when a piece of old iron cookware that is not damaged comes up for sale at an auction or flea market, it commands a healthy price.

A "spider" or "fritter" pan—two views

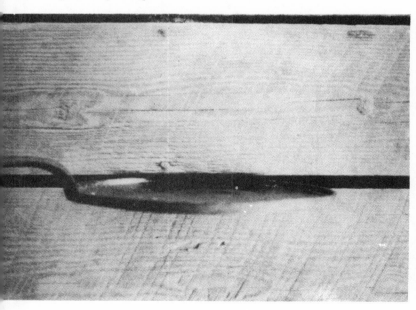

2

Menus

"I don't never make a menu."

Leather breeches with streak of lean
Ham hocks with Irish potatoes
Baked yams
Crowder peas cooked with pickled corn
Cracklin' corn bread with sweet butter
Poke salad and pepper grass stewed together
flavored with streak of lean
Pickled poke salad stalks
Spring onions, tomatoes, relishes
Buttermilk
Dried apple stack cake

This is a typical summer menu used years ago in most parts of Appalachia. Seldom do we see this type of menu used today, but each of the foods listed in the menu is still prepared by people here.

For some people, lunch throughout the week was usually all vegetables with a streak of lean (bacon) in beans as the only meat served. Potatoes, cabbage, green beans, and turnips were the most common vegetables. Supper would be a chicken dish or egg soufflé or beef roast served with greens, squash, peas, and a salad.

For others, a big meal (called "dinner") with meat, bread, and vegetables was served at noon and a light supper prepared in the evening. In that case, there was no meat at supper, it consisting of vegetables left from the noonday meal, bread, milk, and fresh fruit or cooked dried apples.

For still others, there was no consistent pattern at all. As Inez Taylor said, "My favorite foods to cook are fried chicken and macaroni and cheese. I don't never make a menu. Maybe tonight I'd have creamed potatoes, gravy, some green beans, corn bread or biscuits. Maybe tomorrow night I'd have fried potatoes and green beans or soup beans or peas or something like that. Just whatever I want to cook, that's what I cook."

Although most of the cooks we talked with told us that they didn't really plan a menu —they just cooked what food they had on hand at the time—we were still able to collect a bit of information concerning what foods were *usually* served for regular meals, for special occasions, and for crowds.

BREAKFAST

Gladys Nichols on cooking breakfast: "Of course, the old-timers, they'd fly into that kitchen about four o'clock, and by five o'clock they'd have breakfast on the table. I don't like that early risin', but it usually required about a hour to cook breakfast for the family, you know, and get it on the table ready for them to eat. Of course, the old-timers, that's all they knew."

BREAKFAST MENUS

Oatmeal
Meat*
Bread and butter

"That's all we had."— JENNIE ARROWOOD

*Meats include sausage, ham, or bacon.

Eggs
Chicken livers
Gravy
Biscuits

"You boys should have come a little earlier when I had breakfast on the table."
— BESSIE BOLT

Other foods served for breakfast include:

Egg omelet
Corn bread or fritters or biscuit pone*
Fresh creamed corn
Grits
Cornmeal mush
Honey, sorghum syrup
Jams and jellies
Applesauce
Baked fruit
Berries and cream

NOONDAY OR EVENING MEALS

We collected a good sample of menus from our contacts:

Pork tenderloin
Rice or dressing or fried potatoes
Green beans or turnips or greens
Sauerkraut
Blackberry pie

*Fritters (or "flitters") are pancakes made with homemade wheat flour. (See Breads chapter, page 177).

Pork chops, fried or baked
Fried green tomatoes
Potatoes
Biscuits and gravy
Peaches

Fried ham and brown gravy
Sliced onions and green beans
Candied sweet potatoes
Corn bread
Pumpkin pie

Cured ham and red-eye gravy
Baked sweet potatoes and butter
Chicken and broccoli casserole
Rice and gravy
Peas
Applesauce

Fried chicken
Stewed or fried apples
Green beans or peas or greens
Corn
Corn bread or biscuits and gravy

Baked chicken
Rice or creamed potatoes
Baked apples
Biscuits and gravy
Lemon pie or cobbler or jello

SUNDAY DINNER AND HOLIDAY MENUS

Sunday dinner has always been a special time for families in this part of the country. The cooks would have one or two menus that they would generally follow for the Sunday meal or for special occasions such as holidays (Thanksgiving and Christmas) or for when company was invited over.

A special dinner menu consisted of:

Fried chicken and gravy, ham or turkey
Stewed or mashed Irish potatoes or sweet potatoes if available
Boiled corn, on or off the cob
Green beans or lima beans or white half runner beans
Other vegetables from the garden as available
Cooked apples or applesauce
Corn bread and/or biscuits
Pie, cobbler, or a special layer cake

Fried chicken was served in summer when there were young fryers to kill. Chicken and dumplings were cooked in the winter when it was necessary to kill a hen or rooster. Their meat is tougher and requires a longer time cooking.

In the summer when there were plenty of fresh vegetables from the garden, some combination of mustard greens, collards (and sometimes poke salad mixed in), tomatoes, onions, lettuce, cucumbers, peppers, okra, English peas, cabbage, beets, carrots, sweet potatoes, or squash would be served. Cushaws and pumpkins, fresh fruits, and berries were also plentiful during summer months.

During the months when there were no fresh vegetables and fruits, they chose from pickled beans, leather breeches beans, dried field peas, kraut (or fresh cabbage that had been stored in the ground), Irish potatoes, sweet potatoes, and dried apples.

Families would not cook as much meat in the summer. As Bessie Underwood explained to us: "In the summertime, we don't cook a lot of meat. It's in the wintertime that we cook all our meat. It makes you get hotter."

A Typical Sunday Menu at Aunt Arie Carpenter's:

Souse and/or sausage
Chicken and dumplings
Leather breeches
Hominy
Cabbage cooked in a frying pan in the broth from making souse
Potatoes cooked in a Dutch oven
Chowchow
Bread
Egg custards
Peach cobbler

3

Beverages

"Used to you couldn't make it too strong
but what I could drink it."

COFFEE

Coffee and milk were for years the two major beverages in the Appalachian mountains. Lettie Chastain recalls that coffee was primarily an adult drink: "We kids didn't drink much coffee. Mama and Daddy thought milk was what children were supposed to drink, so that's what we drank."

Before the days of freeze-dried and decaffeinated coffee, Gladys Nichols told us how she first prepared the real thing. Said Gladys:

I've parched a many a pound of green coffee. That used to be my job when I was eight or ten years old. Mama would fly into that kitchen at about four o'clock and call me out to parch the coffee. I didn't have a stove to parch it on, either; I did it on the fireplace. I put my coffee beans in a pan and got me some coals out and put them on the hearth. I'd take a spoon and stir that coffee around and around until it turned brown. It's pretty easy done, but if you burned your coffee or scorched it a little it wasn't no good. Then I'd cool it down, put it in that old coffee grinder and grind her up. Put it in the pot, and you've got some of the strongest coffee. If I had it today I'd like it better, but I wouldn't like that extra work. I didn't like that early rising, either, but it usually required about a hour to cook breakfast and get it on the table by five.

41

Coffee beans were once ground in an old hand-turned mill like this one of Gladys Nichols'.

On a wood stove, the coffee-parching process was much the same. As Blanche Harkins said,

> My mother had a large pan that covered the bottom of the wood stove. It fit down in there. She'd put her coffee beans on that pan and put it in the oven. You couldn't have your stove too hot. You wanted to parch the coffee slow. She'd open the stove and take the pan out and stir the coffee around. Then she'd put it back in. When the beans got brown like you've seen the coffee beans you buy in the store, they were ready to take out and grind. She had a grinder on the kitchen wall.
>
> They didn't perk it back then. They boiled it in the grounds. Some people would break a raw egg in their coffee when it boiled. That'd make the grounds settle in the bottom of the pot or kettle, and they wouldn't pour out in your cup. Of course, the egg was cooked in the boiling coffee.

TEA

Through the years iced tea—Southerners drink it summer and winter—has made great advances on coffee and milk and may nowadays be the favorite Appalachian beverage. Once, however, teas were used by the mountain people as beverages, tonics, and remedies. They would gather the roots or barks in the proper season and dry them, and then they would store them for use as the need arose.

Spring was the time to refresh the spirit and tone up the system with a tonic. Spicewood, sweet birch, and sassafras were common spring tonics. The spicy, distinct flavor of sassafras made it a particularly popular tea served hot or cold. Pearl Martin has made sassafras tea her specialty, and an unexpected visit paid to her might find her in the woods behind her house digging roots for this tea.

She has a field behind her house that she keeps bogged down (cleared of brush) to allow her sassafras to grow freely. Left alone, this plant grows into a medium-sized tree with an irregularly shaped trunk, but when Pearl's sassafras reaches bush height, she digs it up for tea.

Pearl told us that she could gather the roots any time of the year without affecting the taste of the tea. However, the roots should be gathered young, so they will be tender.

Pearl chops these young roots from her sassafras and washes them in cold water. Then she scrapes off the outer layer of bark and discards it. Either the roots or the bark can be used in making tea, but Pearl prefers the roots. They can be used dried or green. She brings

Pearl harvests young sassafras from her woods.

Sassafras leaves have a distinctive three-lobed shape.

the roots to a boil in water. The longer they are boiled, the stronger the tea. To make a gallon of tea, Pearl boils 4 average-sized roots in a gallon of water for 15 to 20 minutes. She then strains it and serves it either hot or iced, sweetened with sugar or honey.

Pearl also has her own recipe for sassafras jelly, which is made from the tea itself. To make the jelly, follow the steps for making tea and then mix 1 package of Sure-Jell with 8 cups of tea in a large saucepan. Bring quickly to a hard boil, stirring occasionally. Now add 8 cups sugar and bring to a full rolling boil. Boil hard 1 minute, stirring constantly. Skim off the foam with a metal spoon. Pour at once into hot sterilized jelly jars and seal with paraffin.

Other spring tonic recipes follow:

SASSAFRAS TEA

In the spring, gather roots and tender twigs of sassafras.

Pound the roots to a pulp if they are very big, and wash them with the twigs. Boil them, strain, and sweeten.

SPICEWOOD TEA

The spice bush *(Lindera benzoin)* grows along branch banks. It is best to gather the twigs in early spring when the bark "slips," or peels off easily.

Break the twigs, place them in a pot, cover with water, and boil until the water is dark. Strain and serve hot. Sweeten if desired, with honey or molasses. Mrs. Hershel Keener claims the tea is especially good with pork and cracklin' bread.

In the winter, as Ethel Corn told us, teas were widely served as panaceas:

I was bad to doctor my babies with old-timey remedies because I still think they do more than the doctor's does. I'd give mine ground ivy tea and catnip tea, and I've give the juice out of the onion. That juice out of the onion makes them sleep instead of giving paregoric. Most people give them paregoric to make them rest. But if you bake an onion, squeeze the juice out, put a little sugar in it and give it to a baby, it'll bust a cold out of it. It'll make it relax and rest better than paregoric will, and they is no danger in the onion. I've heard of young'uns being killed by giving them too much paregoric.

You can give a baby catnip tea, and it'll help them bust a cold. Ground ivy tea was a good tea to give a baby for a cold, too. Now, when it comes to measles—they'd use spicewood tea and ginger tea for breaking out measles. And they'd make a tonic out of sarsaparilla. That's to build the blood and give them an appetite. And they'd put wild cherry bark in a tea form and take it.

Back at home, Pearl takes the axe to the limbs and removes the roots that she requires for tea.

Cold mountain water is used to clean the sassafras roots.

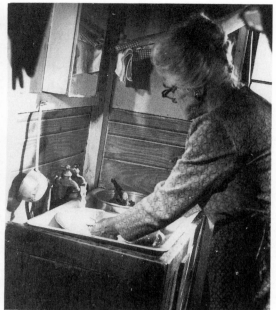

Scraping the roots adds a further degree of cleanliness.

She stirs the boiling roots.

Mountain mint

Catnip

Here are several remedy teas:

MINT OR WHITE HORSEMINT TEA

Gather mint leaves in the summer when the plant is young, just before or just after blooming. Boil the leaves in water, strain, and sweeten with honey. This is used both for an exceptionally pleasant tea, and for a cold remedy.

GROUND IVY TEA

This vine can be gathered in the summer and fall. Make the tea by boiling 6 or 7 leaves in a pint of water. Strain and sweeten to taste.

Ethel Corn said, "Ground ivy does make a pleasant tea for anybody to drink, and old people was bad to give it to babies for colic."

CATNIP TEA

Pour a pint of boiling water over about ½ cup of broken stems and leaves. Let stand several minutes, then strain.

It is best to gather catnip in the spring when it is flowering. Catnip tea is also often given to a fretful child to make him sleep.

RAT'S BANE TEA

This herb, mainly a remedy, may be gathered in the summer or fall. Boil 2 or 3 whole plants for several minutes in about a pint of water. Strain and sweeten.

BONESET TEA

Boneset grows in swampy places, and it is best if gathered in the summer while in bloom. It is quite bitter.

Boneset

Peppermint

3 or 4 leaves boiled in a cup of water will make a strong tea. Strain, sweeten, and drink.

As Icie Rickman said, "You see that yellow weed that grows—boneset? You make tea out of that. My daddy and mother did that all the time. They would get yellowroot, rabbit tobacco, boneset, and all that stuff and boil it, and that is the way they treated us. That's good for a cold."

YELLOWROOT TEA

The plant grows along branches, and it can be gathered in the summer and fall. The roots are brilliant yellow and very bitter when tasted raw.

Put the roots of a medium-sized plant in a pint of water and boil them until the water is colored. The tea will need a good bit of sweetening for most people. It is essentially a remedy.

CAMBRIC TEA

To make cambric tea you take 2 tablespoons of cream and 2 teaspoons full of sugar, pour boiling water in it, stir it, and drink at once. A contact told us, "I don't guess anyone has heard of this, but a school teacher that once boarded at our home drank this tea for breakfast in place of coffee. It tastes real well."

CIDERS AND JUICE DRINKS

APPLE CIDER

After searching for someone to show us how to make apple cider, Ernest Watts volunteered his services. He unearthed his old cider press and mill and brought them to our office. This summer we all gathered around while he demonstrated the process of producing apple cider (for further details, see "Apple Cider," *Foxfire 4*, pp. 449–51).

First we bought a bushel of apples. We were told by Marinda Brown that a good proportion to use is half sweet and half sour apples, but any type of firm, juicy apple will yield cider. To make a more tart or sweet cider, simply add more of the appropriate kind of apple.

Then we collected other cider-making equipment: pans to catch the juice or cider and cloths (cheesecloth is excellent) for straining the final products. Allan Ramey and Tammy Ledford washed, cored, and quartered the apples we used—leaving the peelings on—but whole apples may be used instead.

Apples are fed into the hopper as the mill crank is turned. At this point you may appreciate the advantages of having quartered apples, since whole apples are much harder to grind. The apple pulp or "mash" falls into a container placed under the hopper. If the grinder and press are one piece, as in the diagram, this container should be bottomless so that it may be slid forward to a position under the screw where the apples will be pressed. Otherwise—as with the cider Mr. Watts made—a bucket may be used. In this case, the mashed apples are transferred to a slatted, bottomless tub. Then a wooden disc is fitted into the top of the tub, and the screw—which fits into a metal socket in the top of the disc —is turned by a separate crank. This presses the disc down onto the apple pulp and squeezes the juice out into yet another container. To keep the process going, while one person squeezes the juice, another places a second container under the mill and begins crushing another round of apples. The final step in cider making involves straining the juice through cheesecloth. Gather the ends of the cheesecloth and squeeze the bundle to force the juice through.

The cider may be sipped immediately, refrigerated for use in the near future, or preserved by either canning or freezing. Marinda Brown believes that the canning process takes away the "fresh apple" taste of the juice and prefers to freeze her cider in plastic containers.

Some years ago, Aunt Arie told us how folks used to make cider without a cider press. She said that a wooden trough with holes drilled in the bottom was filled with apples.

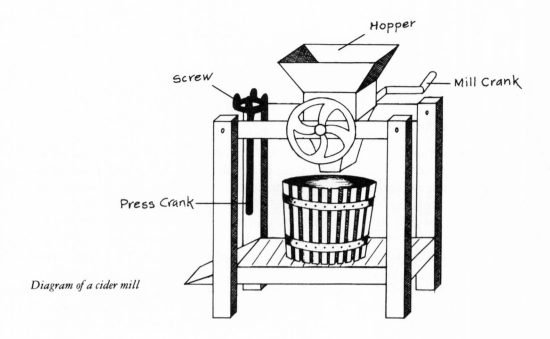

Screw

Hopper

Mill Crank

Press Crank

Diagram of a cider mill

A maul was then used to mash or crush the apples, and a plank was pressed down on top of the apples to squeeze the juice out. This cider was stored in wooden barrels or in the springhouse for drinking. After aging, some was used for vinegar or apple brandy.

MULLED CIDER

BELLE LEDFORD

1 quart apple cider
1 teaspoon whole allspice
1 teaspoon whole cloves

2 sticks cinnamon
6 thin lemon slices, if desired

Combine ingredients except lemon slices in a saucepan. Simmer, covered, for 20 minutes. Remove spices. Serve hot, with lemon slices, if desired. YIELD: *6 servings (about ⅔ cup each)*

Tracy Speed places apples in the hopper as Ernest Watts turns the mill crank.

A bucket of ground apples ready to be pressed into cider

MERRY BREW

BELLE LEDFORD

½ cup firmly packed brown sugar
2 sticks cinnamon
1 tablespoon whole cloves
½ teaspoon whole allspice

1 cup water
2 quarts apple juice
1 lemon, thinly sliced
1 orange, thinly sliced

Combine sugar, spices, and water in a small saucepan; bring to a boil. Reduce the heat, cover, and simmer 10 minutes. Combine with apple juice and serve warm with the lemon and orange slices. YIELD: *2 quarts*

GRAPE JUICE

Mix 2 cups grapes and 1 cup sugar for each desired gallon of juice. Wash grapes and put in a hot sterilized gallon jar. Fill with boiling water. Seal and process by placing in water bath for 10 minutes.

Ernest Watts transfers the apple pulp to a wooden tub.

The wooden disc is placed in the tub, and the screw is wound down until it meets the disc.

Juice is squeezed from the apple pulp as Ernest Watts uses a board for extra leverage.

A pan catches the unstrained cider.

BEERS AND WINES

Quite a few folks in our area enjoy stocking cellars and back shelves with homemade beers and wines. A selection of fruit-based beverages of various strengths follows:

APPLE BEER

Peel apples and dry the peelings in the sun or by the stove. Put them in a crock, and add enough boiling water to cover. Cover the crock and let sit for about 2 days, until all the flavor comes out of the peelings. Strain and drink. You may add some sugar if desired.

Straining is the final step. Here Marinda Brown and Suzy Angier do the honors.

PERSIMMON BEER

To make persimmon beer, gather persimmons and a good number of honey locust seed pods. Wash them both well and place them in a large crock or churn in layers until the crock is full. Pour enough boiling water in to cover them. Cover the crock with something and let it sit at least a week. Pour off or dip out the beer as desired. When drained, the crock may be filled with boiling water again to make a second batch.

Another variation is to gather and mash persimmons and place them in a crock. Pour enough boiling water in to cover them and let them work. Strain off foam, add sugar to taste, and let work (ferment) some more. The beer is supposed to be very potent.

SIMPLE-TO-MAKE GRAPE WINE

Use 5 gallons crushed grapes and 5 pounds sugar. Mix the grapes and sugar together and let work 19 days. Strain, and let work 9 more days.

Strain again and seal up in jars, but don't seal too tightly, as it will work a little more and might blow up.

When it quits working, seal the jars tightly and store in a dark place.

JAKE WALDROOP'S RECIPE FOR BLACKBERRY WINE

Gather 6 to 8 gallons of wild blackberries, wash them well, and put them in a big container. Mix in 5 pounds of sugar, then cover the top of the churn or container with a cloth, tied down so air can get in but insects can't. Let the mixture work for 8 to 10 days.

Strain the mixture through a clean cloth, squeezing the pulp so all the juice is removed. Measure how many gallons of juice you have. For every gallon of juice, add 1½ pounds of sugar. Let it work off. When it stops (when the foaming and bubbling is stopped on top), strain it again, measure the juice, and again add 1½ pounds of sugar to each gallon of juice. When it finishes working this time, it is done and can be bottled. Jake keeps his in an earthenware jug with a corn-cob stopper. He makes grape wine the same way.

Lex Sanders' stock of canned goods includes grape juice (top shelf).

MUSCADINE WINE

Mash ½ bushel of muscadine grapes with your hands, put them in a large churn, and add 2½ pounds of sugar. Let it work for about a week, until it quits.

Strain the mixture to get out the grape skins and impurities. Put back in the churn, add 10 pounds more sugar. Let it work about 8 to 10 days, until it quits and can be bottled. YIELD: *4 gallons*

MARY'S RHUBARB WINE

MARY PITTS

Put into churn:

1 gallon raw rhubarb stalks, sliced in
    ½ inch pieces
5 pounds sugar

1 teaspoon yeast
1 gallon warm water, poured over above
    mixture

Stir well each day for 7 days. Strain and add 1 pound sugar and work 7 days, until it quits and can be bottled. YIELD: *2 gallons*

4

Milk, Butter, Cheese, Eggs

*"Mama'd tell me to pull on the cow's tit to learn
how to milk and that's the way I learned how."*

MILK AND BUTTER

In the past, every home in this area probably had at least one milk cow. Families depended
on the cow for milk, buttermilk, butter, and cottage cheese.

To get the butter and buttermilk, one had to churn. Although there are those who
still do churn in this part of the country, it is quickly becoming a thing of the past.

Inez Taylor is one of the few who still enjoys keeping a milk cow:

You see, mama had four girls and five boys. None of the boys learned to milk. I guess
I was about twelve or thirteen when I learned. She'd go to milk, and she'd have a cow
there that was dry, and I'd get in there and play with it. Mama'd tell me to pull on the
cow's tit to learn how to milk and that's the way I learned how.

I churn about once or twice a week, and I enjoy it. I have two cows, but I just milk
one because one is dry. I get a gallon of a morning and half a gallon at night. You know,
there's a man that buys milk and butter from me, and I told him, "I wish I had a place
big enough and all the cows I wanted and that all I had to do is just fool with cows, because
I love animals."

Tammy Ledford's grandmother Ruth Ledford remembers learning to churn and still enjoys it.

My mother taught me how to churn. It really wasn't hard when I was learning, but churning is never *easy*. Some milk is harder to churn than others. It is according to the kind of cow it is, I reckon. My mother churned a lot—about every other day. I churn about three times a week.

My grandmother had a churn and it was square. It had two big dashers of the thing that went in the middle of it and it had a wheel like thing and you turned it around and around. It had pedals on it like bicycle pedals that you turned with your hands. Gosh, I loved to churn for her 'cause man you could just fly and it didn't take you long to churn. My daughter Liz used to churn all of the time and I was like her. I used to go to Granny's just to get to churn.

After you milk the cow, bring the milk in and strain it into a jar. Let the milk stay in the refrigerator for a few days to let the cream "rise on it."

Inez Taylor told us what she does after the cream rises: "I take a spoon and run it around that cream, and I take it off and put it in a separate jar till I get what I need for a churning. And then I wash and scald my churn out real good and put that [cream] in it."

You need to have the churn at least half full—"about two to three gallons for a good churning," according to Gladys Nichols. After pouring up the cream, let it stand until it gets thick. The time required for the cream to clabber is determined by the temperature of the cream. Ruth Ledford said, "[In the summer] I let it set that night, and then the next morning it's ready to churn." Rittie Webb added that if it's hot weather, pouring a little buttermilk in it will start it to souring. Others told us that in winter it may take as long as three days if it is warmed on alternate sides by the fireplace. Gladys Nichols instructed us to "let it stay where it's warm till it sours, and then it'll clabber and be thick. Then it's ready to churn."

The clabbered cream must be churned as soon as it has thickened. If it is left too long, it will curdle and separate and making butter will not be as successful. On the other hand, good butter will not be made if it is churned too soon—while it is still "blinky milk," or sour milk.

Inez Taylor showed us how to test the cream for churning: "You can tell when it's ready to churn when you pull your churn to the side and it's thick and pulls away from the churn. A lot of people will go ahead and churn it before it's ready, but then their buttermilk is thin. I want mine thick."

Mrs. Ledford told us, "It's according to the temperature of the cream as to how long it takes to churn. The cream can be too cold or it can be too hot. It has to be just right. If it's just right, then it don't take but about twenty minutes [for the butter to start forming].

If the cream is real cold the butter doesn't gather, and you'll have to place [the churn] in a tub of warm water." Otherwise the butter will form small balls, which will not stick together. A small amount of hot water, stirred into the cold liquid with the dasher, will also help to gather the butter.

Inez Taylor explained what to do in warm weather: "Put your churn down in a bucket of ice. I do because I like all the water worked out of [my butter]. When it's warm weather it won't work all the water out without you do that." If the clabbered cream is too warm the result will be soft white puffy butter.

To start churning, Rittie Webb suggested: "Take your dasher—it has to be scalded before you put it in there—and churn it just 'round and 'round like this." Mary Hopper demonstrated the procedure.

The more cream you have the more butter you get. Mrs. Ledford said:

The milk actually doesn't make the butter; the cream does. The butter comes to the top when [the cream] is churned. After you take the butter off, the milk that's left is the buttermilk. You make both butter and buttermilk at the same time. I don't ever churn the whole milk. I just save my cream and churn the cream. You won't have much buttermilk that way but you will have lots of butter.

Once churning is complete, butter can be molded and buttermilk "poured up."

Mary Hopper dipping butter out of churn using her dasher

Ruth Ledford scooping butter out of churn with her hand and into a bowl of cold water

Mrs. Ledford packing butter into mold

Molded butter ready to store in cool place

Inez Taylor pours her buttermilk into jars.

You'll know that the butter is starting to make when you see these little specks coming out of the top. I learned that from watching my mama, I guess. You turn the dasher as you take it up and down. I don't know if everybody does that or not, but I do. I think it helps the butter to gather.

I don't know how long it takes after you see the specks but it usually takes about an hour and a half to do it all. It gets harder to churn when the butter starts to gather, too. You know that the butter is finished making because it all comes to the top.

After the butter is made, Stella Burrell said to "dip the butter off the top [by hand or with dasher], and put it in a bowl in cold water and you wash the milk out of it. Some people use their hands, and some use a wooden paddle. I still have a wooden paddle I used. Work it out till it's firm. You mix about a half teaspoon of salt in it, and then while it is still soft, you mold it or put it in dishes." The buttermilk is "poured up" into jars for storage.

Besides using the clabbered milk for making butter, some people found other uses. Many of our contacts talked about eating the clabbered milk. Terry and Arizona Dickerson have eaten it often. Others dotted it on cobblers for an added flavor.

By placing the butter in the refrigerator, it will get cold and hard. Before refrigerators, contacts remember storing butter and milk along with other foods in their springs or springhouses or in water troughs inside their homes.

Gladys Nichols describes the function of a springhouse: "Where they had a spring, the old-timers would build a little house. And they built a box through that house that would hold water. And they put their milk and butter in containers in this box of water that continually run through there, and that's the way they kept it cool. They didn't have no refrigerator. Mama and Daddy had a springhouse over yonder, and I went and got butter and milk a many a time.''

IONE DICKERSON: "We just had a spring; we didn't have a [springhouse]. We had a spring about two hundred yards downhill from the house. It was cold water, and we put milk and butter in there.''

CHEESE

Mrs. Monroe Reese and Mrs. Thelma Earp are both expert cheese makers. This section begins with interviews with Mrs. Reese and Mrs. Earp in addition to other material from Tedra Harmon, Harriet Echols, and Aunt Nora Garland.

The first person we talked with was Mrs. Reese. She showed us the process she follows for making blocks of cheese that she and her husband like best. On occasion, she has sold some to bring in a little extra money.

She begins with 2½ gallons of refrigerated whole milk from their cow. She pours this

Sometimes local springs are still used—usually when refrigerator is full—for keeping foods cold.

A front view of the springhouse showing how the rocks were carved and laid into the ground

The rocks in the springhouse were carved out by Babe LeCount. This photo shows the precision of Mr. LeCount's work.

The water comes into the large hole (right, see ripples) and runs through the trough into the smaller hole. From there it goes into the building.

all into a large pan and heats it on her wood stove until it is a little past lukewarm. She prefers a wood stove, as it gives a slower, steadier heat.

When the milk is warm, she takes the pan off the stove and adds ¼ Hansen's cheese rennet tablet dissolved in 1 teacup of water, and ⅛ Hansen's cheese color tablet dissolved in 1 teacup of water. Both these tablets are available in drugstores, and directions for their use are listed on the containers.

She lets the milk stand from 15 to 30 minutes until it stiffens and gets jellylike. Then she cuts it with a knife or spatula into tiny squares, also running the spatula under the surface as if cutting it into layers.

This diagram shows the layout of the springhouse and the formation and location of the rocks.

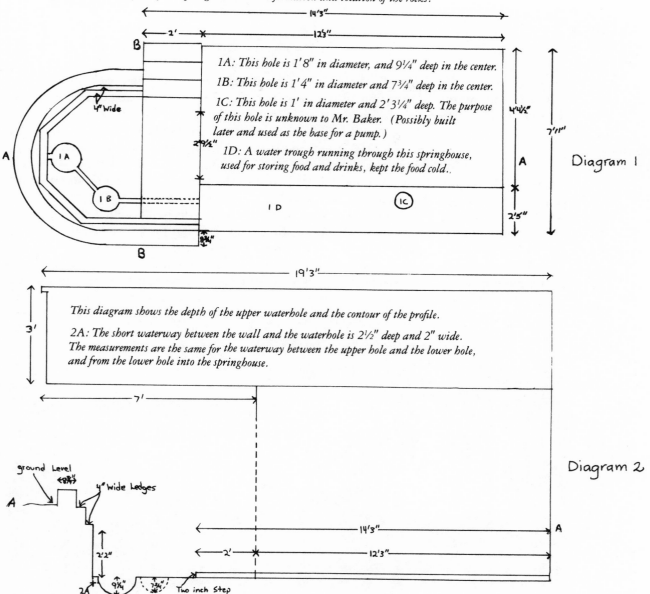

14'3"

12'3"

2'

B

4" Wide

2'9½"

A

1A

1B

1D

1C

8¼"

B

1A: This hole is 1' 8" in diameter, and 9¼" deep in the center.

1B: This hole is 1' 4" in diameter and 7¾" deep in the center.

1C: This hole is 1' in diameter and 2' 3¼" deep. The purpose of this hole is unknown to Mr. Baker. (Possibly built later and used as the base for a pump.)

1D: A water trough running through this springhouse, used for storing food and drinks, kept the food cold..

4'4½"

7'11"

A

2'5"

Diagram 1

19'3"

This diagram shows the depth of the upper waterhole and the contour of the profile.

2A: The short waterway between the wall and the waterhole is 2½" deep and 2" wide. The measurements are the same for the waterway between the upper hole and the lower hole, and from the lower hole into the springhouse.

3'

7'

ground Level

8¾"

4" Wide Ledges

A

2'2"

2A

9¾"

7¾"

Two inch Step

14'3"

2'

12'3"

A

Diagram 2

This diagram shows the steps leading into the springhouse on the left, and the rock wall on the right. The ledges on the wall are there mainly for the decoration, and serve no specific purpose.

3A: Steps leading into the basin of the springhouse

3B: Waterway from the lower hole flowing into the springhouse. (This hole is 2½" deep and 2" wide.)

3C: Ground level is just below the top of the basin.

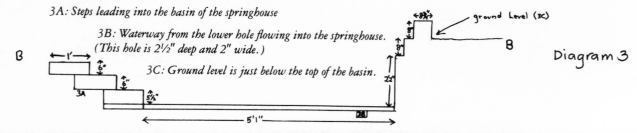

8¾"

ground Level (3C)

B

8"

B

Diagram 3

1'

6"

6"

B

3A

6½"

2'2"

3B

5'1"

Letting it stay there briefly, she then works the mixture until it is all broken up into pieces that are about the size of grains of corn. She works it gently, squeezing the custard-like substance until it is completely broken apart. Then she puts the pan back on the stove and heats the mixture slowly until it is almost as hot as the touch can stand, although not boiling. While reheating, the mixture is stirred constantly so that the curds will stay separated and not melt back together. She then removes the mixture from the stove and lets it cool from 15 to 30 minutes. Next, she strains the contents through cheesecloth in the colander she has ready on her sink. She does not squeeze the mixture dry—she lets it drip naturally; and then she returns the mixture to the pan, adds a heaping teaspoonful of salt, and massages it in well.

Finally she puts the contents of the pan into a homemade press, which she has lined with cheesecloth. Adding weight in stages, she leaves it in the press overnight, or up to 12 hours, to press the cheese down into a firm block. She removes it from the press and dries it for a week in the open air with a cloth underneath the cheese to absorb any additional moisture. She turns it two times a day during this drying process, during which the cake of cheese forms a dry crust on the outside. It should not spoil for a month or more.

Before rennet tablets were available, cheese of this sort was still possible to make.

Mrs. Reese starts her cheese-making process by heating the milk....

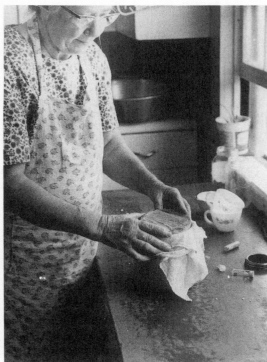

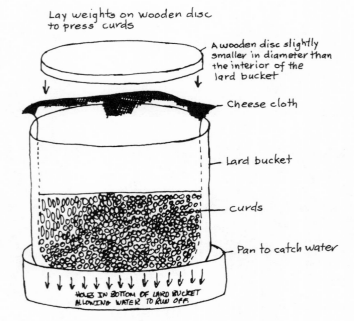

Lay weights on wooden disc
to press curds

A wooden disc slightly
smaller in diameter than
the interior of the
lard bucket

Cheese cloth

Lard bucket

curds

Pan to catch water

HOLES IN BOTTOM OF LARD BUCKET
ALLOWING WATER TO RUN OFF.

Mrs. Reese's homemade press

Tedra Harmon remembers that when they killed a cow for butchering, they would get the stomach out, cut it open, and clean it well. Then they would stretch it out in one piece to dry like a banjo hide. After it was thoroughly dry, they rolled it up and hung it in a bag from a convenient rafter. Whenever his mother made cheese of the sort just described, she would use a tiny piece of the stomach lining (about the size of a thumbnail) to curdle the milk, just as the rennet tablets are used now. He also remembers his mother using a small piece of the stomach lining when making light bread. He remembers it giving the bread a sour taste.

The cheese his mother made was pressed into wooden hoops that were from 12 to 14 inches in diameter. The cheese would be placed up in the attic to dry for 6 to 8 weeks before being cut, and he remembers that the older the cheese got, the better it tasted.

Mrs. Thelma Earp makes a different kind of cheese. It can be eaten right away. In fact, it was so good that we wound up taking half a cake with us in the car and nibbling on it all the way home.

Before we got to her house, she had clabbered the milk and had it waiting in the refrigerator. To do this, she took whole milk, allowed the cream to rise, skimmed it off, and made butter. Then she added 2 to 3 tablespoons of buttermilk per gallon of skimmed milk and let it sit out for 2 days to sour. She put this in the refrigerator to await use.

When we arrived, she went right to work, pouring 2 gallons of the clabbered milk into a pan and heating it on the stove until it was a little hotter than lukewarm. She said it should be pretty hot, but not boiling, and not so hot that it would burn your hands.

Once the clabbered milk was thoroughly heated, she poured it into a strainer made with a cotton cloth pinned over a bucket with clothespins. She then gathered the corners of the cloth and squeezed the whey through the cloth, leaving the curd. "The best thing to do with the whey, now, is feed it to the hogs," she said, laughing.

She then put the curds in a bowl and added 1½ teaspoons of salt and a raw egg. (She prefers barnyard eggs to store-bought ones, as they make the cheese yellower.) She mixed it all in with her hands, readying it for cooking.

Then she put a lump of butter about the size of a large hen egg into a big iron frying pan and melted it. She prefers a wood cookstove because it heats more evenly and slowly.

When the butter was melted, she added curds and kept turning them in the pan over medium heat. When all the curds were melted enough to form a cake, she put them into a dish to cool. As they cooled, they formed a cake.

Mrs. Earp mixing ingredients for cheese

Mrs. Earp's strainer

Final stages in making Mrs. Earp's cheese

COTTAGE CHEESE

We asked Mrs. Harriet Echols to tell us how she makes cottage cheese. Below are her directions, with some additional comments from Mrs. Nora Garland.

To begin the process of making cottage cheese, pour about a gallon of raw (unpasteurized) whole milk into an enameled or metal pan. Any amount of milk may be used. The amount used here is what is preferred by Harriet Echols for her family. Mrs. Echols puts her pan of milk on the back of the wood stove in the winter or on a kitchen table during warm weather, so that it can sour slowly. This process may only take one day, or perhaps two, according to the temperature. Mrs. Echols does not heat the milk at all before it clabbers. (When on the stove, it is not over direct heat—only in a warm place.)

After the milk clabbers, the cream is lifted off and refrigerated. The cream may be used later as sour cream in any recipe.

The skimmed, clabbered milk is then heated over a low fire until it curdles. It is removed from the heat and poured into a colander or cheesecloth to drain all the water. This usually takes a couple of hours. It may also be hung in a cloth overnight. Mrs. Nora Garland remembers that she put the curdled milk into a clean flour sack and let it drain overnight outside.

Both Mrs. Garland and Mrs. Echols told us they would work the cheese by putting it back into a pan or bowl and squeezing it with their hands or a spoon or spatula, getting out any remaining water. Mrs. Echols warned us not to work the cheese too vigorously or get the curds too fine. A little salt may be sprinkled in to taste, and to make the cheese creamier some of the sour cream may be mixed in with it. The cottage cheese is then packaged in small containers and refrigerated. It will keep several weeks in the refrigerator.

CHEESE SOUFFLÉ

MARGARET NORTON

3 eggs, separated
¾ cup grated cheese

Salt and pepper to taste

Beat egg whites with an electric mixer until peaks are formed. Set aside. Mix together grated cheese and egg yolks. Add salt and pepper to taste. Fold the whites into the egg yolk mixture. Pour into a buttered baking dish and set the dish in a pan of cold water to keep the milk and egg mixture from burning. Bake at 350°F for 15 minutes. YIELD: *4 servings*

MACARONI AND CHEESE

1 cup macaroni, boiled
1 cup grated cheese
⅔ cup milk

1 to 2 eggs
Salt to taste
¼ cup soft bread crumbs

Place alternate layers of macaroni and cheese in a buttered baking dish, reserving 2 tablespoons of the cheese for the top. Beat the eggs; add milk and salt, and pour over macaroni. Sprinkle top with remaining cheese combined with the bread crumbs. Bake in a 400°F oven until well browned. YIELD: *4-5 servings*

EGGS

Here are a few egg recipes from Appalachia.

BAKED EGGS

Break number of eggs desired into a buttered baking dish. Cover eggs with cheese, mustard, or curry sauce, etc. Bake in a 350°F oven for 10 minutes. Buttered crumbs may be placed on top before or after baking.

SOUFFLÉ

This soufflé is especially good using broccoli or spinach. Also good served with cheese, tomato, or mushroom sauce.

3 tablespoons butter
3 tablespoons flour
1 cup liquid (milk, stock, vegetable
   water, or cream)

1 cup minced meat, fish, or vegetables
3 eggs, separated
Salt and pepper to taste

Make a sauce out of the first 3 ingredients by first making a paste from the flour and a small amount of the liquid. Gradually mix paste into remaining liquid, add butter and place over heat. When mixture comes to a boil, add minced ingredient. Bring to a boil again and remove from heat. Beat in egg yolks. Cook and stir over low heat until slightly thickened. Remove from heat and add salt and pepper. Cool.

Beat egg whites, and when stiff fold into egg yolk mixture. Pour into an ungreased ovenproof dish and bake in a 325°F oven for 30 minutes. Serve immediately.

VARIATION: Substitute ½ cup cheese for the minced ingredient. YIELD: *6 servings*

DEVILED EGGS

6 eggs, hard cooked
¼ teaspoon salt
¼ cup mayonnaise
1 tablespoon vinegar

Sliced olives, chopped pickles, chopped parsley, diced pimiento, or paprika for garnish

Shell eggs, and once cool, cut in even halves lengthwise with a sharp knife. Carefully remove yolks with teaspoon into a bowl; mash with a fork until very fine and crumbly. Add mayonnaise, salt, and vinegar. Mix well until smooth. Refill hollows in the whites with the mixture. Garnish with olives, pickles, parsley, pimiento, or paprika.

Mary Pitts elaborates: "For deviled eggs, first boil your eggs. If you'll put them under cold water and lay them to one side, I find it's easier to peel the shell off right then. After you cut that egg in two [lengthwise] you take the yellow out and put it in a dish. I put in mayonnaise and chip up a little cucumber pickles, or if I have some relish, I'll use that. Sometimes the vinegar in your pickles is not strong enough, so I add a teaspoonful or more of vinegar—taste it and you'll know how to do it. You can use pickle juice if you want to, but sometimes it makes the yellow too mushy. And then you put salt and pepper in it. Mix that all up good with your egg yellow and put it back in your eggs."

5

Soups and Stews

"I made soup every fall, every summer."

VEGETABLE SOUPS

During the gardening season families enjoy soups and stews prepared from fresh vegetables, a delightful addition to the summer menu, and in order to preserve the taste of these dishes—favorites on cold winter days—they can or freeze them. During early fall it is customary to see kitchens in this area and the local cannery filled with cookers of soup and stew mixtures.

Vegetable soup, a mixture of several vegetables cooked with tomatoes or tomato juice is probably the favorite of soups in this part of the South. People enjoy making it because they can make the mixture to suit their own taste. Two of our contacts told us how they make theirs:

EXIE DILLS: "Yeah, I made soup every fall, every summer. I just used corn and tomatoes and if I had them, shelled beans. And okra. That's all I put in mine. Some uses peas. I don't eat peas, so I don't put peas. You can put potatoes in if you want to, but I just never did. When you go to fix it for the table, you know, you can put cooked potatoes in with it then if you want to."

Lena Shope from the Wolfork Community will be gathering vegetables from her garden until fall.

STELLA BURRELL: "When my boys were growing up, they got tired of just vegetable soup, and I would add beef to it. I would put usually about eight different kinds of vegetables in it—tomatoes with corn and green beans and lima beans, okra and onions and maybe a little pepper. I like vegetable soup with corn bread, but I eat it with crackers a lot now if I don't have the corn bread. That's another quick meal to serve if you've got somebody dropping in."

VEGETABLE SOUP

ADDIE NORTON

2 cups peas
4 cups okra
1 to 2 cups water
2 ears corn, cut off the cob
2 small onions, chopped up

4 cups potatoes, peeled and diced
2 cups carrots, sliced
2 cups shelled beans
2 cups beef, cubed or sliced
3 to 4 tomatoes

With the exception of the tomatoes, boil each mixture of vegetables separately until done. Boil beef until well done and mix with all the vegetables in a large pot. Add tomatoes, needed water, and salt and pepper to taste. Cook together, uncovered, for another 15 to 30 minutes to let flavors mix. Simmer 2 to 3 hours. YIELD: *twenty 1 cup servings*

OLD-FASHIONED VEGETABLE SOUP

3 pounds stew beef
4 cups water
1 cup cubed carrots
2 cups small cubes of Irish potatoes
1½ cups corn
¾ cup okra, sliced very thin
1 cup baby lima beans

½ cup chopped celery
1 medium onion, chopped fine
6 cups tomatoes or tomato juice
2 teaspoons salt
1 teaspoon pepper
½ teaspoon sugar

Cover beef with water and heat to boiling. Reduce heat; cover and simmer 1 to 2 hours until meat on shanks is fork tender.

Let cool and pull meat from shanks into small cubes. Skim fat from cooled stock. Strain stock into large saucepan; add meat cubes and remaining ingredients. Heat to boiling, cover and simmer for 1 hour, or until vegetables are tender. Additional water or tomato juice may be needed if mixture gets too thick. YIELD: *twenty to twenty-five 1 cup servings*

TOMATO SOUP

ANNIE LONG

1 pint peeled, canned tomatoes
2 cups water
1 carrot, cubed
1 small onion, chopped fine
1 bay leaf

2 cloves
1 teaspoon salt
Dash of pepper
4 cups soup stock

Place all ingredients in large saucepan. Cover and cook for 1 hour, or until carrots are tender. Remove cloves and bay leaf before serving. Serve as is or place in the blender and purée before serving. YIELD: *4 servings*

CREAM OF TOMATO SOUP

"That's a good soup. I still use it."–IONE DICKERSON

2 cups canned or stewed tomatoes
⅛ teaspoon baking soda
⅓ cup flour
¼ to ⅓ cup butter or margarine

4 cups fresh milk, heated
2 teaspoons salt
⅛ teaspoon pepper

Put tomatoes in a saucepan, cover, and simmer about 15 minutes. Press tomatoes through a strainer, add baking soda, and stir to mix. For white sauce, add flour to the heated butter and cook a few minutes. Add the heated milk, salt, and pepper. Add the tomatoes to the sauce rather than the sauce to the tomatoes. Have both the sauce and tomatoes hot before combining, and do not cook after combining. YIELD: *6 servings*

CHASE SOUP

GLADYS NICHOLS

This recipe is named for Gladys Nichols' son Chase, who liked it so much.

4 cups ripe tomatoes, quartered
1 small onion, chopped
2 tablespoons flour

2 cups milk
Salt and pepper to taste
Butter or lard

Cook together ripe tomatoes and chopped onion until onion is tender. Blend flour into milk and mix into tomatoes. Add enough salt and pepper to taste. Bring to a boil, then simmer about 5 minutes. Season with butter or lard. YIELD: *6 servings*

SPLIT PEA SOUP

BELLE LEDFORD

2 cups dried split peas
3 quarts water
Ham bone or 2-inch cube of salt pork
½ cup chopped onion
1 cup chopped celery
½ cup chopped carrots

2 cups soup stock or 2 cups milk
1 bouillon cube
2 tablespoons butter
2 tablespoons flour

Salt to taste

Soak peas for 12 hours in water to cover by 2 inches water.

Drain the peas and put in a large kettle. Add water and ham bone or salt pork and simmer, covered, for 3 hours. Add chopped onion, celery, and carrots; simmer, covered, 1 hour longer.

Put soup through a food mill or blend in a blender. Chill and skim off all fat. Add soup stock or milk, if thinner soup is desired. If using milk instead of soup stock, add the bouillon cube, butter, and flour paste to soup stock before adding the milk. Add salt to taste. Cook until thickened and well done. YIELD: *16–20 servings*

CREAM OF BROCCOLI SOUP

BELLE LEDFORD

2 tablespoons butter
1 onion, chopped fine
2 tablespoons flour
5 cups chicken broth
1 pound fresh broccoli, cooked

½ teaspoon salt
¼ teaspoon pepper
½ cup whipping cream
Grated lemon rind from 1 to 2 lemons

Sauté onion in heated butter in a saucepan for 3 minutes, until softened. Add the flour and stir in the chicken broth. Cover and simmer 20 minutes.

Mix together the cooked broccoli and 1 cup of the liquid. Beat or process in a blender until smooth. If necessary, strain to remove strings and lumps. Return purée to the soup mixture in saucepan. Add salt, pepper, and whipping cream, heat to boiling. Serve in warm bowls and garnish with desired amount of lemon rind. YIELD: *6 servings*

QUICK POTATO SOUP

ANNIE LONG

3 potatoes
2 tablespoons butter

Salt and pepper to taste
2 cups hot milk

Peel and cube the potatoes. Cover with water and cook until done. Do not drain—potato water gives additional flavor. Add butter, salt, pepper, and milk. Heat but do not boil. Serve hot. YIELD: *4-6 servings*

CREAMED POTATO SOUP

2 cups sliced potatoes   *Butter to taste*
2 cups water   *½ cup milk*
Salt and pepper to taste   *1 tablespoon flour*

Peel and slice potatoes, cover with water in a saucepan, and add enough salt, pepper, and butter for taste. Boil until tender. Mix milk and flour in a jar and shake until well mixed, then add to potatoes. Let the mixture boil 2 to 3 more minutes, until broth is slightly thick. If the broth becomes too thick, add more water or milk. YIELD: *4-5 servings*

POTATO SOUP WITH CORNMEAL

BELLE LEDFORD

"I make potato soup and I put cornmeal in it. My mother used to make it, and she didn't have any recipe. When [my daughter] Mary Ann was a little girl, every time she got sick, she'd say, 'Grandmother, make me some potato soup.' And [Mary Ann] still cooks it. When I'm at her house, I say, 'Cook *me* some potato soup.'

"She puts about a quart of water and about a quart of sweet milk [regular milk] on the stove and gets it to cooking. Then she puts her potatoes in. I guess she uses about six good-sized potatoes and cuts them up fine. She puts one or two stalks off of the celery in, cut up fine, and you can put onion if you want it. She just puts cornmeal in until she gets it as thick as she wants it. The last time I fixed it, I think I used a half a cup for that much soup. Season it good with butter and cook it. She always makes a big pot full when she makes it, because we all eat it. She makes it much better than I do, too."

MEAT SOUPS AND STEWS

As with vegetable soup, Brunswick stew recipes may be altered to suit one's taste. Many people make it without a recipe, mixing ingredients together to suit their particular tastes. Several contacts told us how they make Brunswick stew.

MARGIE LEDFORD: "I make Brunswick stew—that's some beef and some pork and some chicken and tomatoes and potatoes and some A-1 sauce. It's first one thing and then another. I don't have no recipe."

LETTIE CHASTAIN: "We start cooking ours and put everything in it—corn, tomatoes, chicken, pork, beef, all your seasoning and butter and ketchup. Some people put sage in it, but I don't; and I put barbecue sauce. Put it on to cooking and we put our margarine and stuff in it, but I always just taste of it. It's good if you put some broke-up soda crackers in it, but not too much, just some; then we put our seasoning in until we get it like we want it."

EASY-TO-MAKE BRUNSWICK STEW

CLYDE BURRELL

1 pound chopped or ground beef
1 large onion
2 cups canned tomatoes
1 cup tomato ketchup
½ cup chopped green pepper

2 cups fresh, canned, or frozen corn
1 teaspoon sugar
1 teaspoon vinegar
Salt and pepper to taste

Brown beef and onion together. Add tomatoes, ketchup, and green pepper. Cover and cook slowly for 30 minutes. Add corn and seasonings and stir well. Cook slowly, covered, for another 30 minutes. Stir often and add water if the stew becomes too thick. YIELD: *16 servings*

HEARTY BRUNSWICK STEW

1 pound lean pork
1 small chicken
2 pounds ground beef
3 to 4 potatoes, peeled and diced
2 cups fresh, canned, or frozen corn
1 cup fresh or canned lima beans
2 to 3 carrots, diced
2 to 3 onions, chopped

2 cups chopped tomatoes or tomato juice
Add enough of each for desired taste:
Ketchup
Chili powder
Salt
Black pepper
Ground red pepper
Worcestershire sauce

Boil chicken and pork until done and then grind both chicken and pork; sauté ground beef, then add all 3 to the vegetable mixture. Mix everything together in a large pot and simmer, covered, for 1 to 1½ hours. If canning the mixture, put in pint jars and process them in a water bath for 1½ hours. YIELD: *approximately 10 pints*

BRUNSWICK STEW FOR A LARGE CROWD*

BELLE LEDFORD

10 pounds ground beef
10 pounds chicken
5 pounds pork
4½ gallons tomatoes
4 gallons fresh, canned, or frozen corn
5 pounds onions, chopped fine and boiled
    or sautéed

½ gallon ketchup
1 pound butter
1½ cups Worcestershire sauce
5 ounces Tabasco sauce, or to taste
1 pound cheese (optional)
Salt and pepper to taste

Precook chicken, pork, and beef by boiling each until tender. Grind or cut chicken, beef, and pork into small pieces. Mix with remaining ingredients in a large pot and cook until good and done. Be careful with Tabasco sauce, using only the amount to suit taste. If canning this mixture place jars in a water bath and process them for 2 to 2½ hours. YIELD: 32½ quarts

OLD-FASHIONED BEEF STEW

½ cup plus 2 to 4 tablespoons flour
1 teaspoon salt
¼ teaspoon pepper
2 pounds stew beef, cut into bite-sized
    pieces
2 tablespoons shortening
6 cups hot water

4 medium potatoes, cut into bite-sized
    cubes
4 carrots, cut into bite-sized cubes
½ cup sliced celery (optional)
1 medium onion, diced
1 tablespoon salt
1 cup cold water

Mix ½ cup flour, salt, and pepper and use to coat meat. In a large skillet, brown meat in the melted shortening. Add hot water and heat to boiling. Reduce heat; cover and simmer for 2 to 3 hours.

Stir in the vegetables and salt and simmer 30 to 45 minutes longer, until the vegetables are tender. To thicken the stew, mix together the cold water and 2 to 4 tablespoons flour in a jar; shake until blended and stir into the stew. Heat to boiling, stirring constantly. Boil and stir 1 minute. YIELD: 15-20 servings

*This recipe is easier to prepare at a cannery because of the convenience of large cookers.

HOG'S HEAD STEW

JOANNE CARVER

This recipe comes from the Carver family. Every harvesttime they plunge into a cooking-canning spree that goes for days and leaves them more than ready for the winter. The measurements given below yielded 63 quarts last time around. If you can't handle quite that much, cut proportionally, subtracting or adding other ingredients according to preference.

1½ hog's heads
2 shoulders or hams of venison
4 chickens
1 peck onions
1 gallon Irish potatoes
5 half gallons each of tomatoes, corn,
   peas, carrots

6 large cans tomato juice to thin (broth
   may be substituted for, or added to,
   the tomato juice)
1 package poultry seasoning
Bay leaves to taste
5 pounds salt (or to taste)
Worcestershire sauce to taste
Pepper to taste

Cook the meat until it comes easily off the bones. Cool, remove the meat from the bones, and grind it up (or run through a food chopper) together with the other ingredients. Place the mixture in quart jars, seal, and cook in a pressure cooker for 60 minutes at 10 pounds pressure. Then store away for the lean months.

Her mother's recipe for the same stew, provided us by Brenda Carver, varies somewhat: 1 hog's head, 2 chickens, 4 pounds ground beef, 1 gallon potatoes, 1 gallon tomatoes, 4 number 2 cans each of peas, corn, and carrots. Chop and blend ingredients, can, cook in pressure cooker for 30 minutes.

FISH SOUP

Roast small chunks of fish by cooking them on a stick over the fire. Then boil them in water to make a thick soup. A little cornmeal (gritted or dry) added will help to thicken the soup. Salt and pepper to taste.

6

Salads

*"When you get all that chopped up,
you've got a bowl full."*

Salad combinations vary in the South, although they are not as elaborately prepared as in other regions of the country. Leaf lettuce fresh from the garden is a favorite, and it is not unusual to see cabbage cooked or made into cole slaw practically every day during the summer while it is plentiful in the gardens.

A variety of wild greens is also cooked or served raw in salads. We've included the most popular wild greens in the vegetable section along with the most favored cultivated greens—turnip and mustard greens, collards, and spinach.

Esco Pitts discussed planting the number-one-ranked green salad item, lettuce.

ESCO PITTS: "My mother grew it every year. She had two kinds—leaf lettuce and some that made heads. She planted it very early in the spring, even before the frost quit, because lettuce is a hardy plant. She had a corner of the garden where it seemed to grow better than any other place. Then she had lettuce along in her onion rows."

The old way of preparing the salad makings—lettuce, tomatoes, cucumbers, onions, peppers, and so on—was to slice and arrange a portion of each around a plate, not mixing them together. They were usually eaten as separate vegetables, but mayonnaise or oil was set on the table for those who wanted that extra taste or wanted to mix the vegetables into a salad. We found that several women made their own mayonnaise on a regular basis.

MARY PITTS: "My mother used olive oil to make mayonnaise. In a big, deep bowl, beat your egg yellow good with a rotary egg beater. We used the egg white for other stuff, and then we found out later you could use the whole egg and beat it. Then you put in one half teaspoon of oil at a time. It takes one standing putting that in and the other beating. Put a grain or two of salt in it, and you could tell when you got it thick enough. You could get it as thick as the mayonnaise you buy today. The more oil you put in it the thicker it got. It's real good, and my mother said she'd rather make it often and have it fresh made. You could put it in potato salads and things. We made mayonnaise way back in the thirties when my three oldest children was little. They loved just plain mayonnaise on loaf bread. It tastes different. To me it's better. [Note: Belle Ledford says that plain cooking oil—she suggested Wesson—may be used instead of olive oil. You may season with salt and add a little lemon juice or a little vinegar.]"

MAYONNAISE DRESSING

1 egg yolk
2 tablespoons vinegar or lemon juice or
*   1 tablespoon of each*
¼ teaspoon mustard

¾ teaspoon salt
⅛ teaspoon pepper
¾ cup salad oil

Beat egg yolk and add 1 tablespoon of the vinegar or lemon juice. Add mustard, salt, and pepper. Beat well. Drop oil, a teaspoon at a time, into the egg mixture, beating constantly until ¼ cup has been added. Then add in larger quantities, beating thoroughly after each addition. As mixture thickens, add remaining vinegar or lemon juice a little at a time. Have all ingredients equally cold when mixing. Store in a cool place in clean jars. YIELD: *1 cup*

POTATO SALADS

Potatoes were commonly served, so it isn't surprising that local housewifes invented many ways to use them. There are almost as many variations for making potato salad as there are cooks, and it is still a favorite for taking along on outings. We discovered that potato salad is most often prepared for picnics, covered-dish dinners, and large crowds because the cook doesn't have to worry about the dish becoming cold. It is a vegetable salad that can be prepared to suit almost anyone's taste.

OLD-FASHIONED POTATO SALAD

DAISY JUSTUS

Use leftover mashed potatoes or cook as many potatoes as needed. Mash the potatoes and about 1 cup of chopped onions. Then use 3 or 4 tablespoons of vinegar, and salt and pepper; mix well. Serve on lettuce leaves.

POTATO SALAD

MARY PITTS

"When I make potato salad, I usually peel about a gallon of potatoes and cube them before I cook them. They cook quicker that way. And then I drain all that water off of them and pour them on a tray and let them get cool. While they're cooling, I chip up a big onion and cucumber pickles and six or eight boiled eggs. By the time you get your eggs and all chipped up, your potatoes is nearly cold. And I just salt and pepper it, mix it all up with some mayonnaise, and set it back. When you get all that chipped up, you've got a bowl full."

SLAW

DAISY JUSTUS: "Used to, when we made slaw we'd take the thick cream of the milk and mix it and vinegar together and pour it over the cabbage. That was the way we made slaw. We still put tomatoes or onions in our slaw."

Slaw can be made in as many different ways as potato salad, but the average slaw tends to "keep" longer. In fact, most names for slaw indicate how long they may be kept in the refrigerator. Cabbage is a hardy vegetable, and more recent recipes include instructions for freezing slaw.

SEVEN-DAY COLE SLAW

MARINDA BROWN

Pack in layers in crock:

½ head cabbage, grated
1 carrot, grated
1 medium onion, chopped

½ sweet red pepper, chopped
½ green pepper, chopped
Thin layer of sugar on top

Mix together and bring to a boil:

¼ cup vegetable oil
½ cup vinegar

Sugar and salt (amount depends on how
sweet or sour you want the slaw)

While still hot, pour the mixture over the vegetables in the crock. The peppers are optional, but they make it pretty and give it color. This recipe makes a quart and it will keep on and on, not just seven days.

THREE-WEEK SLAW

BELLE LEDFORD: "It says you can keep it three weeks, but I've kept it in there three months in the refrigerator and set it out for people to eat when they come. They say it's still good."

3 pounds white cabbage
2 onions
1 green pepper
2 cups sugar

1 cup vegetable oil
1 cup vinegar
2 teaspoons celery seed
1 tablespoon salt

Combine chopped cabbage, onions, and pepper. Add the sugar and let stand. Mix oil, vinegar, celery seed, and salt. Bring to a boil. While hot, pour over the cabbage. Toss well and let sit for a few minutes until it becomes room temperature. Store in refrigerator. YIELD: *2 quarts*

CABBAGE SALAD

3 cups shredded cabbage
1½ cups shredded carrots
½ teaspoon salt

1 tablespoon vinegar
Mayonnaise
Orange sections (optional)

Combine cabbage, carrots, salt, and vinegar. Moisten with mayonnaise. Mix by tossing with two forks. Add orange sections, if desired. YIELD: *8 servings*

FREEZER SLAW WITH CUCUMBERS, ONIONS, AND PEPPERS

BELLE LEDFORD

1 gallon chopped cabbage
1 tablespoon salt
4 small onions
4 cucumbers
2 carrots

2 small peppers
1 teaspoon celery seed
2 cups sugar
1 cup vinegar
½ cup water

Mix cabbage and salt. Let stand 30 minutes, then drain. Chop the onions, cucumbers, carrots, and peppers. Add to the cabbage, along with the celery seed. Set aside. Boil the sugar, vinegar, and water for 1 minute. When cold pour over the cabbage mixture, mixing well. Let stand 5 minutes before putting into containers to freeze.

VEGETABLE SALADS

LETTUCE AND ONIONS

DAISY JUSTUS: "Chop up onions and lettuce. Sprinkle with salt. Heat bacon grease in frying pan. Have it real hot. Pour over lettuce and onions and mix well. Serve at once. Good with corn bread and buttermilk."

As more exotic items such as pineapple and French green beans became available in local stores, cooks added them to their salad repertoires:

BEAN SALAD

BELLE LEDFORD

1 green pepper
1 stalk celery
1 large onion
1 can French green beans
1 can green peas

16 ounces white shoepeg (whole kernel)
    corn
1 small jar pimientos
¾ cup red wine vinegar
½ cup oil
1 cup sugar

Chop peppers, celery, and onion into fine pieces; add to other vegetables. Drain well before adding vinegar, oil, and sugar. Keeps in the refrigerator for weeks. YIELD: *10-12 servings*

BROCCOLI SALAD

BELLE LEDFORD

1 bunch broccoli
1 onion, chopped

1 cucumber, sliced, or cauliflower,
    chopped and steamed
2 tablespoons salad dressing

Steam broccoli about 10 minutes, drain, and cool. Add onion and cucumber or cauliflower. Pour salad dressing over mixture and serve. YIELD: *6-8 servings*

CARROT SALAD

2 cups grated raw carrots
2 cups grated tart apples, unpeeled
1 green pepper, chopped

1 sweet red pepper, chopped
1 tablespoon mayonnaise
1 tablespoon peanut butter

Blend together carrots, apples, and peppers. Toss with mayonnaise and peanut butter and serve. YIELD: *8 servings*

CARROT-APPLE SALAD

1 cup grated raw carrots
1 cup chopped celery
½ cup chopped peanuts
Mayonnaise

Lettuce
1 large tart apple, cored and sliced
1 sweet red pepper
1 green pepper, cut in strips

Blend carrots, celery, and nuts with desired amount of mayonnaise. Serve on lettuce, garnished with slices of apples and strips of peppers. YIELD: *8 servings*

CARROT-PINEAPPLE SALAD

1 cup grated raw carrots
1 cup chopped celery
1 slice pineapple, diced

1 cup chopped pecans
Mayonnaise

Blend together the carrots, celery, pineapple, and pecans. Toss with a small amount of mayonnaise and serve. YIELD: *8 servings*

SWEET SALADS

Before the popularity of gelatin, sweet salads consisted of fruit salad made from apples, raisins, nuts, and other fruits in season at the time. The fruits were generally tossed with mayonnaise.

Belle Ledford offers a more sophisticated version of the basic fruit salad:

FRUIT SALAD

1 cup sour cream
1 cup mandarin orange slices, drained
1 cup crushed or chunk pineapple,

drained
1 cup coconut
1 cup marshmallows

Mix together all the ingredients. Let stand 24 hours before serving. YIELD: *8 servings*

With the arrival of gelatin came a whole new series of congealed salads like those printed below, but the Southern cook still seems to prefer keeping salad dishes simple but tasteful.

CRANBERRY SALAD WITH COTTAGE CHEESE

BELLE LEDFORD

1 package orange gelatin
1 cup boiling water
1 can cranberries

4 ounces cottage cheese
½ cup mayonnaise
½ cup chopped nuts

Dissolve gelatin in boiling water and set in refrigerator. Once cooled and starting to thicken, mix in other ingredients. Let congeal well before serving. YIELD: *8 servings*

RHUBARB AND STRAWBERRY SALAD

BELLE LEDFORD

1 large package strawberry gelatin

2 cups hot cooked rhubarb

2 cups sliced strawberries

Dissolve gelatin in cooked rhubarb. Let cool, then add sliced strawberries.

CUCUMBER AND PINEAPPLE ASPIC

3 lemons

4 cups cold water

1 can diced pineapple (about 2 cups),
    drained but juice reserved

2 cups peeled and diced tender cucumbers

1 package plain gelatin

2 cups hot water

Green food coloring

Lettuce

Mayonnaise

Juice lemons and add to cold water. Put pineapple and cucumbers into water. Use pineapple juice to sweeten to desired taste. Dissolve gelatin in hot water and add to mixture. Drop in enough green food coloring to make a delicate green. Turn into mold to jell. Serve on lettuce with mayonnaise.

LAYERED CHEESE AND APPLE SALAD

ARIZONA DICKERSON

1 package lemon gelatin

2 cups boiling water

1 tablespoon lemon juice

1 teaspoon salt

1 red apple, cut into ¼-inch dices

1 teaspoon sugar

3 ounces cream cheese, softened

½ cup walnut meats, broken

Lettuce

Mayonnaise

Dissolve the gelatin in boiling water. Add 1 tablespoon lemon juice, and the salt. Chill.

Combine apple, sugar, and remaining lemon juice. When gelatin is slightly thickened, fold diced apple into half of gelatin mixture. Turn into mold. Chill until firm.

Beat remaining gelatin with rotary egg beater until consistency of whipped cream. Fold in cheese and nuts. Pour over already firm layer. Chill until firm. Serve in squares on crisp lettuce. Garnish with mayonnaise. YIELD: *8 servings*

7

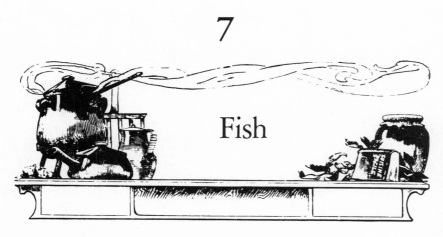

Fish

"They was plenty of fish in the river."

MINYARD CONNER: "One time I was camping in the mountains, and was starving to death! We didn't have nothing to eat but fish. I had my frying pan frying a fish and had one side cooked. I turned it over on the other side to cook, and reached in that pan and pulled that side off and ate, and left the side that was cooking in the pan. I pulled the bones out and ate the other side of that fish when it got done. I was that hungry! Couldn't wait!"

For people who enjoy camping, hunting, and fishing, it is a customary practice to cook fish at the campsite or at least attempt it, as Buck Carver tells us:

"When you go fishing and don't take anything to eat and you're depending on catching fish, I bet you're going to learn how to catch them darn things. Most of the time, when we went camping, we would take meat to fry, to make grease so the fish wouldn't stick to the pan. Most of the time we had a few fish to eat, but sometimes we wouldn't have so many. We always managed to make out with whatever we had, though."

Leonard Jones remembers: "I've camped out many a night. A whole bunch of us used to go together to Fontana [North Carolina]. We'd take a bunch of stuff and cook it. The camping was worth more than the fishing, almost."

Trout is the favorite fish in this area as told to us by many of our contacts, like Minyard Conner, who said, "I think speckled trout is the best eating fish I've had." Bream, catfish,

91

Minyard Conner

Leonard Jones

bass, perch, and pike also rank high on the list as "good eating" fish in this area of the South.

"Stocked" fish, however, are not too popular here. Lawton Brooks echoed what several of our contacts had to say about stocked fish:

> I don't eat them stocked fish. I just don't like [those that have been fed in the hatchery]. I like fish that's never had nothing to eat except just what fell in the creek. Then you got something! You can tell a difference in a fish that ain't never been hatchery fed and the stocked fish any time.

PREPARING FISH FOR COOKING

The technique used to clean fish depends upon the kind of fish it is. Several people shared their techniques with us.

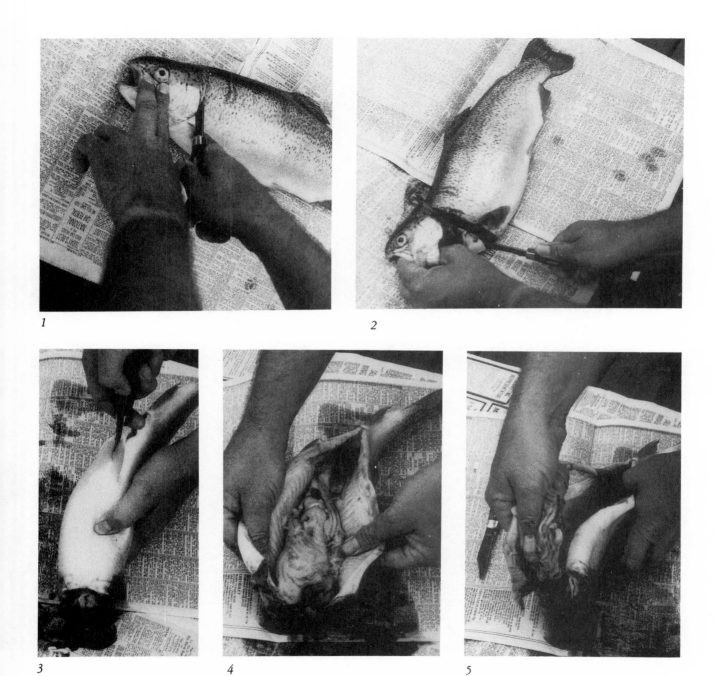

After washing the fish, lay it on a clean work surface—newspapers are good. Insert knife behind the gill and start cutting head off (1). Pull on head by inserting fingers through mouth (2). Holding fish, belly side up, cut forward from the anal fin (3) and pull apart, exposing the entrails (4) and begin pulling them out (5).

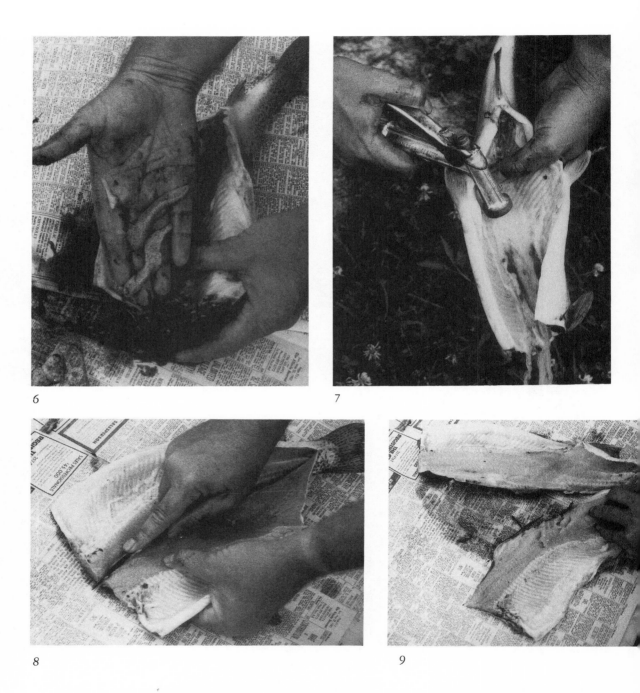

6

7

8

9

Fish eggs come out with the entrails (6). Wash out the inside using pressure from fingers to scrape out the slimy remains (7). The pressure from a water hose is a good aid for doing this step. Slice through the middle of the two sections (8) until you have sliced completely through it to the caudal (tail) fin (9). Then cut one portion off where it is connected at the tail fin.

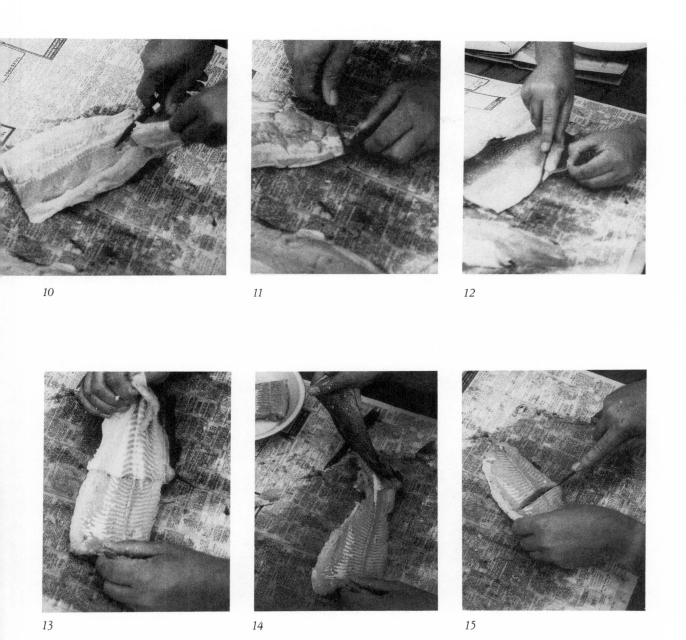

Cut away the backbone (10). Cut off the tail fin and other fins (11-12). To skin the fish portions, pull up skin on one end, being careful not to pull meat with the skin (13-14).
Slice into fillet pieces (15) and you are ready to cook them

CATFISH

LEONARD JONES: "You have to skin a catfish. It ain't got no scales on it. Cut it around the neck, split it down the back and stomach, and take a pair of pliers and pull that skin off. You can skin'em just about as quick as you can scrape'em. If I catch a great big fish of any kind, I skin it. Small ones, I don't."

WILLIE UNDERWOOD: "I clean big catfish by cutting around the head, and then pulling the skin off with a pair of pliers. Small catfish clean pretty easy. Just pour boiling water over them and the skin will turn loose. Then pull it off with pliers."

TROUT AND BREAM

BUCK CARVER: "The rainbow and the brown trout and bream have scales and you have to scrape them. Though the speckled trout has scales, they're so fine you needn't try to scale him. All you do is rub that slime off with some sand." (Blanche Harkins takes the slime off with a scrub pad or a dishrag or luffa-gourd.)

PERCH

BLANCHE HARKINS: "You skin perch. They have scales, but you just cut their heads off and get them started. The skin will just come off to the tail. You cook them the way you do trout. They're really good fresh fish."

PIKE

LAWTON BROOKS: "A pike's bones lays exactly like a trout's. You fix them the same way, only you skin a pike. Generally when you catch a pike, he's a pretty good size, and you just cut around [his neck] and split him down the back. Then take your pliers and you can just pull that skin right off there."

COOKING FISH

There are several methods for cooking fish in this area. The South, being well known for "Southern fried foods," is proud to include fried fish as a Southern specialty and probably a favorite with most people in the area. Willie Underwood told us that almost all the fish "we catch around here can be fried." Other means are used too, however:

LEONARD JONES: "After I take their innards out and cut their heads and fins off, I salt the fish. Then I roll them good with cracker crumbs or cornmeal. I think cornmeal makes a better flavor. Then I put them in the shortening to fry. It's important to have your shortening pretty hot. Then turn them over and let them brown on the other side. I always turn my heat down and cook 'em slow so they get really cooked all the way through. One thing I don't do is to put a top on the skillet. The reason is because it makes the cornmeal soft and easy to come off. Leave the skillet open after you've turned your heat down. I cook stocked fish about twenty-five to thirty minutes, because they're not usually tough or hard to cook. If a fish is real wide, I slice it in two down the back. If you like crisp fish, just slice 'em and cook them quickly." (Blanche Harkins uses her black frying pan and Crisco, and browns the fish rolled in cornmeal ten minutes on a side over moderate heat.)

MELVIN TAYLOR: "Best way to cook fish is to roll them in cornmeal and put them in a good hot pan of grease. Sometimes fry some good salt meat [pork fatback] and cook 'em in that grease."

MINYARD CONNER: "There are a lot of ways you can cook trout—bake 'em, fry 'em, or stew 'em. Now these stockers [stocked fish]—I'd stew 'em and take the bones out and make fish patties out of them because their meat's too tender to hold together to fry." Minyard's wife, Lessie, elaborated: "Take a mess of fish—ten trout or stockers—and boil them with a little grease and salt. When they are real tender, let them cool. Remove bones. Save a little of the juice in which the fish were boiled and add to a cup of flour. Mix in fish, two eggs, and one onion, chopped fine. Make mixture into patties and fry in hot grease until brown on both sides.

"To bake fish, you coat them with a little grease and lemon juice. Heat your oven to about 350 and cook 'em about thirty minutes.

"And I've eat fish eggs. I've caught a lot of big fish with big rolls of eggs under them. Boy, I like them! That's caviar. That's good. That's extra good! Talk about burning you in grease! They'll pop and bust when you're frying them, and they'll burn you, buddy!

"I have never ate the liver out of a fish. I bet that would be really good, too."

SALMON CROQUETTES

MARY ELLEN MEANS

2 eggs	*¼ cup cornmeal*
¼ teaspoon baking powder	*8 oz. can salmon (undrained)*
¼ cup flour	

Mix ingredients thoroughly and drop from teaspoons into hot fat to fry. Watch closely and turn to brown other side. Fry about 2 to 3 minutes on each side. YIELD: *8-12 croquettes*

PRESERVING FISH

Minyard Conner tells about preserving fish in the old days:

Well, I was raised with the Indians. They wouldn't do like the white man does—you know, catch too many of anything and have to throw them away. They'd just catch what they could eat, and that's all they took. If they could eat ten, then that's all they took. They didn't usually try to preserve them.

They was plenty of fish in the river. And it's always been a puzzle to me—we lived on the Oconoluftee River [in Cherokee]. They was over there on the other prong, and where they lived was the Indian territory. When I was a boy, there was what I called "chubs." That was a fish that was five or six inches long. When you'd catch one, he'd say, "Rooork, rooork," and start making a fuss. There was plenty of chubs in both forks of that river, but later on you could hardly catch them in the area where we'd lived, and there was still plenty in that part of the river that was Indian territory. (I guess they were more careful not to catch too many of them at one time, and the white man would get all he could catch, whether he was going to eat them or not. Just fished them all out.)

Well, the Indians would catch them chubs and fry 'em good and brown—just as hard as they could fry 'em—and put 'em in flour sacks and fill up those flour sacks. Just cook them in a frying pan right there by the river where they'd caught them, and they said those would last them two or three weeks. Now that's the only way they preserved them. They'd cook every bit of the grease out of the pan, and get 'em just as brown as they could get 'em, and they was good, too! You didn't have to worry about the bones because they were all cooked up. They'd just cut the heads off and pull out the backbones and ribs. The little ones that were left would just break up. They wouldn't hurt you to swallow.

JAKE WALDROOP: "[Before we had a freezer,] we had some cool springs, and we would put any fish we weren't going to cook right then in a bucket or half gallon jars and stand them under those springs where the cold water would run over them. We could keep them for four or five days or more."

BLANCHE HARKINS: "To prepare fish for freezing, you first clean the fish and cut out their insides and wash them. Don't salt them before you put them in the freezer. Generally, I put enough in one plastic bag—and some people use half-gallon cardboard milk cartons—for one meal. Then I cover them with clear water and seal them up. Being packed in water keeps them from being freezer burned. When I'm ready to cook them, I thaw them in cold running water. I wouldn't think about thawing them in hot water because they would tear all to pieces, they're so tender."

8

Poultry and Wild Game Birds

"Now I like the old-fashioned way of cooking wild turkey."

CHICKEN

Most of the people we talked to about poultry had raised and killed their own chickens for eating. None of them enjoyed the task of "dressing" them—the entire process from killing the chickens to cutting them up—but most of them agreed that poultry can add variety to the menu and is a delightful and economical alternative to beef and pork.

In this section we show a basic method that can be used to dress most birds, and we present a variety of cooking methods. The South is famous for its fried chicken, but we found that the other chicken dishes such as dumplings, pies, and simply roasting or stewing the meat are enjoyed almost as much.

LINDA GARLAND-PAGE: "On a cool foggy July morning my mother called to tell me she and my father were getting ready to kill chickens. I told her to get started and I would be there soon. I ate a quick bite of breakfast, knowing that the episode ahead could do strange things to one with an empty stomach, especially at seven o'clock in the morning.

"When I arrived at my parents' home, they had already killed ten of the fifteen chickens and were busily at work skinning them. I watched them kill the remaining five, as my two sons, Seth and Nolan, who are always entertained by unusual events, looked on.

Marinda Brown comments on killing chickens:

In, I guess, the early forties, we grew chickens (fryers) and furnished some of the summer camps. We furnished the Athens Y camp one time and the boys' camps. Then another time we furnished the girls' camp and some of the hotels around. We dressed sometimes a hundred at a time and took to those camps.

My husband would kill them. We'd tie them up on a line, and he'd go along and cut the jugular vein and we'd let them hang till they dripped blood. That's the way they were killed. We'd hire some of the women in the community to come in on certain days and help dress those chickens. We'd scald them. We had a big old washpot out there to scald the chickens in; then we'd pull the feathers off and dress them out in the house. We did that for several summers. Sometimes we'd let people come in and dress their own chickens if they had a bunch they wanted to clean.

And then later we had this little building out here with running water in it, and we got a chicken picker to pick the feathers off. It was kind of a barrel-like thing, and it had little rubber things [suctions] on it that stuck up so far. And it would turn, and as it turned those suctions would pull the feathers off. It worked good. It would clean the feathers off. You had to be mighty careful and not get your scalding water too hot or it would bring the skin, too, but if you got them scalded just right it would take every feather off. 'Course there were lots of pin feathers that had to be picked off by hand.

Wringing chicken's neck

Chopping chicken's neck for bleeding

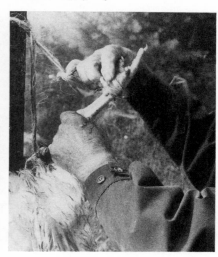
Using a piece of twine, O.S. hangs the chicken up by its feet.

Start by cutting the skin away where the feet and legs connect, pulling the skin away and down the body of the chicken (1), using a knife to cut it away from the joints of the chicken's body where it is connected (2), and cutting it off at the neck (3).

When the skinning is completed cut through the joint where the legs and feet connect (4), leaving the feet to throw into a bucket of feet, feathers, heads, and entrails (5).

4   5

"Now boys, you look at this. Youns are going to be grown sometime and have a family and have to keep them something to eat."

Olene takes the chicken out of the boiling water to hang up for picking the feathers off. After picking off the feathers there remain small ones which are called pin feathers, that have to be singed off by holding them over a flame.

My family likes fried chicken mighty good. That's something I guess we've eaten more of than any other one kind of meat. Since we killed chickens, you know, we could have all we wanted to eat any time we wanted them. I guess we ate more fried chicken and gravy on mashed potatoes or rice than anything. That was about their most favorite.

Blanche Harkins adds: "We used to raise our chickens and we'd kill them, scald them, and dress them. We singed the hair off of them using paper. You have to use a paper bag; if you use paper with dark ink it will smoke and darken the chicken. A paper bag won't do that. Then rinse the chicken good and dress it.

The following method is what most of our contacts call the "old-timey way" of cutting up a chicken. By cutting one using these instructions, there will be four separate pieces of breast: the pulleybone [wishbone], center breast, and two side breasts. For a family that loves white meat, this helps to stretch the supply. Mary Ellen Means describes how to use this method:

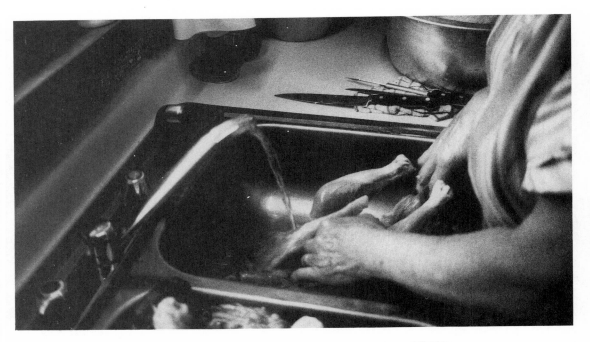

Wash the chickens well and they're ready to start cutting up. Using a sharp knife, cut through skin of abdomen along a straight line from end of breastbone to within ½" of vent. Keep vent small. Insert forefinger into opening made, and circle finger around intestine leading to vent. Lift intestine up, then cut skin about ¾" around and completely encircling vent. Holding carcass with one hand, insert other hand through opening and locate gizzard near center of cavity. Grasp gizzard and draw entrails out of cavity. "You have to soak the cut-up chickens in salt water to draw the rest of the blood out of them. I always soak mine about an hour."

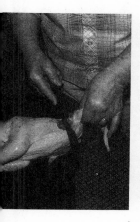  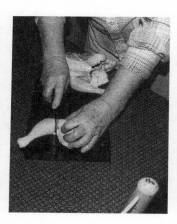 

1   2   3   4

Pull back wing, cutting away from the thigh toward yourself with a sharp knife, remove wing (1). Repeat with other side. Turn chicken on its back and, grasping drumstick, cut the thigh off at joint (2). Thigh and drumstick will be cut off together. To separate, sever at joint (3). With chicken breast side up, grasp at wing end and cut straight down about one-third of the way down the body from the wing end (4). The incision would be approximately one-inch deep. Then cut back until you meet your hand grasping the end. Pull back pulleybone ("wishbone"). and break off at joint (5). Still holding to wing end, cut straight back toward your hand under the cartilage of the breastbone until you reach two joints left from the wings (6). Pull this center breast up and break it off at these joints (7). Turn chicken over. Cut under two knuckles exposed at the neck and down neck to ribs on back of chicken (8). Turn bird back over, and split the exposed cartilage (left over from center breast). down the center (9). Turn over again, grasp knuckles one at a time and pull toward the tail of the chicken (10). This will remove each side breast. Back, ribs and neck remain. Cut at the back of the ribs to make two pieces: neck and ribs; and back (11).

5   6   7   8

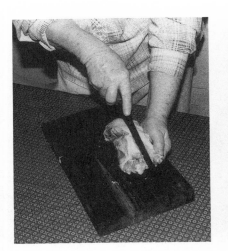
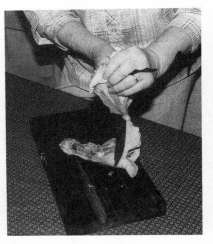

9   10   11

During our visit with Ione Dickerson, she was cooking fried chicken in an iron skillet on her wood stove. We forgot about it while we were talking and it almost burned. She pulled it away from the heat, placed a stick of wood under one side of the pan, arranging the chicken on the raised side so that the grease would drain off. She said disgustedly "Well, pot can't call the kettle black for they're both black!"

AUNT ADDIE NORTON: "Chicken is good fried in a lot of ways. If you buy the chicken at the store already cut and fixed, you thaw it out, naturally. If it's never been frozen I always just salt mine good. Not too much, just enough to make it salty like. Roll it in flour. I use flour or meal. I love my chicken fixed in meal a lot of times instead of flour. Dampen your chicken good before you roll it in meal or flour or whatever you're rolling it in. You got to get it damp so it [the meal or flour] will stick to it, you know. Dampen it with water, milk, anything you want to put in it. Make a paste if you want to fix it that way. A lot of folks do it that way. Just like making up a batter and rolling your chicken in that. Then you use salt and pepper. I just guess at it and put whatever I think that it needs. Then you put it in your grease to fry or you can fry it in the oven. Put in just a little bit of grease and put it in and bake it. 'Course I use Crisco lard. It won't soak into it. I never was very good about frying chicken, I didn't think. Most people said I always had good chicken, though."

BLANCHE HARKINS: "We had a black thick frying pan. Some people called them skillets but they're frying pans. Just put your grease in there. I use to use just pure lard. We'd cut up the chicken, roll it in flour and have your grease hot enough to fry it when you put it in. Let that side brown, turn it over, and brown it. I put a lid on mine. I don't just fry it open. It takes about an hour to fry chicken and not fry it too fast. It won't be tender if you brown them too fast."

EXIE DILLS: "Roll it in meal and gosh it is good! It don't take as much grease to fry it thataway as it does flour. [Gladys Nichols remembers using meal made by grinding up chestnuts.] Pepper it just like you do your flour and roll your pieces in it and lay it in your hot grease. It's good. Then make your gravy in there. Gee, that makes good chicken gravy, I think. Not ever'one has a taste like someone else. I like that."

MARY ELLEN MEANS: "Salt and pepper the chicken; roll in flour. Fry in lard with three tablespoons of butter added to make the chicken brown well. Brown both sides, cover with a tight lid and cook on *low* temperature for thirty minutes. Check in ten minutes to see that it's not burning. After thirty minutes, take the lid off and remove top pieces that have not been submerged in grease. Turn heat up to medium and fry until remaining pieces get crispy. Take out and drain on paper towel and serve."

FRIED CHICKEN

For each pound of chicken mix together the following flour mixture to dip or shake chicken in:

¼ cup flour
1 teaspoon paprika

½ teaspoon salt
¼ teaspoon pepper

Put the flour mixture in a pie plate to roll chicken pieces in or in a paper bag to drop chicken in and shake until coated. Leftover flour can be saved for gravy. Drop chicken pieces into a hot skillet with a ¼-inch layer of lard, shortening, or oil. Turn pieces to brown evenly. Once the pieces are lightly browned, cover, then reduce heat and fry slowly until tender—30 to 45 minutes, depending on size of chicken pieces. Turn often but carefully, being careful not to pierce the chicken with the fork.

BROILED CHICKEN

Lay split bird, skin side down on a broiler rack or in a shallow pan. Brush well with melted butter or other fat. Place under preheated broiler. Broil slowly, regulating the heat or changing the rack position so chicken just begins to color lightly after cooking for 10 to 12 minutes. Turn, then brush with melted butter about every 10 minutes as browning increases. Broil until tender and evenly browned, 30 to 40 minutes according to size. Season to taste.

STEWED CHICKEN

Cover chicken in a pot with water and bring to a boil; lower heat and let cook until tender. Pull the meat off the bone, putting the meat back into the broth. Stewed chicken may be eaten plain; poured over mashed potatoes or dressing; or may be used for making dumplings.

BARBECUED CHICKEN

Cut chicken in half sections or into serving pieces. Place aluminum foil in a shallow pan; place chicken on foil and pour your favorite barbecue sauce over it (try the recipes in our Sauces and Gravies section). Add salt and pepper to taste. Pull aluminum foil over chicken, making sure it is covered tightly and there are no holes for juice to boil out. Bake in 325 to 350°F oven until chicken is tender.

OLD-FASHIONED CHICKEN PIE

OLENE GARLAND

3 cups chicken broth
2 tablespoons flour
1 fryer, boiled and boned

2 hard-boiled eggs, chopped
Salt and pepper to taste
Biscuit dough

Thicken broth with flour. Add chicken, chopped eggs, and salt and pepper. Pour into a large casserole dish. Make up a recipe for biscuits; roll and cut out thin with a biscuit cutter or a glass. Place the biscuits on top of the chicken. Bake 15 to 20 minutes in a 400°F oven.

VARIATION: Leftover vegetables may be added to the broth mixture. Peas and carrots are used by most cooks.

CHICKEN AND DUMPLINGS

ARIZONA DICKERSON

1 chicken
¼ cup rendered chicken fat

3 to 6 tablespoons flour
Salt and pepper to taste

Stew the chicken in water to cover, then remove from the broth; cut it up. Mix other ingredients together and pour into 3 or 4 cups of the broth, stirring constantly until it thickens slightly.

¾ cup sifted flour
2½ teaspoons baking powder
½ teaspoon salt

1 egg
⅓ cup milk

To make the dumplings, mix dry ingredients. Add egg and milk and beat. Drop by small spoonfuls into the boiling chicken gravy. Cover pot tightly and cook 15 minutes. Do not remove the lid while dumplings are cooking. The steam is necessary for them to be light. To serve, spoon out dumplings and gravy together into dish.

ROASTING POULTRY

Poultry should be roasted by dry heat in a slow to moderate oven. The larger the bird, the lower the temperature. Methods for roasting the birds vary as illustrated below. Here are general instructions for roasting time. Remember to adjust time or temperature according to size of bird.

CHICKEN: 300°–325°F oven, 25–30 minutes per pound
TURKEY: 275°–325°F oven, 15–25 minutes per pound
GOOSE: 275°–325°F oven, 20–25 minutes per pound
DUCK: 325°F oven, 25–30 minutes per pound

ROAST CHICKEN OR TURKEY

Wash the bird, rinse, dry well, and stand upright to drain. Rub cavity of bird with salt (about ⅛ teaspoon to each pound) or fill with stuffing. Brush skin all over with melted fat. Place bird, breast side up, on a wire rack in an uncovered roaster. Do not add water or other liquid, and do not pierce the bird with a fork during cooking period. To test for doneness, grasp the ends of a leg bone and wing; if the joints move easily, the ligaments are tender, which means the bird is probably ready to serve. Make gravy from drippings.

ROAST DUCK

Wash the duck, rinse, and dry thoroughly. Either salt the cavity or fill with stuffing. Do not brush with oil. Place, breast side up, on a rack in an uncovered roaster. Do not pierce through the skin of the duck before or during cooking. Test for doneness just as you would for chicken and turkey. Skin should also be crisp. If the duck is very fat, dip some of the fat from the pan during roasting. Serve with gravy made from drippings or with desired glaze.

ROAST GOOSE

Follow the same directions given for the duck except, after stuffing the goose, prick with a fork through fat layers, over back, around tail, and into body around wings and legs before cooking. This helps draw out fat.

GAME BIRDS

ROAST WILD DUCK

1 wild duck
Stuffing of choice

⅔ cup undiluted canned consommé

Prepare the bird for cooking. Fill with preferred stuffing and place on a wire rack in covered roaster. Pour consommé in bottom, cover, and bake in a slow (250°F) oven for 2½ hours, or until tender.

WILD TURKEY

Wild turkey is prepared much like the domesticated turkey. After cleaning, some people cut off the legs and breast (saving them for frying like chicken) and stewing the rest. Others rub the outside with lard, sprinkle it with 2 tablespoons of salt and 1 teaspoon of pepper, replace the liver and gizzard, and bake it for about 3 hours on low heat. After roasting, 2 cups of the resulting liquid are sometimes mixed in a saucepan with 2 tablespoons flour and ¼ cup water and heated to make gravy. Chopped liver and gizzard can be added.

Lon Reid's family used to cut off the feathered wings, spread them out and dry them in front of the fire. When stiff, they were used as fans for the fire.

Gladys Nichols adds: "Now I like the old-fashioned way of cooking wild turkey. And that's to cut it up, parboil it real good, and get it good and done and take it out and put it in an oven and bake it just a little. Or leave it in the pot and make gravy with it, either one. I like them that way better than I do the way they bake them now."

Lizzie Moore continues, "You prepare it just like a tame turkey. I prefer taking the broth out and making my dressing out of biscuit and corn bread. I bake my corn bread, and I bake my biscuit and make as much dressing as I want to. Now generally I think that a wild turkey is not as fat as a tame turkey, and you don't have as rich a broth. But I always put some butter in my broth when I'm making dressing. Then, of course, you've got to put salt, pepper, and sage in. Now some people like the dressing put in the turkey, but I put mine in an extra pan and have the dressing to itself. Then I cut it and set it on the table. And we used to take a wild turkey and slice the meat off its breast in big pieces, roll it in flour and fry it. Now that's delicious. Next time you have a turkey you slice some off and try it. It'll fry just as brown like chicken, but it tastes different."

ROAST QUAIL OR PARTRIDGE

1 quail or partridge　　　　　　　　*½ cup water*
Butter　　　　　　　　　　　　　　*Salt and pepper to taste*

Prepare the bird for roasting. Spread with butter, lay breast side up in an uncovered roasting pan, moisten with ½ cup water; season with salt and pepper. Roast in hot (450°F) oven for 5 minutes, then reduce the heat to 350°F and roast for 20 to 30 minutes longer. Baste frequently. Serve with gravy.

ROAST PHEASANT

1 pheasant (2½ to 3 pounds)　　　　　*Oil*
Stuffing of choice

Prepare the bird for roasting. Fill with preferred stuffing. Place on a wire rack in a covered roaster. Bake, uncovered, in a hot (400°F) oven for 20 minutes. Baste breast generously with oil; cover and bake at 250°F for 2 hours longer, or until tender.

Lizzie Moore claims, "The pheasant breast is the best eating there is."

BROILED QUAIL

Quail　　　　　　　　　　　　　　*Melted butter or margarine*

Prepare the quail and split down the back. Brush each one with melted butter. Place, breast side down, on rack in broiler, broiling 6 to 8 minutes on each side. Brush once again with melted butter. Serve with juice from broiler pan.

FRIED QUAIL

2 quail
2 tablespoons flour
1 teaspoon salt

⅛ teaspoon pepper
2 tablespoons fat or oil
¾ cup light cream

Prepare the quail for cooking and split down the back. Mix the flour, salt, and pepper and roll the quail in the mixture. Brown in hot fat in a covered skillet. Add cream; cover and cook over low heat 20 to 25 minutes longer, or until tender. Make gravy from leftover fat.

PIGEON

BESSIE UNDERWOOD: "We used to cook pigeons. When we was children, we lived on a farm where they was lots of pigeons and you know, they multiply real fast. And they would kill maybe, oh seven, eight, or ten, and we would just fry them."

STUFFING OR "DRESSING"

In this area of the country, people refer to stuffing as "dressing." Most of them prefer cooking the dressing for a turkey and chicken in a pan separately rather than stuffing it inside the bird. They claim that the dressing takes away too much of the moisture and flavor from the flesh of the chicken. When cooking game birds, they do like to stuff the bird, however, in order to absorb some of the wild taste from the bird.

DRESSING

BELLE LEDFORD

2 cups crumbled corn bread
½ cup butter, melted
⅓ cup onion, finely diced
⅛ teaspoon pepper
1½ cups fine dry bread crumbs

3½ to 4 cups stock
3 eggs, slightly beaten
1 teaspoon salt
1 to 2 stalks chopped celery (optional)

Crumble the bread in a large bowl. Melt butter and sauté onion and pepper in it. Add to the crumbled bread. Stir in beaten eggs and add remaining ingredients. Bake in a well-greased shallow pan in a 400°F oven for 15 to 20 minutes.

WILD RICE STUFFING

This stuffing is great for wild game birds.

½ cup raw wild rice
Giblets
1 small onion, peeled
1 tablespoon butter, margarine, or oil

¼ pound sausage meat
1 teaspoon salt
½ teaspoon sage

Place rice in top of a double boiler, cover with water, and soak overnight. Drain, cover, and cook over boiling water for 10 minutes. Clean and wash giblets, then chop with onion into very small pieces. Melt the butter in a skillet and sauté giblets, onion, and sausage for 10 minutes. Add rice, salt, and sage and cook 2 minutes longer. This recipe will stuff a 1½-pound bird.

POULTRY STUFFING

OLENE GARLAND

4 cups firmly packed broken-up stale
    bread
2 teaspoons salt
½ teaspoon pepper
1 egg, slightly beaten

½ teaspoon poultry seasoning
1 tablespoon minced onion
2 tablespoons chicken fat or other fat
⅓ cup hot giblet stock or hot water
Giblets (optional)

Mix all the ingredients except the giblets in a large bowl, blending well with a fork. Stew giblets in salted water until tender. Drain and chop into small pieces. Add to the bread mixture. This recipe is sufficient for a large chicken or small turkey.

CORN BREAD DRESSING

BELLE LEDFORD

3½ cups corn bread crumbs
3½ cups crumbled biscuits
¼ cup butter
3 tablespoons minced onion
1 cup chopped celery
2 teaspoons salt
½ teaspoon pepper

½ teaspoon savory
2 to 3 teaspoons sage
1 egg, slightly beaten
½ cup milk
2 cups hot chicken broth, or more if
    needed

Mix bread and biscuits in a large pan or bowl. Melt butter and lightly sauté onion and celery. Add to crumb mixture; add remaining ingredients and mix well. Bake in well-greased shallow pans in a 400°F oven for 15 to 25 minutes.

9

Pork

*"We used to kill five or six big hogs every
winter."*

For most mountain folk, pork is an essential part of the overall diet, and the popularity of traditional delicacies such as souse meat, scrapple, hog's head stew, and cracklins remains today. Since the hog has never been extremely difficult to raise, it is still found on many farms. Old- and new-timers alike adamantly stand by their belief that virtually no part of the hog should be thrown away. This is evidenced by the recipes that follow, which include such things as the head, tongue, brain, snout (or "rooter"), ears, liver, heart, lungs (or "lights"), skin, intestines, feet, and even the tail. Use of the entire hog is clearly reminiscent of the pioneer traditions of conservation and utility as every part found a creative and practical use.

Billy Long remembered when he and his father raised hogs in the mountains.

When I was growing up and when we was raising our family, we had plenty of scraps. Young'uns are all the time wasting stuff, you know. I can feed a good hog on scraps; I mean feed him *good* on things like potato peelings.

My daddy also had hogs out in the mountains all the time, and I had [them, too] for several years after he died. We'd just turn them out to feed themselves in the woods and go to them all along through the year to look after them. We had them marked, and we knew our mark, too. We had it registered. It was a "over half crop" in the right ear and "split and under bit" in the left. An over half crop was a cut right straight down about halfway on the hog's ear—about two inches—from the end. And for the under bit, we'd just double the ear up and take out a nick—what we called a small fork. Our mark was always pretty hard [to mistake] to me, and it was kind of unusual.

We used to kill five or six big hogs every winter. Now I don't kill one, let alone five. We had a pretty good-sized smokehouse. Daddy just made him a bench and shelves to put the meat on. He'd sprinkle salt on the hams and hang them up; and in the spring of the year, he'd take them down and take the salt off of them. A lot of people wanted to kill hogs by the signs, but my daddy said when a hog was fat and on the land, he was good any time you killed him.

I never was much of a meat eater, but Daddy didn't think you had much if you didn't have meat on the table. I remember he'd tell about eating dinner one time with somebody. When they started eating, the fellow he eat with said, "We're out of meat here. It seems like when you're out of meat, you're just about out of everything." Another old fellow there said, "Yeah, and it's just about that way, too." I never did care that much for it, but when people ate a lot of pork they seemed to live longer than they do now.

PORK RECIPES

Esco Pitts explains how the various parts of the hog were used in his family:

We always fattened our hogs in a floored pen and topped them off on corn. Of course, they could get fat in the mountains eating chestnuts, but the meat from chestnuts would be streaked and flabby. We didn't like it. So we would always catch our hogs and bring them in and pen them and top them off on corn. That'd make the meat solid and firm and produced more gravy, and we liked gravy. I was raised on meat and gravy and sorghum syrup and corn bread.

Then when we killed a hog in the fall, we would dress it and take the entrails out; and my daddy would slice it up into middlings and hams and shoulders, and salt it away in the smokehouse. My mother was a conservative person, and she didn't waste anything. So she would clean the head good—take the eyes out—and put that in a pot and cook it until all the meat come off the bone. She made pressed meat out of that. That was something good to eat. And when my mother would fix a mess of meat to cook, she would peel off the skin, I guess. I have seen her put a bunch of skins in the skillet and fry them good and crisp, and us children would just eat them to beat the band.

And I like hogs' feet. We would take the hoofs off and clean the feet good and cook them. There was more bones in a hog's feet than there is in all the rest of the hog, but it's awful good meat. You can't get much out of it, but it has such a good flavor. You can suck the bone and get what meat you want.

My mother would also take a hog's entrails and split them open. She had a spout off the ground where the water was running down to the branch, and she would take them entrails and wash them off good and clean, put them in the pot, and boil them down to what she called chitlins. And then she would season bread with cracklins and make shortnin bread. You take a pone of cracklin bread warm out of the oven and a glass of sweet milk or buttermilk, and you had a meal that was fit for a king.

For every part of the hog, there are as many favorite recipes as there are cooks. We begin our pork cooking section with the preparation of less well-known pork dishes and conclude with the more conventional ones.

THE HEAD

LETTIE CHASTAIN: "Hog's head is good. You clean the head, boil it, and get the good, lean meat off it. Mother used to make pressed meat out of hog's head and that used to be the best stuff."

Hog's head is also called "souse," "souse meat," "head cheese," or "pressed hog's head." Prepare the raw hog's head as follows: Trim, scrape, or singe off any hairs or bristles that are left. If you intend to use the ears, brains, snout, tongue, or jowls for any purpose other than souse, remove them and set them aside to soak. Otherwise leave them on the head to be ground up. Note that the ears are gristly and when ground up in the souse, they leave white flukes of gristle in the meat. This is not harmful, but some find it unattractive.

Cut out the eyes. The bulk of the head is now halved or quartered with an axe, or left whole—depending on the size of your pot—and while still fresh it is put in a pot of fresh water, usually to soak overnight. This soaking removes the remaining blood from the meat.

After soaking, rinse the head until the rinse water runs clear. Then put it in a pot of clean, salty water and cook it slowly until it is good and tender, and the meat begins to fall off the bones. Then remove all meat from the bones and run through a food chopper. Seasoning depends on your own taste. Some use, per head, 1 tablespoon sage, ½ teaspoon ground red pepper, and salt and black pepper to taste. Others use 1 onion, 1 pod of strong red pepper chopped fine, and 1 teaspoon salt.

Beulah Perry uses a little red and black pepper, an onion, a little cornmeal, sage, and garlic to taste. Evie Carpenter adds a little vinegar, along with sage, black pepper, and onion.

The meat and seasoning are thoroughly mixed and then put into capped jars, a mold, or onto a plate covered with a clean white cloth. Then, if it is not to be eaten immediately, it is put into the smokehouse, where the winter weather will keep it fresh. It can be eaten cold or hot.

Another method is to proceed as before through the seasoning step, then put the mixture in a skillet; place the skillet on the back of the wood stove until the grease is runny. Remove from the fire, put a plate on top of the meat and apply pressure to remove grease. Repeat until all the grease is poured off. Remove the plate, put the meat on a clean plate, and keep in a cold place. Slice as needed.

SOUSE MEAT

DAISY JUSTUS

1 hog's head	2½ teaspoons allspice
Salt	3 teaspoons cloves
4 teaspoons pepper	Vinegar (optional)
2 teaspoons red pepper	

Clean the hog's head by removing snout, eyes, ears, brains, and all skin. Trim off fat. Cut head in four pieces and soak in salt water (½ cup salt to 1 gallon cold water) for 3 hours to draw out blood. Drain off salt water and wash well in cold water. (Heart, tongue, and other meat trimmings may be cooked with head meat.) Cover meat with hot water and boil until all meat can be removed from the bones. Remove all meat from bones. Strain broth and measure. This will make about 6 pounds of meat. Add about 3 tablespoons salt, the other seasoning, 2 quarts broth in which meat is boiled. Mix thoroughly. Add a little vinegar, if desired. Cook mixture 15 or 20 minutes. Pour into a large square pan or a big stone crock. Cover with a clean cloth and weight down. Refrigerate and cut into slices as needed.

May be canned by putting into clean jars within 1 inch of top of jar. Seal and process in pressure cooker 1 hour 15 minutes at 10 pounds pressure.

MINCEMEAT

DAISY JUSTUS

1 hog's head	1 dozen oranges, peeled and seeded
4 cups dried apples	5 pounds sugar
1 pound raisins	1 to 2 quarts grape juice

Clean hog's head as for souse meat (see preceding recipe). Cook until tender, then strain off broth and remove bone. Put into a large pot. Cook dried apples until tender. Add to hog's meat, along with remaining ingredients. Cook as if making apple butter. Simmer and stir until thick enough to be used as pie filling, or eat as is with bread.

SCRAPPLE

Mrs. Mann Norton told us how to make scrapple: "Take the head and take the eyeballs out, and the ears. Then you got all the hairs off of it. You put it in a big pot and cooked it till the meat just turned loose of the main big bone.

"You lifted them bones out and laid your meat over in there and felt of it with your hands to see if they wasn't no bones in it. Then you strain your liquid through a strainer so the little bones would come out. Put your liquid back in a pot and put that mashed meat back in that liquid. Put your sage and pepper in there. Then you stir it till it got to boiling. Then you stick plain cornmeal in there till it's just plumb thick. Then you pour it up in a mold and cut it off and fry it and brown it. Tastes just like fish."

(*See also a recipe for hog's head stew in the chapter on soups and stews.*)

JOWLS

The jowls are fatty, so they are often removed rather than being combined with the souse meat. Some people salt them down and cure them just like hams or middling meat, then save them until warm weather to be boiled in with vegetables. Others grind them up with the sausage meat. Bill Lamb told us, "You fry it. Now you're talking about part of a hog that I love is the jowls. They ain't a better tasting bite of meat in a hog than the jowl is."

TONGUE

Clean by pouring boiling water over it and scraping it. Then boil until tender in a little salt water, with pepper added if you wish. Slice and serve.

BRAIN

Most of our contacts put the hog's brains in hot water to loosen the veil of skin covering them. Then they boil them in 1 cup water, adding salt and pepper to taste while stirring. When cooked, they are mashed with a potato masher and, usually, scrambled with eggs.

Others let the brains stand in cold water for 1 to 2 hours, then drain them and remove any unwanted fibers. The brains are then cooked, as above.

SNOUT

The snout is often cleaned and roasted.

Mann Norton said: "Lot of people throwed away that they called the rooter. Oh, I forbid that. I'd rather have that as any part of the hog. Oh, that's good eating."

LIVER

Most of our contacts used the liver for liver pudding or liver mush. They made it as follows:

1 hog's liver
½ to 1 cup sifted cornmeal to thicken
Salt to taste

½ teaspoon black pepper
2 tablespoons sage
Ground red pepper (optional)

Cut up the liver, wash it well, and remove the skin. Boil until tender in salted water. Remove and run through a colander until fine, or mash well.

Mix the meat with 1 cup of the broth it was cooked in. Bring to a boil slowly, stirring in sifted cornmeal until thick. Also stir in salt to taste, black pepper, sage, and a little red pepper if desired.

Pour into a mold and let sit until cold. Slice and eat. Some eat it as sandwich meat or sliced and fried in bacon fat. According to Lucy, "Liver mush serves as bread and meat for a meal."

HEART

None of our contacts used the heart by itself. Neither did any of them throw it away, though. Some cleaned it and canned it with backbones and ribs for use later in stews. Some boiled the heart, backbone, and lights—lungs—together for stew; and one boiled heart, tail, kidneys, and tongue together for stew.

LIGHTS OR LUNGS

Nowhere did we run into as much difference of opinion as with this item. One said, "It's very good—*very* good." Another said, "Lots of folks like the lights, but I never did."

Another comment was simply, "Feed them to the dogs!" We did get a few recipes: Boil them in just enough salted water to cover them after cleaning them well. Don't use too much water or it will steal some of their flavor. If there isn't any water left when they're done, it's better.

Cook them down to the consistency of a gravy, mash, and serve. They cannot be kept.

Another chopped up the lights with the liver and tongue. She added a chopped onion, red pepper, and salt and cooked until tender.

STOMACH, PAUNCH, OR PUNCH

Cut the stomach free of intestines, split, and wash out well. Scrape it down and put in salt water for 3 days. Then rinse, cut up, and cook like chitlins. Most of our contacts also removed the inside layer when cutting it up prior to frying.

INTESTINES (CHITTERLINGS OR CHITLINS)

Sections of the intestine are put in a jar of salt water and allowed to sit for 3 or 4 days. Then they are taken out, rinsed, washed, and rinsed again. In winter, they can be lightly salted, put up in jars, and kept for a few days before cooking. When cooking, cut up in small pieces and remove any unwanted layers of lining. Then boil in salt water with half a pod of pepper until tender. Dip in a batter of flour, water, and baking powder (and an egg, if desired) and fry; or roll in cornmeal and fry.

FEET

Rake hot coals out on the fireplace hearth. Put the feet on the hearth with the hooves against the coals. When very hot, the hooves can be sliced out of the meat easily, and the remainder of the hair scraped or singed off, and the meat scraped clean. Then put in a pot of salt water and cook; or roast. The feet can also be boiled in salty water until the meat slips off the hoofs. They can also be pickled.

Mann Norton said, "Doc Neville, now he always wanted the feet. I'd pack them in a shoebox just as full as I could get it and mail them to him."

BACKBONES AND RIBS

These can be put together and stewed like chicken parts or barbecued or canned with a teaspoon of salt per quart can.

TAIL

Often the tail was saved for use in stews. One contact made a stew of feet, ears, tail, salt, and red pepper, boiled until tender.

SAUSAGE

Use any combination of lean meat not used otherwise. This includes trimmings of lean meat from hams, shoulders, middling meat, and so on; it can also include the tenderloin, meat from the head, and, if you wish, the jowls. Some people parch their own red pepper in front of the fireplace, crush it and then add it to the sausage.

10 pounds of lean pork	2 tablespoons sage
¼ cup salt	2 teaspoons black pepper
½ cup brown sugar	2 teaspoons red pepper

Run the pork through a sausage grinder, mix in the remaining ingredients well, and fry until browned but not completely cooked since it has to be reheated when served. Pack it into jars halfway to three fourths full while still very hot. Pour hot grease over the top, close the jars and turn them upside down to cool. When the grease cools, it seals the lids shut and the sausage will keep until you are ready to use it. It is usually stored with the jars upside down.

Here are four other ways to keep sausage:

1. Roll the sausage into balls, pack them in a churn jar, pour hot grease over the top, tie a cloth over the lid and set the jar in the water trough of your springhouse.
2. Pack the sausage in sections of cleaned small intestine, tie the intestine off at both ends and hang from the joists of the smokehouse for curing.
3. Remove the ear from a corn shuck. Wash the shuck thoroughly and pack the sausage inside. Tie the end of the shuck closed with string or wire and hang in the smokehouse.
4. Pack in small, clean, white cloth sacks and hang in the smokehouse.

LARD AND CRACKLINS

The fat is trimmed from entrails, hams, shoulders, middling meat, and so on. It may be left out all night in the lard pot so the cold weather can solidify it making it easier to cut.

A black iron pot is used for rendering fat into lard and cracklins.

*The cracklins are dipped out and strained. These will be the main ingredient in the winter's "cracklin' corn bread."
{See recipe}*

In the morning, the fat is cut into pieces about the size of hens' eggs and put in a pot containing just enough water to keep the fat from sticking to the sides when cooked. The pot is then placed over a fire and the fat is allowed to cook slowly. Stir the fat often. By evening, the grease will have boiled out, the water evaporated, and the hard residue, called "cracklins," will have fallen to the bottom. Add soda if you don't want many cracklins. The soda also keeps the fat from smelling while cooking and from tasting strong.

The liquid fat is poured into containers, allowed to harden into lard, and is used all winter for cooking. The cracklins are saved for bread.

FRIED FATBACK

RUTH HOLCOMB: "Try rolling fatback meat in cornmeal and frying that in grease until the meat is done. That's *real* good."

A baked ham ready for Sunday dinner

10

Beef

"Daddy didn't think you had much
if you didn't have meat on the table."

In this region of Appalachia, beef is not a luxury but a staple for most families. At least one cow is kept for breeding in order to raise a few calves each year. Area cattle sales are also popular events where local farmers trade and sell their cattle.

Slaughtering beef was once and sometimes still is done by families with the help of neighbors and friends. Now local slaughtering houses do much of the meat processing which relieves families from the once all-day affair.

As with pork, when slaughtering was done at home, some of the beef was salted down and put into the smokehouse to dry and cure; and much of the remainder was canned. Garnet Lovell's wife, Blanche, told us how she prepares dried beef: Slice off a little piece the thickness of a fifty-cent piece. Let it soak just a little, until it is soft. Roll the beef in flour and fry it; you have a piece of regular steak. Or lay it out in the hot grease and cook it until it is tender and make milk gravy on top of that.

She said, "That is the way they used to do it fifty years ago, and still do it that way today. If you are going to stew it, just throw it in water with vegetables in it."

The fat from the meat may be used in several different ways. Some of it was made into tallow. Garnet said, "We don't do anything with it [ourselves but] it makes good shoe grease, [and] old people used to grease the bottom of kid's feet and chests with it for croup."

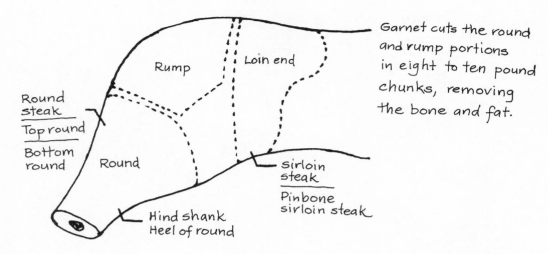

HINDQUARTER

Rump

Loin end

Round steak
Top round
Bottom round

Round

Sirloin steak
Pinbone sirloin steak

Hind shank
Heel of round

Garnet cuts the round and rump portions in eight to ten pound chunks, removing the bone and fat.

BEEF RECIPES

GELATINED BEEF

Simmer together a couple pounds of beef from the neck and some soup bones from the shin, until the meat is very tender. Take it out of the broth, remove all bone, skin, and sinew, and place in a bowl. Pour the broth over the meat. Place a weight on it, and let it all congeal. When ready, slice and serve cold, or rub slices with butter and broil.

MEAT LOAF

GLADYS NICHOLS

"Now that's a cheap meat loaf."

1 pound ground beef
1 pound ground pork
1 cup cracker meal or bread crumbs
7 ounces tomato sauce

1 or 2 eggs
1 small onion, chopped
Salt and pepper to taste

Here is the beef in the smokehouse during the salting process. Only the piece on the left has been salted. The bowl contains the salt Garnet Lovell is using.

After the meat has taken enough salt, Garnet cuts a hole in the center of each piece and slides it on a pole. Wesley Dockins and Alan Mashburn help out. The meat can then be hung above the fireplace to dry. It is then salted—any cloth sack will do—and dried for another week.

Mix together all the ingredients and put into a baking dish. Bake in a 350°F oven for 45 to 60 minutes.

ARIZONA DICKERSON'S MEAT LOAF VARIATIONS

1. Make your ground meat into patties and wrap a strip of raw bacon around each one. Fry them until they're well done. Serve for breakfast.

2. Shape your ground meat into pyramid-shaped cones and bake in a 325°F oven until they're done.

3. Make cones of your ground beef and roll in dry, uncooked rice. Place in a shallow pan and cover with a mixture of tomato juice and stock from chicken. Bake in a moderate oven until done.

COW'S TONGUE

Boil the cow's tongue until tender. Then peel off the outer skin, and boil in salt water until very tender. Slice thin, and serve with mustard or relish.

SUPPER ON A PIECE OF BREAD

MARGARET NORTON

1½ pounds ground beef
1 teaspoon salt
⅛ teaspoon pepper
2 eggs
½ cup bread crumbs

¾ cup sweet milk
Cheese, Swiss or cheddar, cut in strips,
*   enough to decorate*
1 onion cooked in butter
Bread dough for 1 loaf

Mix all (except the bread dough and cheese) together, and shape into an oblong (or to fit whatever baking pan you use). Make bread as if you were making white biscuits, but roll out oblong a little larger than the meat loaf. Place meat loaf on top and bake. If edges of bread get too brown, put aluminum foil under bread and bring up over the edge. Bake 45 minutes in a 325°F oven. Ten minutes before taking out, decorate top with cheese. You can crisscross the cheese and make it really pretty. This is a whole meal in itself—with milk, coffee, or tea.

ROAST

DOROTHY BECK

"In my roast I always flour it good and put it in the roaster. I usually wrap it in aluminum foil. I put a whole onion in with it and I put about a cup of Coca-Cola and a little water over it and cook it slow [250° to 300°F] in the oven."

SWISS STEAK

2 pounds round steak, 2 inches thick
½ cup flour combined with 1 teaspoon
   salt and a dash of pepper

¼ cup bacon or ham drippings
2 cups tomatoes, boiled until tender

Pound flour mixture into both sides of steak. Heat fat in large skillet or casserole dish and sear the steak. Add boiled tomatoes, cover casserole closely, and place in a slow 275°F oven about 2 hours until done. Make a gravy of drippings and pour over steak. YIELD: 6 servings

BEEF STEW

1½ pounds short ribs, shank, neck,
   flank, plate, rump, or brisket
¼ cup flour
1½ teaspoons salt
¼ teaspoon pepper

1 pint stewed and drained tomatoes
2 small onions
1 cup cubed carrots
4 cups potatoes, cut in quarters

Remove meat from the bone, cut in 1½-inch cubes. Mix flour with salt and pepper and roll cubes of meat in it. Heat some of fat from meat in frying pan. Add cubes of meat and brown. Place meat with browned fat into a stewing pot. Add the pint of tomatoes. Simmer until tender (about 3 hours). Add onions, carrots, and potatoes the last hour of cooking. YIELD: 14 servings

PAN-FRIED LIVER

Remove the skin and veins from young beef liver and cut it into ½-inch slices. Season the slices of liver with salt and pepper, then coat with flour. Fry quickly in shallow hot bacon drippings until done. Serve with crisp bacon.

11

Wild Game

"People say I make good squirrel dumplings."

In *The Foxfire Book* (pp. 266–73), there is a collection of methods for killing and dressing wild game. Since then, we have found other people who have given us additional information.

Glenn Worley, from the Turnerville Community in Habersham County, is well known in this area for his hunting skills. We visited with him and his wife, Sara, both of whom graciously shared with us their knowledge of how to dress and cook deer, frogs, rabbits, squirrels, groundhogs, and possums:

"It's a matter of choice how you cut deer up, but most people take all four legs off or either quarter it. If you quarter it, it has to be cut up in smaller pieces later. But most people like to take the legs off. With that they have a big rib section with half the back attached to each piece. And then if you cut that in half you've got two sides. You cut it crossways, making four pieces, two front quarters and two hind quarters. Then it's up to you how you want to cut it. Most people remove the rib section. With that they have split the backbone down the center so they get either rib steaks or filet mignon. It's a section of choice lean meat. Then they usually steak the hind legs and the front legs, and the remainder they make into roasts or barbecue ribs. The neck is a very choice piece—it is all solid meat. The backbone continues on up the neck and that's the only bone in the neck section. From there it's best then to take the meat and put it in a cooler. I would stress to age your deer a little—hang it in the cooler for one to five days—and a lot of the wild goes out, and it becomes drained and it's choice venison.

"You can have a butcher carve your venison. If you prefer steaks, you tell him the thickness and the section you want, and if you want large roasts, he'll do that. Most all people who are in butcher shops know professionally how to prepare deer and will cut it up for you in thirty minutes. They cut it, wrap it, and give you a little basket of scraps that's left. They'll freeze it and package it for you and mark it all, identifying each piece.

"It is not true that deer is tough! The preparation of the deer from the hunter's workpoint to the skillet is really one of the big success factors to having good venison. Most people who cook venison can really do a good job if the dressing and aging has been properly done. I believe that's true in the preparation of all wild game.

"My preference of venison, of course, is steak and roast and barbecued ribs. I never eat boiled deer. Some people make mulligans or stews, but I just don't eat mulligans from anyone's deer. That's one of my peculiarities. Too much goes in mulligans and stews. But I like fried steak primarily. It doesn't take a lot of sauces or additives to make good deer steak; normally they are fine. Fried steak is my choice. Normally deer steaks are cut about a half inch thick and the size will vary like just any other kind of steak—whether it's rib, round, sirloin, T-bone. It all depends on the size of the animal. Cooks usually take them and flour them a little with white flour and put them in a skillet and cook them rather fast over a hot fire."

SARA: Put a little grease in the pan and add pepper and salt—lots of pepper. They're best to eat while they're hot. Deer gets cold real fast.

GLENN: The meat is very firm so it's best cooked and eaten immediately. And cook it at a little faster pace than you cook chicken. Keep the fire up a little bit.

SARA: I'd say medium-high. Now with a roast, it's different. I always marinate my roast overnight.

GLENN: Usually with some wine.

SARA: Or some vinegar water. And put some salt—all wild game needs some salt in the vinegar. It all depends on the deer. If it's an old one I marinate it and then use a lot of onions in it when I cook it to remove some of the wild game taste. When I put it in the oven, I cook it about thirty minutes per pound. If you was cooking a four-pound roast you'd cook it two hours at about 400 degrees. You'd just sorta have to test to see how done it is.

GLENN: Test it occasionally toward the end of that time period, and when it's exactly right call your family together and enjoy.

SARA: You can easily pressure-cook deer. For people who like pressure cooked, that'd be a faster way. I'm sure it'd help to make it tender a whole lot. A lot of people use all the scrap parts to make hamburger from deer. They mix some pork [or beef] with it and grind it up in a sausage grinder. But our favorite way is steaks, and we put all we can in steaks because we just like them best.

GLENN: Now about the only organs people eat is the liver. Fried liver is choice—either just fried alone or with onions. Most hunters will eat that in the woods unless they've brought beef with them. But this is fresh—it's very choice. And some people here eat the heart—it's a firm muscular organ—but there's nothing else eaten from a deer that I know of other than the heart and the liver. Those are the two organs. Leave the rest for a bear or a possum or whatever comes along—one of the scavengers. They'll hunt the entrails up and they won't be there very long.

Glenn continued by telling us how he dresses and cooks his other favorite wild animals:

I caught bullfrogs for years when my father worked for Georgia Power. We always could get them out on the lake or in the river. We gigged them and caught them with our hands. They are delightful. We've had frogs all our lives.

Most times you just lay them out on a board and take a large butcher knife and cut them right above the joint of the hind legs against the backbone. You just cut them totally in two crossways. Just sever the two legs from the rest of the body. Then you take a knife and cut a slit down either leg. Take pliers or pullers and the skin will pull off in one piece down to the web feet. Then you take the same knife and cut their feet off, and the legs are totally dressed. You don't do anything further. There's no organs or anything attached when you cut them loose from the rest of his body. Just get two legs; that's all you want, and that's all you eat.

Then you just dip them in flour and put them in the skillet or pan and fry them in the same temperature you normally would chicken until they become brown. The meat is perfectly white and tender. Add just a little flour and perhaps pepper if you like—but *lightly* of both. The meat is very delicate and very choice. We always eat frog legs. I would now if I could find them!

But rabbits are my choice, I guess, next to venison. Wild rabbits are delicious. When you've been hunting in the woods with a pack of beagles or something to jump them and run them by, you bring them home. They still have their intestines and everything still in, so you take the rabbit out and you put him on your dressing block. Most times I take a sharp knife and cut him off right at the base of his neck. Then I clip off the feet above the footpads. Just clip them off entirely. Then I reach over to the back and make about a two-inch cut crossways in the skin—just the skin.

The skin on a rabbit is rather loose, and you just pick it up and pull it away from the meat. Then insert two fingers in that two-inch cut pointed toward the shoulders and two toward the tail. Then you pull that little cut open, and the skin just gives freely and comes right off the shoulders and tail at the same time, and most times right on down

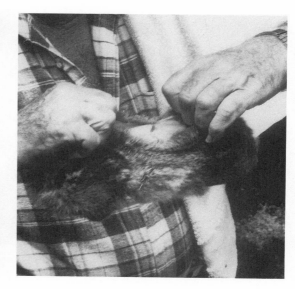

Glynn Worley with a wild rabbit he killed

Make about a two-inch cut crossways in the skin—just in the skin. Then insert two fingers toward the head and two toward the tail, and the skin just gives freely and comes off both ends at the same time.

"He's just clean and beautiful. If there is any hair or if you dropped him or something, you just wash him off."

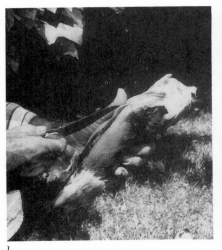 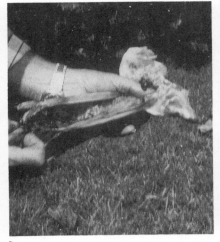 

1   2   3

Then you turn him over on his back and open him up (1)

Remove all his vital organs (2).

The rabbit liver (3, the two small dark patches inside) is absolutely delightful, and that's one of my choice pieces.

Cutting the unwanted skin from the torso of the rabbit (4)

Mr. Worley separating the leg from the ribcage (5)

Cutting the ribcage in half (6)

4   5   6

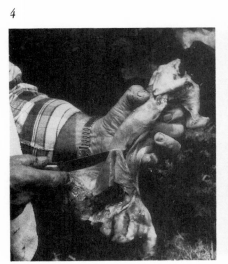 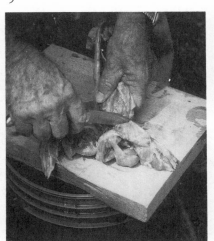 

over the legs. You can pull it off at one time—half goes toward the head and half goes toward the tail—and you've got a totally skinned rabbit.

Then you clip the tail off as a rule, and that's all there is till you open him up. There's very little meat attached to the skin. He's just clean and beautiful. If there's any hair or if you dropped him or something, you wash him off.

Next you turn him over on his back and open him up. Remove all his vital organs. The liver in a rabbit is absolutely delightful, and that's one of my choice pieces. So you open that rabbit up from the base of his neck all the way. His head has been removed in the first operation. You open him up and clean him out good. His organs are exactly like a deer or bear's. They're all attached in a sack, and you pull those out. Split his hind legs apart and split his front legs apart and cut him up into about eight pieces. If he's a big wild rabbit we take a knife and cut crossways through the biggest area of the hind legs about one inch apart. That eliminates the toughness and breaks down the muscle tissue a little bit for frying. And when you flour him to put him in the skillet, you rub a little flour in those cuts and that makes him more tempting. Cook him just like you would fried chicken. He is my favorite! The first time I get a rabbit I'll bring him by and I'll do it for you.

I use the same procedure with a squirrel, but I somehow have difficulty with squirrel. Whereas I can skin a rabbit and never get five hairs from the skin on his body, I sorta wrestle a squirrel pretty much. He's very tough. He's just got the toughest skin of any little animal I've ever tangled with, but I skin him precisely the same way. When you open up the back crossways with the first cut, you tuck your fingers in that skin and pull both ways. You've already removed his head and his feet and sometimes the tail, but when you start pulling that skin on them back, boy, you've gotta have some muscles for that, because he doesn't give easily! But once you do get him skinned out you fry him precisely the same way as a rabbit. The meat is a little tougher, but he's good. Somehow I just don't feel that a squirrel is quite worth the trouble, but there's lots of squirrel hunters in the state that would surely disagree. I love squirrel meat—I guess it's just skinning the squirrel. It's tough for me.

My family has also eaten lots of groundhog, and we like it very much. I first hang him up by the hind feet and I skin him just like the deer or the bear. Cut inside of each leg and cut around the legs, and then I peel him down sorta like a small blanket-type operation. Pull down all the way around him till he's totally skinned out to the front of the shoulders. Throw the neck and the head away. Open him up, and cut all his innards out. As a rule they have a couple of glands, I believe, up in the front shoulder. If you can find them, it's good to remove them. If not, those two pieces of meat won't be as tasty, but he is delightful. He's roasted as a rule—baked whole or roasted. You usually put him in a covered vessel and put some marination in with him in a roasting pan. You can use a cover or heavy aluminum foil. Baste and bake until it's brown, and then he's delightful.

I've eat many possum in my time, too. I used to trap and I've caught big possum. Sometimes I'd put them up in a pen and feed them three or four days and get a little of the wild out of them. Again, just catch them and dress them the same way. Yes, I've eaten lots of possum. They're good. You bake all of them.

Almost all of our other friends in the community have had experience cooking wild game. As Lizzie Moore said,

"My mother and I cooked a lot of wild meat 'cause my daddy was a man that killed a lot of wild game. And then when I married my husband, why, he was a man that hunted a lot. Back in those days you could just get out around here and kill anything that you wanted to and bring it in, you see. They'd kill a lot of squirrels, and when the snow was on was when you generally killed a rabbit. You'd find them sitting in a bed in the snow. They hide, you see. One time my husband [Emory] found a rabbit sitting back in the snow, and it was so much snow on he couldn't find a rock. So he just took his knife out of his pocket and throwed it and killed that rabbit in the snow. They killed coons, possum, deer, turkeys, anything like that."

Many of these friends shared their cooking methods with us.

RACCOON

LIZZIE MOORE: "You know you've got to have raccoon all skinned and dressed first. Then you wash it and cut it up into small pieces, put it in a pot and put cold or warm water over the top. [Bring to a boil] and then you put in two pods of hot pepper and let it cool for an hour in that water. Then you drain all that water off, put water up over it again and put a teaspoonful of vinegar in it. Vinegar is what tenders them and takes that old wild taste out of them. And then you put salt in it, and let it [boil again and] get as tender as you want it to. Stick the fork into it to see if it's as good and tender as you want it. Then you take it out of that water and roll it in meal or flour. I always prefer meal. Just roll it in your meal, have your grease hot in your [frying] pan, and lay that meat all in your pan. Then put some pepper on it, salt it to suit your taste, and let it stay in [the skillet] till it gets as brown as you want it. Take it out, and it's ready to eat. It's lean, dark meat, and it's good."

WILL SINGLETON: "Take one coon any size and clean it. Cut it up and put it in a pressure pot with two cups of water. Then take one-half onion and cut it up on top of the coon along with one pod of hot pepper. Pressure it till it is well cooked, then take it out and put it in a frying pan with grease and put sage and pepper on it. Fry it for about ten minutes and then it is ready to eat."

POSSUM

SAMANTHA SPEED: "Put them on the stove in water and boil them for a long time. When they get tender, take them and roll them in flour or meal and fry them good and brown."

GRANNY GIBSON: "You usually boil possum a while to get it tender and then slice up sweet potatoes and put them around it. Put your possum on top and let it bake with sweet potatoes. Now that is good."

LIZZIE MOORE: "Most people like sweet potatoes and carrots around possum. Just put it in and bake it. I always put a spoonful of vinegar or pepper in with it 'cause then it doesn't taste too wild. A possum is fat. It's not as lean as raccoons. If they're tough, it takes longer to cook them; if they're tender, it doesn't take so long."

SQUIRREL

GLADYS NICHOLS: "People say I make good squirrel dumplings. You just boil your squirrel like you would a chicken. Get it good and done and put your seasoning in it. Then make up your flour like you're going to make biscuits. Squeeze you off a little dough and roll it or cut it out. Have your squirrel boiling and just drop the flour dough in there, pepper and salt it, and boil it till it's good and done. I have got a lot of compliments on my dumplings. And then you can make gravy in your squirrel with just a spoonful or two of flour mixed with milk. Pour it in your pot and cook it. Most people, I think, like the gravy even better than they do the dumplings."

MARGIE LEDFORD: "I like squirrel dumplings and Virge [Margie's husband] likes them. I fix my squirrel dumplings just like chicken dumplings. I stew my squirrel and put seasoning in it. When I boil squirrel I put a piece of fat meat in it, and then when I get ready to make my dumplings I take that fat meat out. The fat meat seasons the squirrel. Roll out your dough and drop it right in the pot with your squirrel."

RABBIT

INEZ TAYLOR: "I have cooked wild game, but I won't eat it. I don't want nothing wild. Not deer, not rabbit—no sir. If rabbits are old you have to boil them, but if they're young and tender you can fry them like chicken. I usually boiled mine till it got tender, then I took it out and let it cool. I roll it in flour, pepper it, and fry it like chicken."

MIKE CANNON: "After you kill the rabbit, skin it and clean it. Bake it in the oven at 350 degrees with butter and wine on it. You can fry it too, like chicken. Dip it in flour and fry it in grease."

WILL SINGLETON: "Take the [rabbit] meat, put it on a cutting board and cut it as thin as you can get it. Put the meat in a pressure pot with two cups of water and pressure it till it's done. Then take it and roll it in flour and put it in a frying pan with shortening and fry it till it's brown on both sides."

LIZZIE MOORE: "You dress a rabbit and when you've got it washed and all, just cut it up into small pieces. I always rolled it in flour or meal—just whichever one you prefer—and put salt and pepper on it to taste. And have your grease hot and just lay that in there, and if you cook it slow it tenders better. I think it's good eating."

DEER

STELLA BURRELL: "I've cooked deer like a steak. We would beat it good like chopped steak and then roll it in flour and fry it. You can smother deer steaks with onions or something just like you do beef steaks to help take away the wild taste. But I've never used the tenderizer on deer, so it would maybe come out a little tough. It would depend on the age of the deer, I guess."

TURTLE

The beginnings of this section go back to the mid-1970s when students Keith Head, Vickie Chastain, and Eddie Connor, along with staff members Suzy Angier and Pat Rogers, took a live mud turtle to Mrs. Vergil Lovell who had agreed to show them how to clean and cook it. They spent the day there, tape recording and photographing the proceedings, and that evening, before returning home, they all sat down with Mrs. Lovell to a turtle dinner.

As sometimes happens, however, the students graduated before they found an opportunity to work up the material they had collected into publishable form. Years later, Pat Marcellino and Kenny Crumley uncovered the fat file folder labeled "turtles" and decided to finish the article. They transcribed the tapes, printed the photographs and, finding that some information they needed was missing, tried to contact Mrs. Lovell again only to discover that in the intervening years, she had passed away. Here is what she said:

[My husband] always got them by the tail. He'd just catch them. Keep their head away from you, though, because they'll bite you, and they are mean, too.

And we've caught them with a hook. But now we had mud turtle hooks—great big ones. I ain't seen one of them in a long time. You can use a regular fish hook, but you have to be awfully careful because they'll get loose from that now. They'll snap it so quick you'll [lose them]. I guess they still have mud turtle hooks in fishing stores, but I ain't seen none since Daddy used them.

Now Verge always, when he was living, I'd go with him and he'd catch a chicken out of the chicken house—just a small little old chicken—chop it in two, and put one half on each hook good. Go back the next morning and he had two mud turtles.

Once we had a man that worked here, and we had a pipe almost like a stovepipe that carried water from the pond to the chicken house. Well, the water kept being cut off, and he'd come to the house and say, "I can't get nothing out. The water's gone and them chickens is starving to death."

So Verge said, "They's something in the pipe up there." So they went up there and worked and piddled and couldn't do nothing with it. So Verge just went in the pond and got down in there and it was a mud turtle about the size of a dinner plate had stopped the hole up!

Now I like to cook these turtles when I clean them, unless I'm going to cut them up and freeze them like you would chicken or any other meat.

When I cook them, I put them on and cook them till they're tender in salt and water. If you want to, you can put a little pod of pepper in. It won't hurt them a bit. Gives that whang to them that they ought to have. Now if you boil the meat too long, it'll just come all to pieces and I don't like it that way. I like to still have the pieces whole where you can pick them up just like a piece of chicken. It's pretty meat, and I don't want it to come off the bone if I can keep it on.

The boiling part doesn't take as long. It depends on the size of the turtle. One great big one I cooked took me nearly four hours, but they usually don't take that long. I always take my fork and test it and see if it's tender enough. When it is, I take those pieces out and fry them in a frying pan—brown them up nice.

Lots of times I've found thirty and forty eggs in them. You know the size of a patteridge [grouse or pheasant] egg, don't you? Like that size. The last one I cooked had thirty-five or forty in it. I took them out and put them in a bowl in there and they filled a pretty good-sized bowl up. I don't care for them too much, though. You can't hardly cook them. They're a kind of rubbery—kind of a watery thing. They don't taste right to me. But now they say they make the best cakes there are, but I ain't done that now.

You'll get enough meat off an average-sized one to feed a good family. I've had them about the size of a dinner plate, and we'll have turtle for supper and two pieces left over to give to the cat! There's plenty of meat in them. I guess two pound and a half in one with any size to it. Lots of times you can't eat a whole hind leg by yourself. There's plenty of eating in it, and it's good meat, too.

12

Gravies and Sauces

"Mighty good for sopping biscuits in."

It is simple to learn to make good sauces and gravies. Bland foods can be made more enjoyable when dripping with a good sauce, and in the mountains, it is a rare meal that does not include a thick gravy or sauce of some sort. These are typical:

CORNMEAL GRAVY

RUTH HOLCOMB

¼ to ½ cup grease from bacon or
    fatback, or lard

1 cup cornmeal
3 glasses water or milk or half of each

Have some grease or lard in a pan on the stove. Get it real hot and add the cornmeal. Stir it until the meal is brown. Stir in water or milk and stir constantly until it's as thick as you like it. That should serve about 4 people.

RED EYE GRAVY

JAKE WALDROOP

"Fry slices of ham in a frying pan. After they are done, remove and add flour to the grease that's left in the pan. Let it brown. Add water or coffee and continue to stir. The coffee will make it a dark brown gravy. You may leave out the flour. Just add coffee to the grease left in the pan after you've finished cooking your ham. Stir it around. The gravy will be very thin, but have an excellent flavor and be mighty good for sopping biscuits in."

Olene Garland offers a variation: "Just fry your ham, pour some coffee over the ham in the pan while the pan is still hot. After liquid comes to a boil, cut down temperature and serve."

SKILLET GRAVY

2 tablespoons flour
2 tablespoons natural drippings
1 cup liquid (water, milk, meat juice,
broth)
Salt and pepper to taste

In a skillet blend flour into drippings. Cook over low heat, stirring until smooth. Remove from heat; stir in liquid. Heat to a boil, stirring constantly. Boil and stir 1 minute. Add salt and pepper to taste. YIELD: *1 cup*

Giblet gravy

GIBLET GRAVY

In 4 to 5 cups salted water cook the gizzard, heart, and neck of fowl until tender, approximately 1 to 2 hours. Add liver toward the last 30 minutes of cooking. Let cool and remove the meat from neck and chop giblets up into fine pieces. Follow the recipe and directions for making skillet gravy, except use broth from giblets for the liquid. Stir giblets into gravy and heat thoroughly.

VARIATION: Boiled eggs may be sliced and added.

EGG GRAVY

EXIE DILLS

1 tablespoon shortening	*1 egg*
1 heaping tablespoon flour or meal	*½ teaspoon pepper*
2 cups milk	*⅔ teaspoon salt*

Melt shortening in a skillet. Add flour or meal. Stir but don't brown. Mix together milk, egg, pepper, and salt and add to the flour mixture. Stir continually over medium heat until the gravy thickens.

FLOUR GRAVY

ADDIE NORTON TOLD US:

"Meat that's been home cured; that's what makes good brown gravy. Meat that's kept in a freezer don't make a good brown gravy."

1 tablespoon grease	*2 cups milk*
1 tablespoon flour	*Salt and pepper to taste*

Heat grease in a skillet. Mix in flour and stir until the flour is smooth. Add the milk, stirring constantly until the gravy thickens. Add salt and pepper to taste. For white sauce, don't let flour brown; for brown gravy, let flour brown to desired color. YIELD: *2 cups*

MEAT LOAF GRAVY

BELLE LEDFORD

¼ cup margarine

½ cup flour

2 cups mashed tomatoes, canned or fresh

1 small can tomato sauce

Brown flour in the margarine. Add tomatoes and sauce. Cook until thick. Pour over meat loaf when done or use later. YIELD: *3 cups*

CREAM SAUCE

STELLA BURRELL

"I've got a cream sauce recipe that you do in a double boiler. It was something that you could do if you had somebody come in and you didn't have something fixed. I think I use about three tablespoons of butter and three of flour. You just add a little bit of flour at a time as the butter melts in the top of a double boiler. It takes about three or four cups of milk to thicken it. Salt and pepper it, too. You can add cheese, beef, chicken, or whatever to that sauce, or you can use it for scalloped potatoes, scalloped cabbage, mixed vegetables, or any way you want to fix it. It's something easy to fix."

VARIATIONS: Cheese Sauce—add grated cheese.
  Egg Sauce—add boiled or raw eggs.
  Meat Sauce—add dried beef, chicken, or turkey.
  Vegetable Sauce—add cream sauce to vegetables—scalloped potatoes, cabbage, etc.

MUSHROOM SAUCE

2 tablespoons butter

4 tablespoons flour

½ pound mushrooms, washed, peeled,
    and cut into quarters, or 1 4½
    ounce can mushrooms

1 cup milk, heated

1 teaspoon salt

⅛ teaspoon pepper

Melt butter, add flour, and cook till a light brown. Add mushrooms and boil until hot. Add heated milk, blending together well. Season with salt and pepper. Cook slowly for 10 minutes. Pour over broiled chicken. YIELD: *2 cups*

BARBECUE SAUCE

1½ cups water
1 cup vinegar
½ cup tomato ketchup
½ cup chopped onion

2 tablespoons Worcestershire sauce or 1
  teaspoon chili powder
1 teaspoon salt
½ teaspoon pepper

Bring all the ingredients to a boil, pour over your meat, and roast in a 350°F oven according to general rules, basting occasionally. YIELD: *3 cups*

TOMATO SAUCE (RELISH)

MARY PITTS

12 large tomatoes
1 green pepper
1 onion
2 cups vinegar
3 tablespoons sugar

1 tablespoon salt
2 teaspoons whole cloves
2 teaspoons whole cinnamon
2 teaspoons whole allspice
2 teaspoons whole nutmeg

Scald and skin tomatoes; chop green pepper and onion. Combine the 3 vegetables in a large pan with the vinegar and sugar. Mix spices and salt and tie in a square of cheesecloth. Drop into tomato mixture. Cook slowly 2½ to 3 hours. YIELD: *4 cups*

MAYONNAISE DRESSING

1 egg yolk
2 tablespoons vinegar or lemon juice
¼ teaspoon mustard

¾ teaspoon salt
⅛ teaspoon pepper
¾ cup salad oil

Beat egg yolk and add 1 tablespoon of vinegar or lemon juice. Add mustard, salt, and pepper. Beat well. Drop the oil, a teaspoon at a time, into egg mixture, beating constantly until ¼ cup has been added. Then add in larger quantities, beating thoroughly after each addition. As mixture thickens, add remaining vinegar or lemon juice (half of each may be used), a little at a time. Have all ingredients equally cold when mixing. Store in a cool place in clean jars. YIELD: *1 cup*

13

Vegetables

"They will melt in your mouth if you're a hillbilly."

The different kinds of vegetables grown here by the settlers in the early 1800s are still prevalent today, with some variations in particular varieties, such as many of the hybrid types that have been introduced in recent years. The Jerusalem artichoke, which many people used to cultivate, appears to be the main exception, as it isn't grown very widely here now.

BEANS

Of all vegetables native to our region, beans were the most popular and prevalent. New varieties of hybrid beans have replaced the old. Several of our contacts remembered their favorites, no longer grown here:

FLORENCE BROOKS: "There's altogether a difference—people ain't got none of the old-fashioned bean seed they used to have. People's stuff used to be a whole lot better than what it is now. The beans ain't near as good as they used to be. We had what we called greasy-back beans—I've not seen any of them in years. They were little white beans in a white pole bean. You can eat the greasy-back bean either green or dried. For a dried bean, after they get dry on the vine, you pick them, put them in a sack, and beat them out with a stick. The beans fall out of the pod.

"We planted green beans and cornfield beans. We always planted the cornfield full of them, so we'd have beans that'd dry up and we'd have our own soup beans."

HARRY BROWN: "We didn't have any half-runners back in those days, we had cornfield beans. We'd pick them after they got large enough. We'd take them and break them like we were going to cook them, and set down with a big needle and string them on a thread. [We called them] leather breeches. People didn't can so much like they do now."

As Harry Brown notes, some years ago leather breeches were indeed a solution to

At Andy Webb's, leather breeches hang to dry.

preserving beans before the popularity of canning jars (see the food preservation section for pickled beans [pages 270–72], another favorite long-term way to keep beans). His wife Marinda contributed her method of making leather breeches:

"Leather breeches is something that people used way back in the past, and it's a simple food that has lots of nutrients. I guess a lot of people practically lived on it way back years ago. You gather the beans in an early stage when the pod begins to get sort of full. You string them just like you would string beads, with a needle and thread. Then tie that and hang them up on the wall and let them dry. They're a little tough and brittle when they dry, but they'll keep there all along until you use them up. When you get ready to cook them, soak them overnight. You can break them, but most people just take them off the string and cook them just like you would green beans—the pod along with the bean—with a piece of bacon or fatback. They're pretty good. Of course, they don't taste anything like green beans. I keep mine, and my bean seed if I ever save any, either in the refrigerator or freezer because the weevils get in them."

Daisy Justus gave her recipe for making leather breeches: "String and break green beans as if you were going to cook them. Spread thinly and dry thoroughly or thread a big needle with no. 8 thread and string them up. Dry until they rattle and put them in a cloth bag, tied securely. Keep dry and on sunny days put them in sun for a while. To cook these beans, wash well and put them in warm water to soak overnight, then cook as any dried beans. Cover beans with water, add salt and a piece of salt pork. Bring to a boil, then cook slowly for two or three hours. The longer they cook the better they are. If you use a pressure cooker, cook for about thirty minutes, then remove; cover and cook them dry."

Rittie Webb also discussed leather breeches: "We usually cook leather breeches all day. We boil them hard for a while and then run the water out of them to get the dried taste out. Then we add more water and cook them with a piece of meat all day. They are good. We'd have green beans, pinto beans, or leather breeches. We'd change around on beans."

There were almost as many "best ways" to cook green beans as there were women who talked with us:

GRANNY GIBSON: "Green beans are the best in an old black pot. I just put them in a pot with some water and some grease or a piece of pork and cook them three or four hours —not all day. I usually have them for dinner on Sundays.

ADDIE NORTON: "Pick a mess of green beans from the garden. String and break them into one and a half- to two-inch pieces. Wash them thoroughly afterwards. Put bacon or streaked pork meat for seasoning into a pot. Add the beans and add water to cover the beans. Cook until the beans are tender. You may want to add more water along to keep the beans from burning, but you want to have most of the water cooked out when they are done."

ARIZONA DICKERSON: "My mother always cooked her beans in a iron pot on the fireplace. They're not good if you don't cook them down to the grease. A lot of people don't know how to cook beans. They leave water in them. I cook mine down to the grease, but not burned."

DAISY JUSTUS: "I peel Irish potatoes and put on top of my green beans—cook them together. I let the beans get practically done before putting the potatoes in. Some people put small pods of okra on top of the beans instead of potatoes."

LOLA CANNON: "I barely cover the beans in water. I add salt to taste. Then I add a little sugar. If you'll add half as much sugar as you do salt, it improves the flavor of your green beans."

OCTOBER BEANS

GRANNY GIBSON

"The mountain people used these beans as a substitute for soup beans, which don't grow here. They can be eaten fresh when young and tender, but people usually dried them, shelled them, and stored them for later use. To cook, parboil beans for five minutes, using about a quart of water to a cup of beans. Drain the water, rinse the beans off, and add another quart of water per cup of beans and [salt] pork about big as your fist (sliced). Cover and simmer until tender."

SOUP BEANS

RUTH HOLCOMB

"I cook soup beans. I pour two cups of ketchup into one quart of beans and add one teaspoonful of sugar. I put raw bacon and sliced onions on top of the beans and cover with water. I salt the beans to taste and cook them until they're done."

Connie Chappell with her amazing gourd bean

GOURD BEANS

A truly unusual "bean" was introduced to us by Connie Chappell. She grows something called the gourd bean. It looks like squash, but it is longer and green. Some people say it tastes like squash, but Mrs. Chappell says the gourd bean has a better taste. Mrs. Chappell lived in Scataway just outside of Hiawassee, Georgia, when she found out about the vegetable:

> I found out about the gourd bean about forty something years ago. We were working for a man hoeing corn, and [his wife] had some fixed for dinner. We ate them at that man's house that day for dinner, and he give us seed of them, and we planted them, and I've been growing them ever since. I don't know if you can freeze and can them. I haven't tried, but I don't like squash frozen; so I know I wouldn't like them. Some people call them guinea beans, but we know them as gourd beans.
> You can cut a mess off of one when it's young and the place will just heal over and

keep growing. I have grown them to be four and five feet long, but this year mine haven't got that long because of the dry summer. They're easy to care for. You just plant them and work them like anything else. You don't have to dust them or anything like that. The best time to plant them is early in the spring when you plant your garden. You can use almost any kind of soil [laughs] but you can't plant them in red soil. I use regular fertilizer, but you can use manure if you ain't got fertilizer for them. You have to have something for the gourd bean to run on. I usually have mine growing on the hog lot fence. Then they are ready to pick in a month or two. The best time to pick them is when they're eight to ten inches long, when they're young and tender.

[To cook them] you just take and peel the outside peeling off, and wash them in the sink in cold water. Let the water run over them, then get a towel and dry them off and slice them just like you do a squash, and fry them. When you cook them, put them in your grease and fry them like you do regular squash. I fry them in just a little Crisco or just any kind of grease I've got. They taste different from squash—they've got a better taste, and the taste is not strong.

To get the seed you just have to bust that hard shell with something. They're just like gourd seed; if you take them for seed, let the frost hit them. The vines usually run to be very long. They ain't a bug bothered them this summer. The pigs have though. The pigs tore the vines nearly all up [laughs].

BEETS

Beets were often raised for pickling (see food preservation, chapter 16), but they could be eaten in various other ways. Lucy York said, "Beets can be stored like cabbage. When ready to prepare them, scrub them and boil, adding a small amount of vinegar to the water. Cook until tender."

HARVARD BEETS

OLENE GARLAND

1 tablespoon cornstarch
½ teaspoon salt
½ cup mild vinegar or 6 tablespoons
   vinegar and ¼ cup cream

3 cups cooked sliced beets
½ cup sugar
2 tablespoons butter

Cook and stir the first 4 ingredients in the top of a double boiler. When clear, add the beets and place the pan, covered, over hot water for ½ hour. Just before serving, heat the beets again and add the butter. YIELD: 6 servings

SAUTÉED BEETS

Peel and slice raw beets. Place slices in butter in a frying pan. Cover and let simmer about 20 minutes. When tender, season with salt and pepper.

CABBAGE

Cabbage is another standard fall vegetable in the mountain diet. It is locally grown in quantity for sale to grocers. Several women offered cooking tips:

RUTH HOLCOMB: "Wash cabbage thoroughly and cut into squares. Put into a pot and cover with water. Add salt to taste and season with meat or bacon grease. Boil until cabbage is tender—about two hours."

ARIZONA DICKERSON: "Don't cover cabbage when cooking as this keeps odor in. Cook without the lid."

LUCY YORK: "After the cabbage has been cooked tender, you can pour the water off and fry the cabbage in a pan with some bacon grease."

FRIED CABBAGE

1 head cabbage, chopped   *Salt and pepper to taste*
4 teaspoons lard or other shortening

Put about an inch of water in a large frying pan and bring to a boil. Put all the cabbage and lard in, season it, and cover. Simmer for about 25 to 30 minutes.

See recipes for slaw in Salad section.

CARROTS

Granny Gibson says, "I never have cooked carrots too much, but I usually just cut them up and boil them. They're supposed to be good for your eyes."
Carrots were first eaten raw or boiled, but they eventually found their way into

modern casserole dishes. These are a recent introduction, however. As Dorothy Beck says, "They didn't even know what casseroles was when I was growing up."

CARROT CASSEROLE

ARIZONA DICKERSON

1 pound carrots, cooked and mashed
1 small onion
1 small green pepper
½ cup milk
⅓ cup sugar

1 cup cracker crumbs (half for topping; half in mixture)
½ cup soft butter (a little for topping; remainder for mixture)
Salt and pepper to taste

Mix together all ingredients, except for the topping. Pour into a casserole dish. Add crumbs and butter on top. Bake in a 350°F oven for 30 minutes until brown. YIELD: 5 servings

CORN

Corn was one of the most important crops, used as a staple for both people and their animals. They ate it fresh on or off the cob. They used it dried to make cornmeal, parched corn, hominy, and grits and sprouted it to make moonshine. They also raised and dried popcorn. The dried fodder (leaves) was used to feed animals, and the shucks could be used to bottom chairs, or could be made into mats, scrub mops, hats, horse collars, and various other things.

Florence Brooks recalled some of these diverse uses for corn: "Up there on Scaly Mountain, we didn't waste nothing. We used every blade of fodder and every top, every shuck. We'd always cut our tops and pull our fodder along about September. They let us kids out of school for two weeks to do that. Then after about three frosts we'd start gathering it. And we used corn for eating and grinding into meal."

Some folks ground corn by hand with a homemade "gritter" (similar to a manufactured grater, but more coarse). Inez Taylor was one of these: "I make gritted corn for Daddy a lot now. I just take the corn where it's too hard for anything else, and I put it on a gritter and grit it. Then I just put salt and a little sugar in it, put it in the pan and cook it just like corn bread."

Diversions from the daily routine were few, and families took advantage of every opportunity to turn work into a social event. Corn-harvesting time was no exception, as

Bessie Underwood notes: "We used to have corn shuckings when I was a young girl. You had to cook then, but you just cooked up big pots full of chicken and dumplings, beans, potatoes, cobbler pies, baked sweet potatoes, and stuff like that."

Jake Waldroop adds: "We'd get our corn gathered up in the fall of the year, and then we'd have corn shuckings. We'd ask in ten or fifteen men. We'd get in women folks, too, and they would bunch in and get supper. They'd kill chickens and we'd have fresh meat. They'd make pies and custards and fix the awfullest dinner or supper ever you saw. We'd get the corn all shucked out, and they'd dance till daylight."

Most of the time corn was prepared simply. Granny Gibson told us: "Whenever I was growing up we'd go to the field and get just regular old field corn. Just cut it off and put it in the pan and fry it; or you could boil it, either way. I thought it was good. Sweet corn's took its place now. It's good, too."

Some basic corn recipes follow.

BERTHA WALDROOP: "For boiled corn on the cob, shuck and silk your fresh corn. Put the ears of corn in boiling water. When the water returns to a hard boil, put the lid on the pot and continue to boil for ten to fifteen minutes more."

LUCY YORK: "Cut fresh corn off the cob. Put it in a frying pan with a small amount of butter or grease. Add water, if needed, and cook a short time—just long enough to get it tender."

INEZ TAYLOR: "I remember my mother's fried corn. She cut it off the cob real thin, and she'd put her some butter in one of those old iron skillets and put the corn in that hot butter and just stir it till it thickened. Lots of times she'd put it in the oven and it would brown on the top and the bottom. There's nobody could cook it like she did."

BLANCHE HARKINS: "Parching corn—shell dried corn off the cob in the fall or wintertime. Toast it in the oven like parching peanuts."

It was possible to create relatively complicated concoctions using only readily available ingredients and a little imagination:

Skin the corn with homemade lye. Cook corn by boiling. Cook dried beans. Put corn and beans together in same pot, cook some more. Add pumpkin if you like, and cook until pumpkin is done. Add to this a mixture of cornmeal, beaten walnut and hickory nut meats, and enough molasses to sweeten. Cook this in an iron pot until the meal is done. Eat fresh or after it begins to sour. Some of this may be fried in hot grease. This mixture will not keep very long unless the weather is cold.

The arrival of the supermarket caused the creation of more sophisticated recipes like the one Arizona Dickerson shared with us:

CORN AU GRATIN

ARIZONA DICKERSON

2 egg yolks, well beaten
1 cup cooked corn
1 small onion, chopped
1 small green pepper, chopped
2 tablespoons shortening

1 cup cooked rice
½ cup grated cheese
Salt and pepper to taste
Dash of paprika
Strips of bacon

Mix together beaten egg yolks and corn. Sauté onion and green pepper in the shortening and add to egg and corn mixture. Lightly fold in cooked rice. Place half of mixture in a baking dish, add ¼ cup cheese, salt, and pepper, then remaining corn mixture. Cover with remaining grated cheese. Dust with paprika and lay strips of bacon across the top. Bake in a 400°F oven for 20 minutes, or until bacon is cooked. YIELD: *6 servings*

GARDEN GREENS

While cultivated collards, turnip greens, and mustard varieties have been known to escape or naturalize and grow wild in old garden plots, it was common practice to plant them in late summer and early fall with other cool weather crops. People also planted late cabbage and turnips for storing through the winter, and the fall garden assured them of a good supply of fresh greens after the warm-weather crops finished coming in.

Esco Pitts elaborates: "For a fall crop, we planted turnips and cabbage in September. Sometimes we'd put out late multiplying onions in the fall (around September) and have onions all winter. We buried the turnips along with the cabbage to keep them through the winter. Usually, my mother planted [collards] in the fall of the year. Around the latter part of July or the first of August, she'd sow a collard bed, and when they come up a good size to transplant, she'd have a row in the garden. Collards are not much good till the frost bites them—it makes them better to eat."

Turnip and mustard greens still appeal widely to the Appalachian palate. Ione Dickerson said, "My son didn't like turnip greens, so I gave him a nickel a bite to eat them. He got rich fast like that [laughter]! It's a funny thing—he loves greens now. Dr. Neville told me one time, 'If they don't eat it when you put it on the table, put it on again until they *do* eat it!' "

RUTH HOLCOMB: "Wash the greens thoroughly. Put them in a pan and cover with water. Put top on the pan and bring greens to a boil. Scrape new potatoes and boil on top of the greens. Add salt to taste. Cook until tender, one to two hours. Season with bacon grease or butter."

GRANNY GIBSON: "I've tried raising spinach, and I never could do nothing with it. It just wouldn't grow for me. Mustard greens and turnip greens do good, though. You have to boil them with grease in them. I usually cook mine with peanut oil or some kind of oil made out of sunflower seeds, but people used to just cook it with fatback."

MARGIE LEDFORD: "I don't like poke salad, but I love turnip and mustard greens. You put a piece of meat in the water when you cook your turnip greens and cook them good and tender. When you get them tender, drain the water out of them. A lot of times I take and cook mine in a pot of meat grease. Now that's what makes them good. Have you some grease in one of them big skillets and put them in there and slow fry them where they won't scorch or anything till they are real good and tender. Mix up some seasoning in there, and they will melt in your mouth if you're a hillbilly! Most hillbillies like turnip greens."

RITTIE WEBB: "Let mustard greens cook about thirty minutes and season them. You don't have to fry it if you put the seasoning in while it's in the pot. Of course, a lot of people do fry it. Leonard used to eat his raw."

HOMINY

While the making of hominy was not exactly an easy undertaking, it was yet another way in which the taste of common corn could be altered to add variety to the Appalachian diet.

Hominy is served as a starchy vegetable, like rice, and is made from the kernels of dried corn. The outer husks of the kernels are removed by boiling the shelled corn in lye water. It is usually prepared outdoors in a large cast-iron pot over an open fire. "Granny" Gibson briefly explained this time-consuming process:

"People used to tie ashes and corn in a sack and boil them a pretty long time in an old iron pot. The water going through the ashes makes lye. That's what makes the outer part of the corn kind of scale off, and what you have left is hominy. You just wash it and wash it to get the lye out, and then you put it back in the pot with just pure water and cook it until it gets tender. Keep adding water to it because it just keeps swelling. Then you take it out, put some grease in it and fry it. It takes all day to make it, but it was good."

A more detailed account of how to produce homemade hominy follows:

The first thing that must be done in the making of hominy is to prepare the lye. It is made by pouring water through oak or hickory ashes that have been saved from the fireplace.

During the demonstration by Bessie Kelly, the ashes were placed in a large metal barrel, which had a spouted hole in the bottom. Several gallons of water were slowly poured over them. The water soaking through the ashes leached out the potash, or lye, and this dripped into a plastic container. (Plastic, iron, or porcelain can be used, but not aluminum, as the lye will corrode it.) This should take about 2 hours. (For more detailed information about ash hoppers, see *The Foxfire Book,* p. 156, and *Foxfire 4,* p. 478.)

Two gallons of shelled corn are put into a large iron wash pot and the 2 gallons lye added. Then 2 gallons of water are added. More water is poured in as needed to keep the corn covered and to prevent its sticking to the bottom of the pot. The lye-corn mixture must cook until the skins start coming off the corn. This usually takes 4 to 6 hours. Stir the mixture occasionally to prevent sticking. All the corn is then removed from the pot, the lye water poured off, and the pot washed out. Thoroughly rinse the lye off the corn. Place corn back into the clean pot and cover with clear water. Boil the corn again until

Hominy was most frequently made in an old cast iron wash pot.

A barrel used for dripping lye when making hominy

*The final, ready-to-eat product is brought up
on the paddle used to stir the hominy.*

the skins come completely off. The hominy comes to the top of the pot and can be scooped out, ready to eat plain or fried in butter. If you want to preserve the hominy, it can be frozen or canned.

HOMINY

1 cup hominy   *4 cups boiling water plus 1 teaspoon salt*

Drop the hominy into the salted boiling water in the top of a double boiler. Place over hot water and steam, covered, for 1 hour, or until tender. Serve with cream or melted butter.

Rittie Webb uses "bought lye" today for making hominy: "My mother used to make hominy out of homemade lye, and I have too. It makes it taste better than this lye we buy. It gives it a kind of sweet taste. Of course, now I use the bought lye. You take about a gallon of water and put it in an iron kettle and let the water start boiling. Then you put the lye in. I use about a teaspoonful of lye to a quart of water. When the water starts boiling, get the lye dissolved good in there, and then put in the corn. I put in about a half a gallon of corn, and that way you make enough. Then you stir it with a wood-handled spoon. Make sure the skin is all off of it, and take it out of the kettle and wash it real good about three times in a [different] pan. Wash the kettle, too. Put the hominy back in the kettle, in some clean water and boil again. You have to stir the hominy pretty often, till it comes to the top and you can see it. [It will] make your water get thick. Then it swells up and it will make your kettle full directly. I start cooking my hominy early in the morning and it takes me all day to get it cooked enough. By night, it's all right to eat. It's a job to make hominy. I like to eat it right out of the kettle. Most of us put it in a pan with some bacon grease, salt it, and fry it just a little before we go to eat it, and that gives it a good taste."

OKRA

Another popular vegetable was the prickly pod called okra.

FRIED OKRA

Slice the okra about ½-inch thick, roll in meal and salt, and fry in grease until light brown and crispy.

OKRA AND GREEN BEANS

BELLE LEDFORD

"I steam okra on the top of green beans. Just before your green beans get done, pick out the tender, young okra pods. Cut their stem ends off, but don't cut into the okra. Put them on top of the green beans and let them steam while they finish cooking. Don't stir the beans, or you'll stir the okra down in them."

ONIONS

Onions are most frequently fried:

FRIED GREEN ONIONS

BELLE LEDFORD

"My mother used to fry green onions [spring onions or scallions]. When they were young and tender, you could eat the tops, too. She'd cut them up and fry them all together, the tops and the onions."

SCALLOPED ONIONS

Wash onions and boil until tender. Drain well and layer onions in a baking dish. Sprinkle each layer with soft bread crumbs, grated cheese, salt, and paprika. Pour hot bacon drippings over the onions. Bake in moderate 375°F oven until top is brown.

BOILED ONIONS

Place whole, sliced, or skinned onions in a boiler, covering them with salted water. Boil onions until tender. Drain well. Serve with melted butter or drop into a boiling white sauce.

Some people much preferred the taste of ramps to any type of cultivated onion, and the controversy continues even today. It seems that people either love or hate the strong-scented plant. One gentleman said, "They're not for ladies or those who court them." And Ethel Corn said, "Now a lot of people still go into the mountains and get ramps to cook and eat. I don't see how they could because you can smell anybody that's took a bite of one a half a mile away before they get there. But some people are crazy about them. They'll even get them and put them up for the winter and freeze them."

Ramps—onion-like wild plants—are eaten by some brave people as a cold remedy.

"Down in south Georgia they's sights of these old wild onions. Now they smelled *good* to what a ramp does. Ramps stinks worse than what wild onions does." Others, as Maude Shope noted, "go crazy for a mess of ramps in the spring of the year."

LESSIE CONNER: "Wash them clean, cut them up fine just like you would onions, put them in some grease, salt them, and fry them. When they get about done, break you two or three eggs in them and scramble them. I like them, but they'll knock you down. You can smell them in the house for weeks! Minyard's got about fifteen quarts of ramps out there in the freezer now."

Minyard Conner says, "Every time I get sick I always eat them." But Addie Norton argues, "I never could stand them, and I never did gather them. There was plenty of wild onions just a mile off. You can boil them, and they just nearly make you sick they're so strong. And they say ramps is lots worse."

You may want to try them for yourself, using the following recipes:

FRIED RAMPS

NORA GARLAND

"There are red ramps and white ones. White are best. Put them in a pan with water and cook until tender. Drain and fry in grease along with tunafish and eggs."

CLIFFORD CONNER

"To clean them, pull off the outer skin around the bulb. Chop a good bit of ramps with about five eggs into a frying pan, and fry them with about three heaped tablespoons of grease. Fry them hot and fast because of smell. Add a little salt, pepper, eggs, or potatoes in with them for flavor to your own fancy. Most important, go into solitary in the woods somewheres and stay for two or three weeks because nobody can stand your breath after you've eat them."

RAMPS

HARLEY CARPENTER

"Chop up young leaves fine. You can eat them raw or cook them and add vinegar when ready to eat."

Other suggestions included coating with bread crumbs and frying in butter, boiling with a piece of fatback or adding to soups and salads.

POTATOES

SWEET POTATOES

Sweet potatoes also have a flavor reminiscent of pumpkin and some squash but were often more widely grown:

ESCO PITTS: "When he dug his sweet potatoes, my father always let them dry in the sunshine. Then he'd bring them in the kitchen and put them back of the stove. He'd sort out all the small, long, stringy potatoes that weren't big enough to try to eat."

LUCY YORK: "You may boil your sweet potatoes until they are tender. Then peel them, mash them up, and add sugar and butter to taste. Or you may peel them raw, slice into quarter-inch pieces, and fry in hot grease until tender."

RUTH HOLCOMB: "Wash sweet potatoes and rub them dry with a cloth. With the peels still on, lay them in a pan that is greased lightly. Wash and dry cabbage leaves and lay them on top of the potatoes. Put in a hot stove and bake until soft and tender. The cabbage leaves hold the steam in."

BAKED SWEET POTATOES

Today people use this same recipe but with the addition of orange or lemon juice and cinnamon.

6 to 8 sweet potatoes, cooked and peeled　　*¼ cup honey*
4 tablespoons butter

Place potatoes in a baking dish. Combine butter and honey and pour over potatoes. Bake in a hot (400°F) oven for 15 to 20 minutes, basting frequently.

HONEY SWEET POTATOES

⅔ cup honey　　　　　　　　　　*1 teaspoon salt*
½ cup butter　　　　　　　　　　*8 to 9 sweet potatoes*

In a well-greased baking dish, spoon the combined honey, butter, and salt between layers of sliced sweet potato. Bake in a moderate (350°F) oven for 30 minutes, basting frequently.

SWEET POTATO SOUFFLÉ

ARIZONA DICKERSON

1 cup milk
1 tablespoon butter or margarine
½ teaspoon salt
2 tablespoons sugar
2 cups cooked sweet potatoes, mashed

2 eggs, separated
1 teaspoon nutmeg
¼ cup raisins
¼ cup nuts, chopped

Scald milk. Add butter, sugar, and salt. Stir until butter is melted. Add to sweet potatoes. Stir until smooth. Beat yolks and whites of eggs separately. Stir yolks into potato mixture, and then add nutmeg, raisins, and nuts. Fold in stiffly beaten whites and pour into buttered baking dish.

If desired and obtainable, arrange 5 marshmallows over the top. Bake in a moderate (350°F) oven for 20 to 25 minutes or until set. Use as main course or dessert. YIELD: 6 *servings*

FRIED SWEET POTATOES

Inez Taylor remembers her mother's fried sweet potatoes. "She'd put just a little grease in the pan, and she'd slice them [sweet potatoes] just like you do Irish potatoes. She'd put them in the pan and put a cup of sugar on them. Then she'd dampen that sugar with water and put those in the oven till they browned."

IRISH POTATOES

Irish potatoes are a real staple in the Appalachian meat-and-potatoes diet. They are baked, fried, mashed, put into pies, and eaten with gravy and dumplings.

ADDIE NORTON: "Irish potatoes, everybody eats Irish potatoes in North Carolina. I don't know about everywhere else, but everybody here eats Irish potatoes about every meal. I told my daddy one time, I said, 'I've eat potatoes till I don't think I'll ever want any more,' and I never have wanted any more.

"And I could then fry some of the best Irish potatoes I believe I ever seen, and you know how I done? Done the hard way. I put them on and boiled them and took the skin off of them, and then I mashed them up while they was hot. I mashed them up with salt and pepper and worked that salt and pepper in them, you know, and then I made them up in patties and put them in a pan of grease and fried them. You can't find nothing no better than that if you love Irish potatoes. They would just get as brown as they could be on both sides. They was good, even if I did cook them.

"I bake Irish potatoes. I also peel them and boil them, then mash them, adding salt, pepper, butter, and milk to make them creamy. To fry them I slice three or four potatoes very thin, like potato chips; put in a frying pan with hot grease, and season with salt and pepper. Cover, and cook until light brown, turning occasionally."

LOLA CANNON: "A good-sized potato will bake in the wood stove in about two hours."

IONE DICKERSON: "My grandmother used to make this recipe. Cook and mash potatoes and brown sausage. In a casserole dish place a layer of potatoes and then a layer of sausage until both are all used. Bake until bubbly or cooked through at 300 degrees for fifteen to twenty minutes or until done."

RUTH HOLCOMB: "For gravy and potatoes, I peel small new potatoes and boil them until they are tender. I mix three tablespoons of flour in two cups of milk and pour this into the potatoes and cook them two or three more minutes, until that gravy's thick. Take from stove and stir in one tablespoon butter and a dash of black pepper and salt to taste."

POTATO CROQUETTES WITH CORNMEAL

BELLE LEDFORD

"In making potato croquettes, most people use flour, but I like the cornmeal. You take cooked potatoes. You can use leftover stewed or creamed potatoes, but if I was just going to begin from the first, I'd cook about four or five medium-sized potatoes. Put one egg in that, and if you wanted two eggs, you could put two in it. I dip out between a fourth and a half cup of cornmeal in my hand and add that with about a half a teaspoon baking powder. Then put in about a tablespoon or two of chopped onion. That cornmeal and the egg helps it to hold together. Sometimes you have to put a little milk in it to moisten it up if it's too dry. Make it out into little cakes and fry them in grease."

IRISH POTATO PIE OR DUMPLINGS

RUTH HOLCOMB

"Peel and slice Irish potatoes. Cook in a boiler with enough water to cover the potatoes. After they are tender, leave them in the water and add one tablespoonful of butter and pepper to taste. Roll out a biscuit dough and pat it thin. Lay this on the potatoes and juice. Bring the potatoes to a boil and continue boiling for five to ten minutes, until the dumpling is cooked through. It is a good idea to stick holes in the dumpling with the tines of a fork so that the boiling juice will bubble through and help the dough to cook evenly. It is ready to serve when the dumpling is no longer doughy, but has the consistency of a biscuit inside."

IRISH POTATO DUMPLINGS

1 quart potatoes, peeled and quartered
1½ to 2 quarts water
Salt and pepper to taste

1 tablespoon butter or margarine
1 cup milk
1 recipe for biscuit dough

Peel and quarter potatoes. Put them in a pot, cover with water, add salt and pepper and butter. Boil until the potatoes are tender. Add milk. Roll biscuit dough out ¼-inch thick, cut in 2-inch squares, and drop into the rapidly boiling water in which the potatoes are cooking. Cook dumplings 1 minute, remove the pot from the heat, and serve hot.

PUMPKINS

Lucy York describes preparations for pumpkins and cushaws: "Peel and slice them up. Cook in a small amount of water until soft like applesauce. They can then be served as a vegetable. They have a sweet taste, but more sweetening could be added, if desired. Usually sorghum syrup is used."

FLORENCE BROOKS: "We used to eat slices of pumpkin fried in grease."

FRIED PUMPKIN OR SQUASH BLOSSOMS

MARGARET NORTON

1 egg
½ cup flour
½ cup milk

Pumpkin or squash blossoms
Grease for deep frying

Make a thin batter using egg, milk, and flour. Dip the blossoms in the batter and fry in deep hot grease. Serve as you would any vegetable.

SQUASH

Many varieties of squash were cultivated in the mountains. Some of these were served as vegetables, but others had a chameleon quality that varied according to the kind of spices and flavorings added to them (see Cushaw Pie, for example, in "Desserts").

HARRY BROWN: "Everybody planted their cucumbers and squash on the tenth day of May —they called it Vine Day. You can plant squash earlier, but old people always planted squash, kershaws, and Hubbard then. Kershaws are pulp filled and grow great long. They're white and have a neck to them kind of like crookneck squash, only great big. They were really good to fry like sweet potatoes or to slice up and put butter and sugar on them. Just put them in the stove and bake them."

When local people say "squash," they generally refer to yellow crook-neck summer squash. The following preparation ideas were contributed with this type in mind:

HATTIE WATKINS: "When you're frying squash, you can put in some green tomato slices or okra rolled in cornmeal, and cook it all at the same time."

BELLE LEDFORD: "I dip my squash in cornmeal when I fry it. Don't many people fry squash just one layer at a time in a pan and brown it on each side. My children liked it better that way. After they got large enough to be cooking themselves, I'd say, 'I'll fix one pan full. If you want more, you can fix more. You can fix as many as you want to.' It takes a long time to stand over it and fix it that way."

ARIZONA DICKERSON: "If squash are small, slice crossways like you would tomatoes for sandwiches. If they are large, slice longways into quarters; then slice into quarter-inch pieces. Roll the pieces in cornmeal or flour and salt and pepper. Fry in a pan with a small amount of oil or grease. Turn over when browned. Remove and drain on brown paper when cooked on both sides."

SQUASH SOUFFLÉ

ARIZONA DICKERSON

3 tablespoons butter or grease
1 cup hot milk
1 cup fine dry bread crumbs
2 cups cooked squash
½ teaspoon salt

⅛ teaspoon pepper
1 tablespoon grated onion
2 eggs, beaten
1 cup grated cheese (try different cheeses to vary the dish)

Melt the butter in the hot milk and pour over bread crumbs. Mix with the squash, salt, pepper, onion, and eggs; pour into a buttered baking dish and sprinkle the cheese over the top. Bake in a 350°F oven for 20 to 30 minutes. YIELD: 6-8 servings

Granny Gibson describes a way of preparing winter squash: "There's different ways to cook squash. You can stew them or fry them or bake them. Edith out here bakes hers sometimes. You just cut them [lengthwise] through the middle, lay them in the pan, put some butter on them, and bake them in the stove. They're good."

TOMATOES

ESCO PITTS: "I never saw a tomato till I was ten or twelve years old. My daddy wouldn't hardly go to the table if there was tomato on there. He said they wasn't a hog would eat them and so he wasn't going to eat them. Tomatoes was something we never saw in our young days."

Despite skeptics like Esco Pitts's father, tomatoes, onions and carrots soon became common garden items.

FRIED GREEN TOMATOES

LOLA CANNON

"Pick tomatoes before they start showing any sign of ripening. Wash and slice tomatoes;

roll in a mixture of flour or meal and salt and pepper and fry in hot fat. Brown on both sides."

BERTHA WALDROOP: "Use green tomatoes before they show any sign of ripening. Wash and slice just as you would for tomato sandwiches. Roll the slices in cornmeal and flour or a mixture of the two. Heat grease in a frying pan and put the slices in. Salt and pepper them. Then turn them over to brown on the other side. When browned, remove and drain on brown paper or paper towels and serve."

STEWED TOMATOES

Remove skins and slice tomatoes into a pot. Place over the heat and let stew in their own juice 15-20 minutes. Add desired amounts of salt and pepper; add some butter. Stew for another 15 minutes.

TOMATO PIE

4 cups canned tomatoes
1 cup milk

½ cup sugar
Pie dough of choice

Pour tomatoes into a pan that can be placed in the oven. Add salt to taste. Stir in sugar and milk. Make up a dough just like for a cobbler pie and roll or press the dough out.

Bring the tomato mixture to boiling on top of the stove. Lay dough on top of the tomatoes, letting the juice boil through. Boil until dough is done (cooked through). Then put in a 350°F oven to brown on top, about 5 to 10 minutes.

TURNIPS, RUTABAGAS, PARSNIPS

Turnips were a popular by-product of greens, and rutabagas and parsnips were prepared much the same way.

FLORENCE BROOKS: "We raised great big turnips—people don't raise turnips like they did then. Old people had great large turnips back then, and they had them all the winter. Lot of times they'd have to plow those old turnips up and push them aside to plant again in the spring. And my father went to the field with a big basket [to gather the cast-aside turnips] and we'd put on pots of them to eat."

BELLE LEDFORD: "I stew or steam rutabagas until they're done, mash them, and put a little butter in them. I don't fix them often, but I have a son-in-law that likes them. When he visits if it's in season I cook them for him because he doesn't get them at home."

MARGIE LEDFORD: "I don't like parsnips, but, now, I like rutabagas. I cook them just like turnips. Get a piece of meat and put it in there and get it to boiling; then put the rutabagas in. I put a little bit of sugar in them."

RUTH HOLCOMB: "Wash and peel parsnips. Put in a pan with a piece of ham bone or other meat. Cover with water, add one teaspoon sugar and salt to taste. Boil until almost dry, about three hours. They are then ready to serve."

EXIE DILLS: "You can fry them or you can boil them. Take them backbones you know, and put a bunch of them on top of the parsnips and cook them. They was pretty good, I thought."

WILD GREENS

Greens are among the foods best loved by adults—and sometimes most carefully avoided by children. In the spring before garden greens could be picked, many women would take to the woods and creek banks to locate wild greens. Ethel Corn was one of these:

"I'm bad for wild salads [greens]. You could cut crowsfoot—it grows in the mountains on branches and streams. And cochan grows all up and down these branches, and people'd eat that. It made a delicious salad. People always cooked poke salad and eat it, too. I have even knowed people to pick briar leaves, peppermint, and pepper grass and cook it together. Now, I never did try that because that didn't sound too good to me. And then there's this white rabbit plant and that groundhog plant that they'd cook back when I was just a young'un. Old people went for wild salads more than they did raising salad."

Many wild greens have been used by mountain people since pioneer days, when the use of wild plants was a necessary supplement to the daily diet. Nowadays the consumption of wild plants is a matter of choice rather than need, but many folks still insist that everybody's system needs the personal "spring cleaning" offered by wild plant foods. Others argue for the high vitamin and mineral content of most wild plants. Here we include a few of the favorite and most talked about greens. A more complete discussion of wild plant foods grown from spring through fall may be found in *Foxfire 2*, pages 47–94, and *Foxfire 3*, pages 274–353.

A mature pokeweed plant

POKE

It is sometimes misleading when people from other areas of the country hear Southerners speak of poke "salad." Poke is not usually used as a raw salad ingredient. Because of the wild taste of this green, most people parboil it and rinse it well before cooking it. Poke shoots resemble asparagus and are probably eaten more frequently than any other wild food in the mountain areas. Many country doctors supported the theory that "poke salad eaten in the spring revives the blood." Dr. Neville said to be sure to eat at least one mess of poke each spring, and Dr. Dover said, "Anybody that gets sick from eating poke, I'll treat them free." Local people tended to follow the advice, and, as Carrie Dixon said, "My ma used to send us young'uns looking for it as soon as the frogs started croaking in spring."

It is a fact that parts of the plant are toxic, however, and readers would be well advised to avoid the root, the berries, and the stalk and leaves of the mature plant, cooking only the young shoots (four to six inches high), as they first emerge from the ground. These are safe when cooked, and generally prized:

BESSIE BOLT: "My mother told me that an old doctor said that if you eat three messes of poke in the spring it would doctor you free of any fevers. It killed all the poison from the stomach and body. The way I cook poke is I boil it, squeeze it out and put oil in it. I don't use lard or meat grease. Cut an onion up and put it in there and just turn it over a few times so the onion cooks, and it's ready to serve. It's good, too. I like poke salad. When I was a girl I knowed where all the poke stalks growed, and Mother'd send me to get the poke salad. I used to didn't care so much for it, but I got to liking it. Now I'd rather have it than most anything on the table—chicken stew, eggs, or any kind of meat."

RITTIE WEBB: "Boy, I've eat a lot of poke salad. You put your poke in a pot and hard-boil it. Then take it up and run some cold water over it. Mash the water out of it, and put it in a pan of grease. Let it start to fry, and when it's about done break an egg in it, stir it up, and fry it some more. That poke is so strong that if you don't wash it good and cook it till it's done, it will make you sick."

BOILED POKE

RUTH GIBBS

"Collect tender young shoots of poke in the spring when they are six to eight inches high. Do not cut them below the surface of the ground as the root is poisonous. Wash and cook the leaves and stems together, parboiling two times (pouring off the water each time after boiling a few minutes). Boil in third water until tender, salting to taste. Drain and top with slices of hard-boiled egg."

FRIED POKE AND EGGS

LOVEY KELSO

"Cook two pounds fresh tender greens by bringing them to a hard boil for ten or fifteen minutes. Drain and wash well. Put three tablespoons grease in an iron fry pan, and add salt. Fry greens. You can scramble three eggs in it, serve hard-boiled eggs over it, or cook with a streak of fat and some streak of lean."

POKE AND ONIONS

MRS. DILLARD THOMPSON

"Cook in boiling water the same as turnip greens. When tender take the dark green leaves, chop them up and add little spring green onions."

ZESTY POKE SALAD

ADDIE NORTON

"Wash well and parboil for ten minutes. Rinse three or four times and then fry in fatback grease until tender. Season with salt and pepper or add pepper sauce or apple vinegar. The young stalks are also eaten. They are sliced and peeled, rolled in cornmeal or flour, and fried until tender. You may also pickle stalks in warm vinegar and spices."

FRIED POKE STALKS

ETHEL CORN

"Cut whole poke plant off level with the ground when young or four to seven inches high. Wash and slice like okra. Roll in a mixture of salt, pepper, and flour and fry in grease until brown on the outside and tender on the inside."

COCHAN

Cochan (or tall coneflower) is another popular wild green. Its leaves are edible when young and tender, and it is prepared much like poke. Lizzie Moore is an authority on cochan:

Cochan is a wild [plant]. *You'd* say it was a weed [laughter]. But it grows out on the branch banks and in real rich ground. It has a forked leaf, and it's always great long. After it gets grown it has a yellow flower on it like this Golden Glow. Some people likes it and some don't.

I was the one that used to fix the cochan dinner for ten or fifteen or twenty. I guess you seen that in the [Clayton *Tribune*] if you ever used to read the *Tribune.* I used to fix it for Irene Bynum and Connie Green, Vera Mincemoyer and all those people. Their

Kenny Runion holds a newly gathered mess of cochan.

mother always cooked that cochan for them when they were children, and they liked it so good they always wanted me to fix it. We kept it up for years.

We always had the cochan dinner here in about April or May. I'd get out and pick a half a bushel or just as much as I could. I'd put it in the cooker, slice fatback or streak-of-lean meat, and put it in the cochan and, after I got it cooked down some, put salt in it. Let it boil about thirty minutes, drain that water off, and put some more water back in it. It's got a kind of flavor, you know, and when you drain that [water] off, it's much better. And what they always wanted to eat with that was little tender onions, corn bread, and pickled beets. I've had a crippled arm this time, and I can't get out and pick it, so I haven't fixed a cochan dinner. It takes a long time to pick that much when you have to get out on the branch banks or somewhere like that.

CREASES

Granny Gibson told us, "Creases is another salad-like stuff that grows out mostly in the cornfield. You cook it just like turnip greens." The leaves of creases are sharp-tasting, very like watercress, and can be cooked or used raw in salads. It is gathered young, within days of its appearance.

BOILED CREASES

ARIE CARPENTER

"Put in a piece of middling meat in the morning to boil. Boil for at least two hours or as long as it takes to get it tender. Take the grease off the meat, add it to a pot of water, and bring to a boil. Add cleaned creases and boil for thirty minutes."

FRIED CREASES

NEAROLA TAYLOR

"Fry fatback meat in a heavy pot, preferably an old black dinner pot. Have creases clean and washed. Take meat out, leaving grease in pot. Shake out creases and drop in hot grease, stirring and mixing thoroughly with grease. Add just enough water to keep from burning or sticking to pot. Add salt as desired, and cook about twenty minutes, or until tender. Stir often."

OTHER WILD GREENS

Wild lettuce, dandelion, lamb's quarters, dock, sheep sorrel, and watercress are other common spring greens that may be found in damp woods or by streams. When cooked, their preparation follows the basic salad and greens variations of other wild plants we've mentioned. These greens are sometimes cooked together, and sometimes eaten raw in salads.

TURNIP GREENS AND CORNMEAL DUMPLINGS

DOROTHY BECK

"We used to take the turnip greens out of the crock and set them to boiling. We would make a dough out of cornmeal and onions just like you do hush puppies and drop them in that turnip green broth like a dumpling."

14

Breads

"He's married a woman that can't even cook corn bread."

After the invention of the gristmill, people could take the grains of corn, wheat, and rye, which they grew themselves, to be ground into meal, to be later used for bread making. Although wheat and rye were used for making bread, that cornmeal was and still is the most versatile meal commodity in the kitchen.

Cornmeal, grits, and hominy are all made from corn that is not harvested until after autumn frost, when the husks and the kernels of corn are hard and dry. The ears are either gathered and stored, or shucked (husked) and the kernels shelled off the cobs. The kernels can be made into hominy, or they can be stored in cloth sacks in an airy area through the winter until they are ground. If left on the cob, they can be shelled at the time of grinding.

When going to the mill, most people prefer to take one or two bushels at a time so their meal and/or grits do not stay on the kitchen shelf over a long period of time. If not used, they may become stale, and weevils will get in both.

Many people in this area still raise their own corn for grinding; and although there are several gristmills still operated by water power in the area, most of them have been somewhat modernized, as has the one Ruby Frady operates in the Persimmon Community. Mrs. Frady agreed to talk with us about her mill, and when we went to see her, she had her mill in operation.

In 1955 Mrs. Frady and her husband, Lon, began operating the mill that he had built over a stream in the Persimmon Community. Together they ground cornmeal for the people of the surrounding area until Lon died in 1967. Since then Ruby has continued to run their mill alone, serving a handful of customers who "don't come regular." Some days she doesn't grind any meal; on other days she might grind two or three bushels or perhaps only one "turn," which, Ruby tells us, is a bushel—the smallest amount she'll grind. A 65-pound bushel of corn weighs, after grinding, about 48 pounds. For grinding this amount Ruby charges a dollar and a half. "Some of them," she says, "want to pay first, but all of them don't want to pay. They want me to take a toll out, or take out so much meal for running it."

With her small fees, Ruby has to buy both gasoline and diesel fuel for her mill, which is run by two motors. She starts on gas and then turns over onto diesel, using a switch similar to a Jeep ignition. While getting the motor to crank is sometimes a chore, Ruby says that the most difficult part of the job is pouring the corn into the hopper. She says, "It's a pretty hard job grinding a whole lot at the time, but I don't mind it too bad when it ain't cold, just for a few turns."

Lester Baker told us about a gristmill once operated in the Oak Grove community: "The gristmill down here on the creek was last run in the early 1960s. Jimmy Howard bought it and was the last one to run it, and that's been fifteen or twenty years ago. My dad ran it, but my granddaddy and my uncles were the main ones that ran the mill. We had all these mills down here, and all except for the sawmill and shingle mill were pulled by water power. They were pulled by steam engine. When we lived down there we'd go grind corn any day anybody came. We didn't have no certain day to grind. We would take the toll out, and that was the way most people paid. An eighth of a bushel is what we got for grinding a bushel. We had a little box [down at the mill], and it'd hold about a half a gallon. Take that out twice for a bushel, and if they had a half a bushel we'd only take it out one time. If anybody wanted to pay with money they would, but I don't remember how much. People came from all over the community and some from over the mountain to have their corn ground here. They'd bring five or six bushels of corn in a wagon."

(EDITOR'S NOTE: For more information about gristmills see *Foxfire 2* [pages 142–63] and *Foxfire 6* [pages 285–86].)

CORN BREAD

Like most other older people in the area, Rettie Webb's grandparents cooked their cornbread in a Dutch oven in the fireplace: "I remember my grandpa used to get my grandma to make corn bread in the fireplace. It'd cook good if you got good [hot] coals and a good fire. We used to eat corn bread every day, and older people lived on it. My daddy lived on it and he lived to be ninety-three years old. It's got good stuff in it. We used to take corn bread and put buttermilk over it and eat it."

Later, of course, there were wood cookstoves, and corn bread continued as a staple —and one item all women had to know how to cook. As Margie Ledford said, "The first thing I learned to cook was corn bread. There was about ten in our family altogether, and it took a pretty good pone of bread to fill them up with just 'taters, butter, corn bread, meat, and milk. I think corn bread tasted better cooked in a wood stove. Maybe that was just my belief, but I really do think that if you had a good hot wood stove and put your corn bread in there, it seemed like it tasted better."

During hard times families depended on cornmeal for their main source of food when other products were unavailable. We heard several stories much like the one Stella Burrell told us: "I can remember during the Depression when we wasn't able to have flour, and my mother was sick in the hospital. I can remember having corn bread for breakfast, and my daddy would fix cornmeal gravy oftentimes. We did eat a lot of gravy; we called it 'sawmill gravy.'"

Gladys Nichols told us about one of the earliest methods for making bread: "We used to dry the corn for roastin' ears. Then we shucked it and baked it in the oven. Then you could grate it off the cob, put you a little soda and salt and a little buttermilk in it and bake it. That's called 'roastin' ear bread.'"

Another contact gave us instructions for making gritted meal chestnut bread, another old recipe that is seldom used today: "Gather the corn just past the roasting ear stage. Grit the raw corn on a metal gritter. Remove the chestnut meats from the hulls, scald, and remove bitter skins. Cook in water until tender. Pour boiling chestnut meats and water into gritted meal (be careful with the amount of water lest dough become too soft), fashion into hand-sized pones, wrap with corn blades or hickory leaves, drop into a pot of boiling water and cook until done (an hour or so)."

Practically every person we talked to gave us their recipe for corn bread.

CORN BREAD ON A WOOD STOVE

RUBY FRADY

3 cups freshly ground cornmeal
½ to 1 teaspoon salt

½ teaspoon soda
½ cup milk

Sift freshly ground [not self-rising] cornmeal into a large bowl. Add salt and soda, mixing well, and then the milk. Mix thoroughly and pour into a greased pan. Bake in a 450°F oven until golden brown (approximately 20 to 30 minutes). When brown, take out of oven, let cool for a few minutes, and turn out the bread by inverting the pan. YIELD: *6-8 servings*

CORN BREAD

ANNIE LONG

2 cups cornmeal
1 teaspoon soda
1 teaspoon salt

1 egg, beaten
2 cups sour milk
2 tablespoons melted lard*

Sift cornmeal to get bran out. Measure the cornmeal, soda, and salt and sift together. Mix in beaten egg, milk, and melted lard. Pour into a hot greased iron skillet and bake in a 425°F oven. YIELD: *6 servings*

QUICK AND EASY CORN BREAD

BERTHA WALDROOP

2 cups self-rising cornmeal
1 egg

Milk or water

Mix cornmeal and egg together. Add enough milk or water to make a thick batter and beat. Grease a pan and bake at 425°F until brown. YIELD: *4-6 servings*

MAYONNAISE CORN BREAD

HATTIE WATKINS

1 cup self-rising cornmeal
1 cup self-rising flour
½ cup milk

1 egg
1 tablespoon mayonnaise

*Melt lard in the skillet and this leaves the pan ready for baking.

Mix together all ingredients. Pour into a greased pan or skillet and bake in a hot (425°F) oven. YIELD: *4-6 servings*

CRACKLIN CORN BREAD

To add a different flavor to corn bread, cooks learned to use cracklins. Granny Gibson told us: "You can put cracklins in it. That's what I like—cracklin bread. You know when you kill a hog you've got all kinds of fat and stuff. You have to cut it up and put it on the stove and cook it out to make your lard. You have to keep it stirred, and it'll fry down to the cracklins. That's where your cracklins comes in at. Put them in with your corn bread whenever you go to cook it. That makes it good."

QUICK AND EASY CRACKLIN BREAD

RUTH HOLCOMB

2 cups self-rising cornmeal   *1 cup milk*
1 cup cracklins

Mix cornmeal, cracklins, and milk together. Pour into a greased pan and bake in a hot (425°F) oven until done, 20 or more minutes.

BUTTERMILK CRACKLIN BREAD

2 cups cornmeal   *1 cup buttermilk*
2 teaspoons salt   *½ cup cracklins*
1 teaspoon soda   *Lukewarm water (optional)*
½ teaspoon baking powder

Mix together the cornmeal, salt, soda, baking powder, and buttermilk. Mix cracklins into the mixture. If it is too dry, use some lukewarm water to make it the right consistency for corn bread. Bake in a 425°F oven for ½ hour, or until brown.

CORNMEAL RECIPES

Belle Ledford told us about learning to cook and the ways she has learned to use cornmeal through the years: "I couldn't even cook corn bread when I was married. Doc Page's mother came to visit me, and she was talking about cooking. I said, 'Why, I can't even make corn bread.'

"And she went up to Howard's [Ledford, her brother-in-law] and said, 'I'm sorry for John Ledford. He's married a woman that can't even cook corn bread!'

"And I couldn't, but I just kept trying. I got recipes and tried to follow them and I eventually learned.

"[Now] I use cornmeal for other [cooking, too]. In cooking my fish, I roll the fish in it. And I use it in making potato croquettes. I dip my squash in cornmeal when I fry it; [and when] I make potato soup, I put cornmeal in it. I use corn bread in making my turkey dressing and chicken dressing." *(For Belle's recipes, see the appropriate sections.)*

Another use for cornmeal is in making cornmeal mush, most often used as a breakfast cereal. Stella Burrell remembers when her mother made mush: "My mother used to make cornmeal mush sometimes at night, too, and as a child I've helped her stir that over a fire in the fireplace, but that'd be when she was the supervisor, you know [laughing]. It was mostly made with just water and meal, and I'm sure she salted it. We ate it with milk, but I've known people to put sugar or butter in it. It'd be something similar to grits."

CORNMEAL MUSH

RUTH HOLCOMB

1 cup cornmeal   *Pinch of salt*
2 cups water

Sift meal. Bring water to a boil. Add a pinch of salt. Pour meal into the boiling water and continue cooking. Stir until thick. Put mush into a cereal bowl. Serve with sweet milk or buttermilk, and if desired add butter and sugar. YIELD: *3-4 servings*

CORNMEAL DUMPLINGS

RUTH HOLCOMB

"Use beef broth to cook these dumplings in. Remove the stewed beef and have only the liquid. Bring it to a rolling boil. Add salt to taste. Make up a cornmeal dough, the same kind you would use for corn bread. Roll it into little patties, about two tablespoons to each. Drop these into the boiling broth, one at a time. Bring the broth back to boiling and cook the patties—or dumplings—for fifteen minutes. Stick a fork into them to test for doneness. They are ready to serve when cooked."

GOOD OLD-FASHIONED CORN LIGHTBREAD

ADA KELLY

1 quart cornmeal mush	*¾ cup sugar*
Salt to taste	*¾ cup lard*
Cold water	*Cornmeal*

Cook cornmeal mush until thoroughly done; add salt to taste. Remove from heat and add cold water until cool enough to stick a finger in without burning. Then add sugar, lard, and enough cornmeal to make a good thick batter. Set aside until it ferments (overnight). Add enough meal to make a stiff batter. Bake in a well-greased 8-inch skillet in a moderate (350°F) oven until brown. Remove from the pan when cooled.

CORN CAKES

2 cups cornmeal	*1 tablespoon melted butter or lard*
1 heaping tablespoon flour	*2 eggs, beaten*
1 teaspoon salt	*Buttermilk*
2 teaspoons baking powder	

Sift together dry ingredients. Add butter and beaten eggs. Mix in enough milk to make a thin batter, being careful not to let it get too thin. Pour out into a hot griddle and flip onto other side when brown. Amount of batter poured out depends on desired size of cakes. Good with butter and syrup.

CORN PONES

2 cups cornmeal	*1 tablespoon lard*
1 teaspoon baking powder	*Milk*
½ teaspoon salt	

Mix together cornmeal, baking powder, and salt. Cut in lard and add enough milk to make a stiff batter. Form into pones with hands (or add some milk and drop from the end of a spoon), and place in a greased pan. Bake in a 425°F oven for 20 to 30 minutes.

CORNMEAL MUFFINS

1 egg, well beaten
1½ cups buttermilk
2 cups cornmeal, sifted

1 teaspoon salt
1 teaspoon soda
Melted lard

Mix together well-beaten egg and ¾ cup of the buttermilk. Add sifted cornmeal, salt, remaining ¾ cup buttermilk, and soda. Place pans (iron preferred) on top of range or stove; place in each division a teaspoonful of melted lard and let come to boiling point; when a blue smoke rises, fill each division half full of batter. Let rise while on top of the range, then place in a 400°F oven and bake until golden brown.

HUSH PUPPIES

1 cup self-rising flour
1 cup cornmeal
⅛ teaspoon salt
¼ teaspoon soda

1 egg
1½ cups buttermilk, or as needed
1 medium onion, chopped
Fat for deep frying

Sift together flour, cornmeal, salt, and soda. Add egg and buttermilk until it's the right consistency to hold its shape when rolled into a ball. Mix in onion, then roll into balls about 1 to 2 inches across and drop in deep hot fat. Fry until they're brown and crispy. Let them drain a bit on some paper and serve hot.

RYE BREAD WITH CORNMEAL

1 cup wheat flour
1 cup rye flour
½ cup cornmeal
1 teaspoon salt

1 teaspoon baking powder
3 tablespoons shortening
Buttermilk
½ teaspoon soda per cup of buttermilk

Sift together wheat flour and rye flour, cornmeal, salt, and baking powder. Cut in shortening. Add enough buttermilk to make a firm dough, adding ½ teaspoon of soda per cup of buttermilk. Mix thoroughly, then roll out to about ½-inch thick. Cut as you would biscuits, place on a greased sheet, and bake in a 450°F oven for 10 to 12 minutes.

GRITS

Grits are a breakfast cereal very common in our part of the South. They are made from corn that is not harvested until autumn after frost, when the husks are dry and the kernels of corn are hard.

Grits, a coarser grind than cornmeal, may be ground on the same millstones with the stones set a bit further apart. Some millers have told us that they have two different sets of millstones, one for grits and one for cornmeal.

One of our contacts remembers that her mother would take out a portion of ground corn and sift it to separate the grits from the meal. The "meal" that went through the sifter would be set aside and used for bread. Everything that did not sift through—the grits and the hulls—was then poured into a bowl or pot to be washed. It was covered with water and the trash and hulls floated to the top and were discarded. The grits settled to the bottom. Some contacts still recommend washing their grits, and some prefer to let the grits soak overnight before cooking them for breakfast. Others feel this isn't necessary.

To cook grits, add them to a pot of boiling water. The proportions are 1 cup grits to 4 cups water. Add salt to taste, usually ½ teaspoon per cup of grits. Cook at a moderate heat, low simmer, for about 30 minutes, or until grits have absorbed the water and are the consistency of applesauce or oatmeal. Stir often to prevent their sticking to the pan. Water may be added during cooking if you think they are too dry or haven't cooked long enough.

Grits are usually served on a plate for breakfast with butter or gravy, or for lunch or supper as a vegetable with butter, gravy, or cheese melted over them. They may be cooked the night before and heated the next morning, adding water if needed for the proper consistency.

BISCUITS

Exie Dills talked about biscuits: "I was eighty-five the twenty-second of October, so it's been eighty years since I started making biscuits. At first I was so little I couldn't reach the table to work my dough. Mommy had a bread tray and I'd put that on the floor and

The Frady gristmill

The hopper is the V-shaped, funnel-like attachment on top.

Mrs. Frady waiting for ground meal to come out of the hopper

Ground meal shooting into trough to be bagged and weighed

make up my dough on the floor. I made up biscuits that way a many a time, and there never was one refused to be eat. And I don't say it to be bragging, but I've never been beat in making biscuits yet."

Through the years biscuits have become almost a ritual for the morning meal in this area of the South. Stella Burrell told us her mother "always made homemade biscuits for breakfast." Even when loaf bread became common she made biscuits, because "she didn't like toast."

Gladys Nichols still makes biscuits using her hands to roll them out: "Most of the time I stir them up with my hands and knead the dough until I get it kneaded real good. And then I squeeze my biscuits off and roll them out with my hands. [Squeeze off enough dough for one biscuit, roll dough between palms and flatten, then place on baking sheet.] I don't use a roller like most people do, 'cause I can make them faster than I can roll them out. I don't make little bitty ones either; I make great big ones."

Biscuits cooked with plain flour must have salt and soda added. When self-rising flour became available, cooks like Lucy York discovered it to be more convenient: "I use self-rising flour; don't have to bother too much about baking powder and so forth. It's a little more convenient."

Others found it more difficult to switch to self-rising flour.

As Inez Taylor reminisced: "I never did cook too much when I was at home. Mama usually done most of the cooking, and Daddy done a lot of it. Daddy could make better biscuits than Mama could. He always got up to make biscuits every morning and every night for supper until they started buying self-rising flour. Then he never would make no more biscuits, because he wanted to put all the stuff in it hisself [laughter]."

Self-rising flour soon became widely accepted by cooks, and eventually it was considered to be the number one staple on the kitchen shelf. Not many cooks today use plain flour for making biscuits. Inez Taylor told us: "I *cannot* make bread out of plain flour. I either get too much soda or too much salt."

Addie Norton explained to us how she has made her biscuits throughout the years.

I just sift my flour, usually about two or three cups or however much I want to make. Then I put in about three big, good, deep tablespoons of lard and mix that all up till it's fine like, just in little balls. You know how it does when you mix it up. Then I put milk, enough to dampen my dough. Work it pretty well and roll her out and cook her. I don't never time them. I just—when I think they've been in there long enough—go look at them and see if they're brown; then I take them out. It takes about fifteen or twenty minutes if your stove's not too hot. About ten minutes will usually cook them if they're not too thick when you roll them out. Lots of people love thin biscuits and a lot of them love them up like that. When they're right thin it don't take long to cook them.

Gladys Nichols showed us the bread tray she had made more than forty years ago. It is made out of basswood, which is very light and will not crack easily.

Now I use the self-rising flour. I didn't used to. Back then a lot of times it wasn't made up like it is now. You had to add your own soda and salt and stuff in it and your buttermilk. And I made them with my hands. They wadn't none of them little rolled-out ones; they were made out with my hands. I didn't roll them out then, I patted them in the pan. I don't ever put my hands in the dough any more because I make them littler and I can make them with a spoon. But now to make the biggest biscuits anywhere in the world, make them with your hands. You take your hands, you squeeze that lard, you get it all the same way, gets all through it good, and it ain't in wads and things like that. You get that all stirred up good, you know, all just alike, then put in your milk and mix it together right on for a long time. And then try and put it on your board before it gets too hard. I don't like those dry biscuits. I make mine just dry enough to hold them together so I can roll them out and cut them. And you have some good biscuits.

Fay Long takes her browned biscuits out of the oven of her wood stove.

When Addie was asked how many biscuits she had to make to feed her four boys she exclaimed, "Fifty of a morning! If one or two of the young'uns was sick, they would leave one or two maybe. Hardly ever. Sometimes I'd have enough for the baby to have one or two before dinnertime, you know, and the rest were gone to school. But that's what it took to feed them of the morning—fifty biscuits. It took a great big half a dishpan full of flour nearly, quite a little bit of flour. And I had a great big dough board that Daddy made me. I've cut it in two one time and then cut off another piece off of it. It was great big, but now it's short. I'd pat out my biscuits on that board and put them in the pan. I had two great big pans. I could put twenty-five biscuits in one pan and twenty-five in the other. You know, when you get your biscuits cut out you got a little wad of dough left? Well, I'd just take and roll it out kinda thick and put it in there, you know, not cut it into biscuits. And my boys would quarrel over that little pone of bread. They thought it was better than the rest [laughter]."

Like corn bread, biscuit recipes were shared with us by a majority of our contacts.

BAKING POWDER BISCUITS

2 cups flour
½ teaspoon salt
1 tablespoon baking powder

⅓ cup lard or shortening
½ to ¾ cup milk

Sift flour, salt, and baking powder together. Work in lard or shortening with fingers or fork. Gradually add the milk until mixture is well blended. Put out on a floured cloth, roll, and cut. Place on a baking sheet and bake in a 400°F oven for 10 minutes. YIELD: *16 biscuits*

QUICK BISCUITS

BESSIE UNDERWOOD

½ cup lard or other shortening
3 cups self-rising flour

1 cup milk

Work lard into flour, using a fork, until crumbly. Pour in milk and mix together into a good batter. Put out on floured surface, roll out, and cut. Bake in a 400°F oven for 10 to 12 minutes. "That makes fourteen biscuits and that does us all day."

SODA BISCUITS

NORA GARLAND

"I've had some awful good biscuits off a wood stove. Just as brown. I got the prize at the fair for my biscuits. Mix together four cups self-rising flour and a pinch of soda; add two tablespoons lard or other shortening and mix until meal-like. Add one cup milk and make into good dough. Put out on floured surface, roll and cut out. Bake at 425 degrees for eight to ten minutes." YIELD: *32 biscuits*

MAYONNAISE BISCUITS

HATTIE WATKINS

This recipe does not rise as much as others. It makes a perfect dumpling if you roll it out and let set for 10 to 15 minutes. Drop into lightly thickened gravy and cook with the lid on for 15 minutes.

2 cups flour
2 tablespoons mayonnaise

Water

Sift flour into bowl. Stir in mayonnaise and add only enough water to make a moist dough. Roll and cut into rounds. Bake in a 400°F oven for 15 minutes. YIELD: *16 biscuits*

ANGEL FLAKE BISCUITS

MARY PITTS

1 package dry yeast
2 tablespoons lukewarm water
5 cups sifted flour
3 teaspoons baking powder
1 teaspoon soda

¼ cup sugar
1 teaspoon salt
1 cup shortening
2 cups buttermilk

Dissolve yeast in water. Sift together dry ingredients; cut in shortening. Add yeast and buttermilk to the dry mixture. Knead enough to hold together and roll dough to a thickness of ¼ to ½ inch. Cut with a biscuit cutter and fold in half. Place on a greased pan. Bake in a 400°F oven for 12 minutes. YIELD: *40 biscuits*

"RIZ" BISCUITS

ARIZONA DICKERSON

1 package dry yeast
1 cup warm buttermilk
½ teaspoon baking soda
2½ cups flour

1 teaspoon salt
2 tablespoons sugar or more, if desired
½ cup lard

Mix yeast with warm buttermilk. Add soda. Cut the lard into the dry ingredients. Slowly mix liquid mixture into dry ingredients. Roll out on a board and cut out biscuits. Let stand long enough to rise. Then bake about 12 minutes in 425°F oven. YIELD: *24 biscuits*

EASY PAN BREAD

OLENE GARLAND

"This is a good recipe to use if you don't want to make the mess or take the time to roll your biscuits out. Mix up desired biscuit recipe, adding more milk than usual to make a thinner batter. Pour into a greased baking pan and cook at 425 degrees until light golden brown."

PAN-FRIED BREAD

OLENE GARLAND

"Mix up desired biscuit recipe, and using a large spoon, drop batter into patties in a heated frying pan with ¼ inch of grease or oil and let cook and brown slowly one side, then turn and brown slowly on second side. Corn bread can be mixed and cooked the same way."

FRITTERS OR "FLITTERS"

Mix up biscuit dough, place on a floured surface, and roll out about ½-inch thick. Place in a pan and bake in a hot (425°F) oven for 15 to 20 minutes.

NOTE: Many people do not bother to roll out the dough but pat it down evenly into the pan with their hand.

DUMPLINGS

Cooks could create more interesting dishes using the biscuit dough for dumplings in stewed fruits, vegetables, and meats; crusts for vegetable, meat, and fruit pies; and a variety of desserts (see chapter 15).

DUMPLINGS

MARY ELLEN MEANS

4 cups flour*
⅓ cup lard or other shortening

1½ to 2 cups water

Mix together flour and lard. Add water and mix thoroughly. Toss dough on a floured surface until coated with flour. Divide into 4 balls and roll dough out, 1 ball at a time, to about ¼ inch or thinner. Cut in strips and cut strips into 2-inch pieces. Add a few pieces at a time to boiling broth. Cook, uncovered, making sure that the whole dumpling is under the liquid part of the time. Cook about 5 to 10 minutes. YIELD: *4 or 5 large servings*

BUTTERED DUMPLINGS

FAY LONG

2 cups self-rising flour
2 teaspoons baking powder
½ cup shortening
½ cup instant nonfat dry milk (or 1 cup
    milk, more if softer dough is desired)

1 can clear chicken broth plus ½ can
    water (omit extra ½ can if milk is
    used)
Pepper to taste

Mix flour and baking powder; cut in shortening. Add milk to make a dough. Roll out and cut into desired shapes. Drop into boiling broth mixture, which has been seasoned with pepper. Reduce heat to medium and cook until dumplings are tender.

*If using self-rising flour, heat water so dough will rise before you cook it.

After mixing up her recipe Ruby uses her hand to scoop the batter into a hot skillet.

After letting it cool for a few minutes she inverts the skillet, which releases the bread easily into her hand.

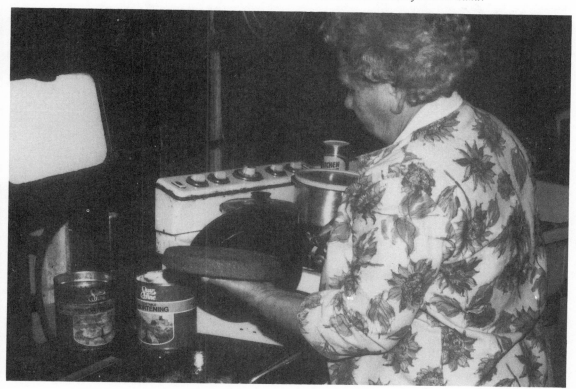

Cooking corn cakes takes longer than baking corn bread, but many people prefer them over baked corn bread.

YEAST BREADS AND ROLLS

In earlier times, yeast used in bread making was not always easy to come by. Many women used the yeast they had on hand in combination with other ingredients to produce more yeast, which they dried into small cakes, thus ensuring a handy supply at all times.

Lettie Chastain told us about her mother making yeast and yeast bread, and about the hard work women had to do to keep the family going: "My mother used to make loaves of yeast bread, and she'd start with a little cake of yeast. You'd make yeast in cakes then. She'd have a pan about as big as a dishpan, and she'd let her dough rise about three inches. She'd shut it up in the safe [cabinet used for storing food], and we'd go to the field and work. When we'd come back to the house that night, it'd be all rose up. Then at dinnertime we'd have that great big old loaf of bread to eat on. That would save time, you see. We had homemade flour. It wasn't as pretty and white, but it was good. It would make big old thick pies and stuff, and it sure was good on those wood stoves. Mother made cobblers —chicken cobbler, potato or apple cobbler. In the summertime women had it hard. They had to go to the fields every day, do the canning and then on Saturday do the washing and the ironing—all that besides cooking.''

Three of our contacts told us how they used to make their own yeast but pointed out that, because homemade yeast often fails, it is more sensible and convenient to buy the packaged kind in the stores.

Dorothy Beck's version: "Boil three potatoes with the jacket on them, and you take fresh peach tree leaves and boil them until you boil all the strength out of them. Then you take the leaf part out and take your potatoes and mash them up in that peach leaf juice and then you add cornmeal to it to thicken it. Sometimes you can put a small cake of bought yeast in it. Then you roll it out in little patties the size that you want for a batch and lay them out in the sun to dry. I used to work at the Earl House and Mrs. Earl used to make all her yeast. She never bought any, and that's the way she made it.''

Mary Pitts describes another method of making yeast at home: "Peel and boil three medium Irish potatoes with a handful of peach leaves or hops. Remove the potatoes and mash; strain water in which they were boiled back into potatoes. There should be approximately three cups of potatoes and water. Let become tepid.

"Dissolve two yeast cakes [packages] in one-third cup of water and add to mixture. Add one teaspoon sugar, one-quarter teaspoon salt, and set in warm place to rise overnight. Next morning stir into the yeast sufficient cornmeal to make a very stiff mixture. Let rise again from one and a half to two hours. Now add more cornmeal to make a stiff dough, roll out until one-third inch thick, cut into squares about two inches large, dry in shade, turning until dry and hard. Do not allow to sour, but turn daily until firm. Compressed yeast may be used as a starter. In recipe use one yeast cake for one quart of flour. Two cakes or more may be used if a shorter [cooking] time is desired."

HOMEMADE LIQUID YEAST

BELLE LEDFORD

8 medium-size potatoes
1 quart lukewarm water or water in
    which potatoes are cooked

½ cup sugar
1 tablespoon salt
1 package dry yeast

Boil potatoes and mash fine. Add water. Add sugar, salt, and yeast, which has been dissolved in lukewarm water. Let stand in a warm place for several hours. Pour into half-gallon glass fruit jars, filling about two-thirds full. Cover but do not seal. Put in cool place. Use 1 cup, or ½ cup if you have plenty of time, in place of yeast cake.

As with biscuits, the dough for yeast rolls may be pinched off and rolled between the hands or they can be rolled out on a floured surface using a rolling pin, the latter being the method that Rittie Webb uses. She then cuts them out and places them in her buttered iron skillet. In another iron skillet she melts butter and dots a small amount on top of each roll.

Rettie Webb

MARY'S ROLLS

MARY BROWN

1 package dry yeast
⅓ cup warm water
1 cup warm milk
⅓ cup melted butter or shortening, plus

more for dipping rolls
¼ cup sugar
1 teaspoon salt
3½ to 4 cups flour

Dissolve yeast in warm water. Mix together warm milk, melted butter, sugar, and salt. Mix together the yeast and milk mixture. Gradually stir in flour. Mix for 5 minutes. Cover the dough and let rise until doubled in bulk. Roll out dough and cut with a biscuit cutter. Dip each round into melted butter and place in a pan. Cover with a cloth and let rise for 1½ hours. Bake in a 350°F oven for 30 minutes. YIELD: *25-30 rolls*

EASY REFRIGERATOR ROLLS

MARY PITTS

2 packages dry yeast
1 cup warm water
1 cup hot milk
1 cup shortening

⅔ cup sugar
2 teaspoons salt
3 eggs, well beaten
7 to 8 cups flour

Dissolve yeast in warm water. Mix together hot milk, shortening, sugar, and salt in a large bowl and let it cool. Once cooled, add yeast mixture and the eggs. Mix in 4 cups flour, then stir in 3 to 4 more cups flour until the dough can be handled easily. Place dough in a greased bowl, cover, and refrigerate. The dough will keep 4 to 5 days. When ready to use, cut off amount needed and roll out ½-inch thick. Shape into desired pieces. Place on a baking sheet and let rise in a warm place for 2 hours. Bake in a 400°F oven for 15 to 20 minutes. YIELD: *approximately 5 dozen rolls*

POTATO REFRIGERATOR ROLLS

BELLE LEDFORD

1 cup milk
½ cup sugar
⅔ cup shortening
1 teaspoon salt
1 cup mashed potatoes

1 package dry yeast
½ to 1 cup lukewarm water
2 eggs, well beaten
5½ to 6 cups sifted flour
Melted butter

Scald milk in a large boiler. Add sugar, shortening, salt, and mashed potatoes. Stir to mix and let cool. Dissolve yeast in lukewarm water and add to cooled milk mixture. Using a heavy spoon or potato masher, mix the yeast and eggs into this mixture and then begin adding the flour, a cup at a time. Mix well. Do not let rise.

Place dough in a greased bowl; turn it once to grease the surface. Cover and chill at least 2 hours or up to a week. About 2 hours before serving, take out the amount of dough needed and shape the dough as desired on a floured surface. Place in a buttered pan. Brush butter on top of each roll. Place in a warm place and let rise for about 1 hour, or until doubled. Bake in a 400°F oven for 15 to 20 minutes, or until light golden brown. YIELD: *approximately 5 dozen rolls*

LIGHT ROLLS

ANNIE LONG

1½ cups milk
⅓ cup shortening
2 tablespoons sugar
2 teaspoons salt

1 egg, well beaten
2 packages dry yeast
½ cup lukewarm water
5 to 5½ cups sifted flour

Scald milk and mix with shortening, sugar, and salt. Let stand until warm, then add beaten egg and yeast, which has been dissolved in the ½ cup lukewarm water. Gradually add flour. Put on a floured surface and knead for a few minutes. Place in a greased mixing bowl and let rise until doubled. Roll out on a floured board, cut into rounds and dip into melted butter before placing in a pan. Let rise until doubled. Bake in a 400°F oven for 15 minutes. YIELD: *approximately 5 dozen rolls*

EASY HOT ROLLS

MARY PITTS

2 packages dry yeast
½ cup cold water
1 cup milk
2 tablespoons shortening

2½ teaspoons salt
2 tablespoons sugar
4½ to 5 cups flour
Melted butter

Dissolve yeast in cold water. Set aside. Put milk, shortening, salt, and sugar in a pan and heat only enough to melt shortening. Cool and then add yeast. Gradually stir in flour until you have a good stiff dough. Put on a well-floured board and knead for 3 to 5 minutes. Place in a greased bowl, cover, and let rise until doubled. When doubled, punch down and let rise again. Place on a floured board and roll out. Cut into desired shapes and dip in butter before placing in a pan. Let rise again until doubled. Bake in a 375°F oven for 15 to 20 minutes. YIELD: *approximately 4 dozen rolls*

WHOLE-WHEAT PANCAKES

MARY PITTS

These pancakes will be "near 'bout big as a saucer."

2 cups whole-wheat flour
2 tablespoons brown sugar
1 teaspoon salt

1 package dry yeast
1 egg, beaten
2 cups milk

Mix together all dry ingredients, including the dry yeast. Add beaten egg to milk and slowly add the mixture to the dry ingredients. Stir well. Cover bowl with a towel and set in hot water for 1 hour. When ready, dip out the batter, using a ⅓-cup measure and fry in a greased pan. YIELD: *approximately fifteen 3-inch pancakes*

BLUEBERRY MUFFINS

MARINDA BROWN

2 cups self-rising flour
1 cup sugar
½ cup melted butter or margarine

2 eggs
1 cup blueberries

Mix together flour, sugar, butter, and eggs only until flour is well moistened. Do not beat. Fold in blueberries. Pour into greased muffin cups and bake in a 350°F oven for 15 to 20 minutes.

VARIATION: 1 cup of grated apples in place of blueberries—mix together 1 cup chopped nuts, ½ cup brown sugar, and 1 teaspoon cinnamon and sprinkle on top of the muffins before you bake them.

MOLASSES SWEET BREAD

2 cups flour
½ teaspoon salt
1 to 2 teaspoons ginger
2 teaspoons baking powder
¼ teaspoon soda
1 teaspoon cinnamon

⅓ cup melted butter
1 cup molasses or ⅔ cup molasses and
½ cup sugar
¾ cup buttermilk
1 egg

Sift together dry ingredients and add melted butter and the molasses. Mix well, adding buttermilk and egg. Pour into a loaf pan and bake in a 350°F oven for 45 to 50 minutes.

QUICK AND EASY DOUGHNUTS

BESSIE UNDERWOOD

2 cups self-rising flour
¼ cup sugar
1 egg

¼ cup milk
Shortening for deep frying
Confectioners sugar (optional)

Sift flour and sugar together. Add egg and milk to make a workable dough. Roll out and cut with a doughnut cutter. Drop in hot shortening. Turn when brown, and when the other side is brown take out and drain on paper towels or brown paper. May sweeten by sifting confectioners sugar over them. YIELD: *approximately 16 doughnuts*

CAKE DOUGHNUTS

ANNIE LONG

3 cups sifted flour
2 teaspoons baking powder
⅔ cup sugar
½ teaspoon nutmeg
1 tablespoon shortening

2 eggs
½ cup milk
Fat for deep frying
Confectioners sugar
Cinnamon (optional)

Sift together sifted flour, baking powder, sugar, and nutmeg. Add shortening by kneading in with fork or fingers. Stir in eggs and milk. Roll out; cut and drop in hot fat. Turn doughnuts when they rise to the top and turn brown. Watch carefully, and when brown on the second side take out with a slotted spoon. Drain on paper towels or brown paper. While still warm, drop into confectioners sugar, plain or with cinnamon. YIELD: *approximately 20-25 doughnuts*

YEAST POTATO DOUGHNUTS

1 cup sieved cooked potatoes (warm or cold)
1 cup liquid, reserved from cooking potatoes
¾ cup shortening
½ cup sugar
1 tablespoon salt
1 package dry yeast

¾ cup warm water
2 eggs, beaten
5 to 6 cups flour
Oil for deep frying
Glaze:
1 cup confectioners sugar
1 tablespoon milk
½ teaspoon vanilla

Mix potatoes, potato liquid, shortening, sugar, and salt. Dissolve yeast in warm water; stir into potato mixture. Stir in eggs and enough flour to make dough easy to handle. Turn dough onto a lightly floured surface; knead until smooth and elastic, 5 to 8 minutes. Place in a greased bowl; turn greased side up. Cover. Let rise until doubled, 1 to 1½ hours. (TIP: Dough can be stored in the refrigerator 3 days before using. Refrigerate in the greased bowl immediately after kneading. If dough rises in the refrigerator, punch down and cover with a damp towel.) Pat the dough out on a lightly floured surface to ¾-inch thickness. Cut doughnuts with a floured 2½-inch cutter; let rise until doubled, about 1 hour. Heat oil (3 to 4 inches) to 375°F in a heavy pan. Fry doughnuts until golden, 2 to 3 minutes on each side. Drain on paper towels. Glaze doughnuts while warm. Store doughnuts at room temperature, covered with a towel. YIELD: *approximately 5 dozen doughnuts*

OLD-FASHIONED GINGERBREAD

This recipe is at least a hundred years old, according to one of our contacts.

½ cup sugar
½ cup butter
1 cup molasses
2 cups flour
½ teaspoon soda

1½ teaspoon ginger
½ teaspoon cinnamon
½ cup sour milk
½ cup raisins (optional)
½ cup chopped nuts (optional)

Cream together sugar, butter, and molasses. Sift together dry ingredients and beat into the sugar mixture alternately with sour milk. Mix well. Fold in raisins and nuts, if desired. Bake in a greased and lightly floured 13 × 9-inch pan in a 300°F oven for 1 hour.

ARIZONA'S GINGERBREAD

ARIZONA DICKERSON

2½ cups flour
2 teaspoons soda
½ teaspoon salt
1 teaspoon cinnamon
1 teaspoon ginger
½ teaspoon cloves

2 eggs, well beaten
½ cup sugar
1 cup molasses
½ cup vegetable oil
1 cup boiling water

Sift dry ingredients together twice. Set aside. Combine beaten eggs, sugar, molasses, and oil. Mix well. Add to dry ingredients and blend. Add boiling water and stir until smooth. Pour into an oiled shallow baking pan. Bake in a 350°F oven for 40 minutes.

PUMPKIN BREAD

MARY PITTS

4 cups cooked mashed pumpkin
4 cups sugar
1 cup oil
1 teaspoon vanilla
4 eggs, beaten
5 cups flour

4 teaspoons baking soda
1 teaspoon salt
1 teaspoon cloves
2 teaspoons cinnamon
1 cup chopped nuts
1 cup raisins

In a large mixing bowl, using a wooden spoon to mix with, combine pumpkin, sugar, oil, vanilla, and beaten eggs. Mix well. Sift together dry ingredients and add to pumpkin mixture. Stir until well blended. Fold in the nuts and raisins. Pour into 3 or 4 greased loaf pans or, for a moister bread, use several coffee or bean cans, ungreased. If using cans, pour each can half full of batter. Bake in a 350°F oven for 1 hour.

NUT BREAD

3 tablespoons butter
1 cup sugar
2 eggs
2½ cups flour
3 teaspoons baking powder

1 teaspoon salt
1 cup milk
1 cup chopped nuts
1 teaspoon vanilla

Cream together butter and sugar. Add eggs and beat well. Sift together dry ingredients and add to butter mixture alternately with milk. Fold in the nuts and vanilla. Pour batter into a greased loaf pan and let rise for 30 minutes. Bake in a 350°F oven for 45 minutes.

CINNAMON ROLLS

2 teaspoons salt
2½ tablespoons sugar
1 cup milk
1 package dry yeast
5 tablespoons melted shortening
2 eggs, slightly beaten

2½ cups sifted flour
Soft butter
Sugar and cinnamon to sweeten
Confectioners sugar
Water

Dissolve salt and sugar in ½ cup of the milk and mix yeast with the other half. Combine the 2 mixtures and leave in warm place for 30 minutes. To this mixture add the melted shortening, slightly beaten eggs, and flour to make a stiff dough. Put in a covered bowl and leave in a warm place again for 30 minutes. Then beat the dough thoroughly in the bowl. Roll out dough on a floured surface about ⅓-inch thick. Spread with soft butter and sprinkle sugar and cinnamon on top. Then fold over in 3 folds, and cut in strips, about ¾-inch thick. Place close together in a greased shallow pan and let rise until doubled in bulk (about 30 minutes). Bake in a hot (400°F) oven for about 10 to 20 minutes. When lightly browned, remove from the oven, and while still warm in the pan pour a sugar topping (confectioners sugar thinned slightly with a small amount of water) over the rolls. YIELD: *approximately 20 rolls*

15

Desserts

"The best sweet potato pie you ever put your tooth on."

"There was ten children in my family, so it was a pretty big chore for Momma to make a dessert for so many, but she was always wanting to treat us." This comment, by Olene Garland, echoed the thoughts of many Appalachian cooks with regard to desserts.

In the days of near total self-sufficiency, the cook was limited, of course, to desserts made of ingredients that could be raised and processed on the farm. For example, one of our contacts said, "Mama always had a skillet full of peanuts or sweet potatoes ready for us when we came home from school." Sugar was not available as a sweetener, but nearly all families raised sorghum cane, and boiled the cane juice down into syrup, which made an effective substitute (see *Foxfire 3,* pp. 424–36). With a little extra effort and some butter, made of cream from the family cow, a candy could be produced that was not only delicious but also fun to make.

Ruth Ledford, who said she learned to make cane syrup candy from her mother, invited us to her home to reproduce the experience:

"Get your molasses—real cane syrup, store bought don't work so well—and you put it on and cook it until when you hold it up it spins a thread. Then you take it off [the heat] and pour it out into a buttered bowl and cool it; then just roll it up [in a ball]. Then grease your hands with butter and then you just pull it. Now it takes two people to pull it. One can't pull it. You're supposed to pull it till it gets so hard it won't pull no more. [Pulling it] makes it get harder, and whenever you get it pulled you take it and twist it like that and just put it out on a [well-greased plate] or a piece of wax paper and cut it into little pieces."

Mrs. Ledford reminded us that cool weather is the ideal time to make any kind of candy, especially syrup candy. If you try to make it during warm weather, it will not harden as well.

There are more candy recipes later in this chapter, which is organized to begin with desserts made with the simplest ingredients—those available to Appalachian cooks of several generations back—to desserts that require more sophisticated ingredients. This organization reflects the increasing availability of refined and packaged foods in recent years.

POPCORN BALLS

LESSIE CONNER

On many farms, families also raised popcorn. Gathered dry in the fall, shelled off the cob, and popped over the fire in the living room fireplace, it could be used alone as a dessert of sorts, or combined with homegrown syrup to make popcorn balls. Lessie Conner taught us how:

Jessie Conner shows how to make popcorn balls.

In order to make the popcorn balls, she said, a large iron skillet is needed, along with two large dishpans or bowls (one for the popped corn and one for the finished popcorn balls), one mixing bowl for the cooked syrup, and several kitchen spoons.

To make the syrup for the popcorn balls, pour a quart of sorghum in the large iron skillet to heat on the stove. The reason for the large skillet is that the syrup boils up, and the reason for an iron one is that it heats evenly and will not burn the syrup as readily as another type of pan. Mrs. Conner said, "You can tell when the syrup is ready because it forms a 'hair' when dripped down from the spoon." When the syrup gets to the stage where the hair will not drop off the spoon, it is ready. It will take about 5 minutes to get to that stage. Pour the syrup into the mixing bowl to cool for several minutes. It should come right off the heat and preferably right out of the pan when it's completely cooked, or it will get brittle when it cools. Cover your hands with butter to keep the syrup from sticking to them while forming the balls. It is better to use cold rather than warm popcorn, because the syrup will stick better.

Mrs. Conner demonstrated two methods for forming the popcorn balls. The first method is to carefully place a small amount of popcorn into the palm of one hand and carefully (because the syrup could still burn) spoon about a tablespoon of syrup on top of it. Then pack the popcorn and syrup mixture together by hand. Use additional butter on your hands after making a few balls or the syrup will start sticking to them. The second method is to add 1 or 2 teaspoons of baking soda to the syrup while it is boiling. The soda makes the syrup bubble and foam up, giving more candy to work with. Then pour the syrup into the mixing bowl and on top of that pour the popcorn. Stir that up with a wooden spoon and scoop it out with your hands to form the balls. After each popcorn ball is made, place it in a large dishpan or on waxed paper to cool.

HONEY

People also used honey by itself as a dessert and as a sweetener when it was available.

Lucy York told us: "If somebody found a honey tree, several families would go in together, cut the tree down and divide the honey up between them all."

Her brother, Terry Dickerson, remembers: "One time somebody found a tree full of honey way up in the cove of old man John Garland's place, and I reckon they got permission to go up there and chop it down. I guess there was eight or ten of us went up there and cut that tree down and when it fell, the hollow part where the honey was split plumb in two and that honey poured out all over the place. But we were still able to get a good bit of it and I remember carrying it home in buckets. That honey was just as white and pretty as what you see in the stores today." (For more information about honey see *Foxfire 2*, pp. 28–46.)

ICE CREAM

By combining milk with honey or syrup as a sweetener and fruits and berries as flavorings, families discovered methods for making ice cream, but until ice became plentiful they were limited to making ice cream only during the winter. The most common method for making ice cream was through the use of snow. Several contacts told us how to make snow cream:

"Gather the snow carefully with a large spoon, keeping the snow fluffy. Place some of the snow in a large bowl; add milk—small amounts at a time—and stir into snow until it is at a nice thick consistency. Add enough honey or syrup to sweeten and add fruits or berries to flavor if desired."

Olene Garland explained another way her family made ice cream during the winter months: "We used two regular water buckets—which were lard buckets, a ten-pound and a five-pound bucket—and we would chip ice off the shoals from the falls—Sylvan Lake Falls—and chip it up fine enough to pack between the two buckets. We would pour the ice cream mixture into the smaller one; set it down inside the larger bucket; pack ice between the two and turn by the bail [bucket handle]. You had to put the lid on the bucket with the milk in it. We used to do that a lot. Sometimes we didn't have to go to the trouble to get ice from the falls—it was so cold we could often get ice by chipping it out of our water buckets."

SYRUP ICE CREAM

MARY PITTS

3 cups dark corn syrup
6 tablespoons cornstarch
3 eggs, well beaten

2 cups whole milk
Cream or additional whole milk
1 teaspoon vanilla

Mix first 4 ingredients and cook in a double boiler until thick. Let cool, then add enough cream or whole milk to make 2 quarts. If you use cream, beat it well before adding it to the boiled mixture. Add the vanilla. Put in old-time ice cube trays (take sections out) and freeze. You may use any shallow (1-inch) aluminum tray.

Mary adds: "When it got icy—before it got hard—I'd take it out and beat it good and put it back in."

The ingredients for desserts (such as various kinds of fruits and berries, milk, cream and butter and eggs) were all common but it was not until the introduction of brown and white sugar, white flour, nutmeg, cinnamon, and the like that they came into their own as real dessert treats. With the arrival of white sugar in local stores, for example, ice cream became more popular. Harriet Echols said, "We had ice cream parties, too—usually on Saturday night. See, most everybody had four or five cows, and we'd get about five ice cream freezers and invite the youngsters in, and we'd get in the parlor and get around the organ or piano and sing and play."

HAND-FREEZER ICE CREAM

2 quarts milk
2 to 3 cups sugar
2 tablespoons vanilla

Crushed ice
Rock salt

Pour milk, sugar, and vanilla into the freezer container; cover, then pack the freezer with ice and salt. Turn the crank slowly at first, faster as the mixture thickens. Crank until it's almost too hard to turn. Eat right away, as it doesn't keep well.

VARIATION 1: You may also add 2 beaten eggs to the milk mixture before putting it in the freezer.

VARIATION 2: Add 1 cup of any mashed fresh fruit, such as strawberries, peaches, blueberries, blackberries. For chocolate you may add ½ cup cocoa to the sugar before adding it to the milk.

LIME SHERBET

MARY PITTS

1 package lime gelatin
1½ cups sugar
1 cup boiling water

Rind of 1 lemon
Juice of 2 lemons (¼ cup)
1 quart milk

Dissolve sugar and gelatin in boiling water. Add rind and juice. Chill this mixture, then add milk. Put into a 13 × 9-inch pan with a cover and freeze. Stir frequently. It freezes in 2 to 3 hours.

THREE-OF-A-KIND SHERBET

ARIZONA DICKERSON

Juice of 3 oranges
Juice of 3 lemons
3 bananas, mashed

3 egg whites, beaten stiff
3 cups sugar
3 cups water

Mix juices with bananas, and fold in beaten egg whites. Heat sugar and water until sugar dissolves. Let cool then mix with fruit and egg white mixture. Place in freezer. Stir often as it cools.

SYRUPS

The introduction of cocoa and various flavorings meant that new types of syrup could be made. Olene Garland told us, "Mama always had chocolate or maple syrup made up for us to have with hot buttered bread or plain cake, or we would use the chocolate syrup to make chocolate milk." Mrs. Garland shared those syrup recipes with us:

MAPLE SYRUP

This syrup will crystallize after a period of time if not used.

2 cups sugar
1 cup water

1 tablespoon maple flavoring

Mix sugar and water in a saucepan and heat to boiling, letting it boil for 1 minute. Remove from heat and add maple flavoring. Let cool before pouring into a container for storage.

CHOCOLATE SYRUP

OLENE GARLAND

"We would use this syrup for making chocolate milk, add to hot milk for cocoa, or just pour it over hot buttered biscuits or plain cake."

2 cups sugar
1 cup cocoa

1 cup water
1 tablespoon vanilla

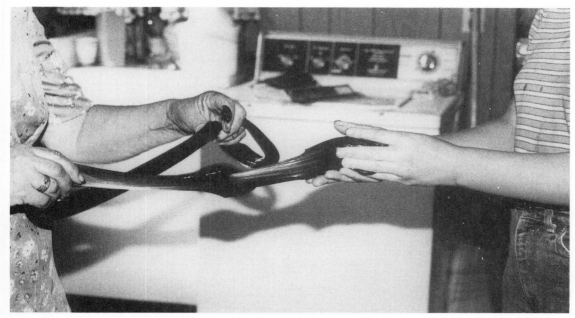

Pulling taffy

Mix together all ingredients except vanilla in a saucepan and bring it to a boil, then turn down heat to medium and let it boil for 1 minute. Take it off the heat and add vanilla. Cool and pour into a quart jar for storing in the refrigerator.

CANDIES

The appearance of sugar, salt, and other such products also meant that the repertoire of types of candies could be expanded. The following are several our contacts agreed to share with us.

MOLASSES CANDY

1 cup molasses
1 cup water

Dash of salt

Combine all ingredients and boil (do not stir) until it reaches the hard-ball stage. Remove from the fire and let stand until cool enough to hold in well-greased hands. Using a small amount at a time, pull the candy back and forth between the hands. After pulling for some time, it will change from a brown to a yellowish color, at which time it is done.

SALT-WATER TAFFY

1¼ pounds sugar
1¼ pounds white corn syrup
2 cups water
1 tablespoon butter

2 teaspoons salt
½ teaspoon flavoring (peppermint, maple, almond, etc.)
Food coloring

Put sugar, syrup, and water in a saucepan and stir until boiling begins. Continue boiling (do not stir) until it spins a thread. Take from fire, add butter and salt, and pour into buttered platters. When cool enough, pull. Add flavoring and coloring while pulling. Cut into pieces and wrap each piece in waxed paper.

COCOA FUDGE

ANNIE LONG

1 cup white sugar
1 tablespoon cocoa

½ cup milk
¼ cup butter

Mix sugar and cocoa together. Stir in milk and boil gently over medium heat for 30 minutes, or until mixture reaches the soft-ball stage. When the syrup forms a ball in cold water, remove from the heat and add butter. Cool, then beat until thick. Pour into a buttered dish and cut when cool.

POTATO CANDY

MARGARET NORTON

1 large potato
Salt

1 box confectioners sugar
Peanut butter

Peel and boil potato. When done, mash up with a fork, add a little salt, and pour in a box of confectioners sugar. This makes a stiff dough. Roll out on a dough board that has been well floured in a layer ¼-inch thick. Spread peanut butter all over top. Roll up like a jelly roll (make 2 rolls if you like). Put this in the refrigerator. Cut with a knife and serve. Good any time.

GRAPEFRUIT RIND CANDY

MARY PITTS

"I used to make grapefruit rind candy by the big platters full. Soak the rinds in water for a couple of days, and then put them on to parboil. You've got to boil the rind and get it hot so the lining'll come out easy. When they get tender you can pull every bit of that tough lining out of them and just leave the rind. Boil one cup sugar and one cup water until it comes to a syrup. When your rinds get tender, slice them in pieces about as long as your fingers and drop them down in that syrup. Let it cook slowly until the rinds absorb all that syrup. The kids just loved them. And I'll tell you, now I've got a bunch of grandkids that loves to eat when they come to Granny's house. We love to see them come."

CHOCOLATE CANDY

ANNIE LONG

2 cups sugar
1 to 3 tablespoons cocoa
⅛ teaspoon salt

2 tablespoons light corn syrup
⅔ cup milk
½ to 1 teaspoon vanilla

In a large saucepan mix together sugar, cocoa, and salt until well blended. Gradually stir in syrup and milk. Cook over medium heat until dissolved, stirring constantly. Place a lid on the pan for about 3 minutes. This allows steam to wash the sugar crystals from the sides of the pan and prevents the candy from being grainy. Let the candy mixture boil until a soft ball will form when dropped in cold water. Keep testing it until the chocolate can be picked up with the fingers. Set off the heat and add vanilla. Let the mixture cool and then stir until thick. Place in a butter dish or platter. Cut into small squares when firm but not cold. YIELD: *16 pieces*

OLD-FASHIONED FUDGE

MARY PITTS

2 cups sugar
¼ teaspoon salt
6 tablespoons cocoa or 2 ounces melted
    chocolate

½ cup water or milk
¼ cup corn syrup or honey
2 tablespoons butter
1 teaspoon vanilla

Mix together in a saucepan sugar, salt, and cocoa. Add milk and syrup gradually. Boil gently, stirring often, until mixture reaches the soft-ball stage. Drop in butter and let cool before beating. Add vanilla. Beat until the mixture thickens and is hard to stir. Pour into a buttered dish. Cool before cutting into serving pieces. YIELD: *approximately 20 pieces of candy*

SEAFOAM CANDY

2 cups brown sugar
½ cup water

2 egg whites, beaten stiff
½ cup chopped nuts (optional)

Boil sugar and water together approximately 5 minutes, or until mixture reaches the hard-ball stage. Then pour mixture into the beaten egg whites and beat until it holds its shape. Add nuts, if desired. Drop by teaspoonfuls onto a greased plate. Let cool before serving. YIELD: *approximately 16 pieces of candy*

PEANUT BRITTLE

3 cups sugar
1 teaspoon vinegar

1 cup peanuts

Melt sugar in a pan with vinegar, being careful not to let it burn. When melted, add peanuts, stirring as little as possible, and pour on a buttered platter; break up when cold.

DIVINITY

MARY PITTS

2⅓ cups sugar
¼ cup light corn syrup
½ cup water

½ teaspoon salt
2 egg whites, stiffly beaten

Mix together all ingredients except egg whites. Bring to a boil until it spins a thread when dropped from a spoon. Pour half the mixture over beaten egg whites. Let remaining mixture come to a boil again, add to previous mixture and beat until stiff. Drop from a teaspoon onto wax paper or into a greased pan. YIELD: *approximately 24 pieces*

HONEY CANDY

1 cup instant nonfat dry milk   *1 cup honey*
1 cup plain or chunky peanut butter   *½ teaspoon vanilla*

Mix together all ingredients and shape into balls. Refrigerate before serving. YIELD: *approximately 24 balls*

SWEET DUMPLINGS AND FLAPJACKS

Probably no other ingredient so changed the dessert scene, however, as refined white flour. Some of the resulting desserts were amazingly simple, such as Ione Dickerson's strawberry dumplings: "You make strawberry dumplings just like you do chicken dumplings. Just have your strawberries boiling good. Of course you have to put water, sugar, and butter in that, and just drop your dumplings in it like you do any other dumplings. When you make dumplings, it is just as good as a baked cobbler with a crust."

Other recipes were only slightly more complex. As Olene Garland said: "After I got married and had children, I used the same recipes my mother had used. I understood the value of easy and quick recipes for a large family because I had eight children of my own. My children are all married now, and my daughters live nearby. They don't have big families but they work and stay busy so they use those recipes and shortcuts, too. The recipes are so quick and easy to do, and children are *always* happy to get a little something. You know, it doesn't take much to make children happy anyway.

"Sometimes if Mama didn't have a dessert for us kids she would fry what we called 'flapjacks' which was really just turned-over bread fried up real thin. She'd roll them in granulated sugar while they were still hot and we would put butter on them, lap them over like a sandwich, and eat them like that. Sometimes we would pour syrup over them, but they were good just with the butter.

"Another easy dessert for Mama to prepare for us was cinnamon rolls. Whenever she would make up biscuits, she'd save some dough to make the cinnamon rolls with. She'd roll out the dough real thin, sprinkle a generous amount of a sugar and cinnamon mixture over the entire surface of the dough, then she would sprinkle slices of butter on top of all that, then roll it up, slice it, and cook them. They were real easy to make and good to eat."

Bread puddings were one of the earlier desserts and one of the most convenient when there were leftover biscuits available.

BREAD PUDDING

RUTH HOLCOMB

2 cups fine crumbs from leftover biscuits
1 egg
1 cup sugar

2 tablespoons milk
1 tablespoon butter

Put the biscuit crumbs in a bowl. Add egg and sugar and mix thoroughly. Add milk and butter. Beat well. Pour into a greased pan and bake in a 350°F oven for 15 to 20 minutes. YIELD: *4 servings*

ARIZONA'S BREAD PUDDING

ARIZONA DICKERSON

4 cups milk
4 eggs, beaten
1 tablespoon vanilla

2 cups bread crumbs
2 tablespoons butter
Nutmeg

Mix milk, eggs, and vanilla together in a saucepan. Place over heat until hot but not boiling. Line a baking dish with bread crumbs mixed with melted butter. Pour mixture over the bread crumbs. Sprinkle top with nutmeg. Place the baking dish in a pan of hot water in a moderate (350°F) oven and bake for 45 minutes.

DAISY'S BREAD PUDDING WITH APPLES

DAISY JUSTUS

4 homemade biscuits, crumbled
1 egg
1 cup sliced and cooked apples
¼ cup grated coconut

1 cup milk
1 cup brown sugar
¼ cup chopped nuts (pecans or walnuts)
1 teaspoon vanilla

Raisins may be used instead of apples, or use both if you wish. Mix all ingredients and pour into a buttered small casserole dish. Bake in a 350°F oven for about 1 hour, or until a knife comes out clean 1 inch from edge of the dish. YIELD: *4-6 servings*

BLACKBERRY PUDDING

OLENE GARLAND

2 cups blackberries
½ to 1 cup sugar
2 cups water

4 to 5 homemade biscuits, crumbled
Butter

Bring blackberries, sugar as needed, and water to a near boil in a buttered baking dish. Add the crumbled biscuits and stir. Dot with butter and sprinkle with sugar, if desired. Bake in a 400°F oven until thick and glossy on top.

LEMON MERINGUE PUDDING

MARY PITTS

"This is a kind of bread pudding. Use leftover biscuits. You have to put that topping on it to get the kids to eat it. Had to fancy it up a little, but they always went back for seconds."

2 cups bread crumbs
4 cups milk
½ cup butter
1 cup sugar

4 eggs, separated
Juice and rind of 1 lemon
3 tablespoons confectioners sugar

Soak bread crumbs in milk. Cream butter and sugar. Add beaten egg yolks, lemon rind, and all but 1 teaspoon of the lemon juice. Mix with bread crumbs. Pour into a baking dish and bake in a 350°F oven for 45 minutes, or until firm. Cover with a meringue made from the egg whites beaten with the confectioners sugar and remaining lemon juice. Return to the oven and brown the meringue lightly.

FRUIT DESSERTS

BAKED APPLES SUPREME

6 large apples
½ cup brown sugar
½ cup raisins
1 teaspoon cinnamon

⅛ teaspoon salt
1 cup water
½ cup coconut

Wash and core apples but don't peel. Place in a baking dish. Fill apples with sugar, raisins, cinnamon, and salt. Add water to the baking dish. Bake 30 minutes in a 350°F oven, basting frequently. Sprinkle with coconut and bake 10 minutes more. Serve warm or cold. YIELD: *6 servings*

BAKED APPLES WITH HONEY

8 large baking apples   *1¼ cups water*
Desired amount of nuts   *½ cup honey*

Wash and core apples. Place nuts inside apple cavities. In a saucepan combine water and honey and bring to a boil. Let cook slowly for 5 minutes. Remove from heat and pour over apples. Bake in a moderate (350°F) oven for 45 minutes, or until apples are tender. Baste occasionally. Cool and serve.

VARIATION: When other products such as flavorings, spices, raisins, coconut, and other fruits became available, this recipe was added to; for instance, raisins were mixed with the nuts and lemon juice and cinnamon were added to the honey and water mixture. YIELD: *8 servings*

APPLE FLOAT

DAISY JUSTUS

1 quart sweetened applesauce   *2 teaspoons vanilla*
2 or 3 eggs, separated   *Nutmeg (optional)*

Pour applesauce into a bowl. Add egg yolks and vanilla; beat well. Beat egg whites until stiff, then fold into applesauce. May be sprinkled with nutmeg, if desired. YIELD: *8 servings*

APPLE FLUFF

IONE DICKERSON

"My mother used egg white in applesauce. Beat the egg white stiff [gradually adding sugar to it] and flavor it if you want to. Then mix your egg white with applesauce. Apple fluff, that's what we called it."

SPICY BROWN BETTY

1 cup sugar
¼ teaspoon cinnamon
¼ teaspoon nutmeg
¼ teaspoon salt
2 cups bread crumbs

3 cups pared, cored, and sliced apples
¼ cup water
3 tablespoons lemon juice
Grated rind of 1 lemon
2 tablespoons butter

Blend sugar, spices, and salt. Arrange a third of the crumbs in a greased baking dish. Add half the apples. Sprinkle with half the sugar mixture. Repeat the process, finishing with a layer of crumbs. Mix the water, lemon juice, and grated rind and pour over. Dot with butter. Bake for 45 minutes in a 350°F oven. YIELD: *8 servings*

PINEAPPLE CASSEROLE

½ cup margarine
¾ cup sugar
2 eggs, beaten

1 8 ounce can crushed pineapple
Crumbs from 4 slices of white bread

Beat margarine and sugar together; add beaten eggs and pineapple. Fold in bread crumbs. Put into a buttered dish and bake in a 350°F oven for 40 to 50 minutes. YIELD: *4-6 servings*

PINEAPPLE FRITTERS

CONNIE BURRELL

2 cups self-rising flour
1 teaspoon baking powder
Pinch of salt
¾ cup milk
1 16 ounce can crushed pineapple,

drained but juice reserved
Fat for deep frying
¾ cup sugar
3 teaspoons butter
2 tablespoons all-purpose flour

Sift together dry ingredients, then mix with milk to make a workable dough. Put out on a floured surface and roll out thin. Cut dough in circles, using a saucer to cut around (as demonstrated by Blanche Harkins making fried apple "half-moon" pies, also following her instructions for shaping the pies once the pineapple is placed on each circle of dough; see following recipe). Fry in hot fat, turning several times till done. While cooking, stick a fork through each fritter once so the inside will cook. When fully cooked, place on paper towels or brown paper to absorb the oil. Mix the pineapple juice, sugar, butter, and all-purpose flour in a pan and bring to a boil. Pour over the pineapple fritters.

"HALF-MOON" PIES

"Half-moon" pies, one of the most popular desserts, are made by cooking and thickening sweetened berries or fruits such as strawberries, blueberries, blackberries, peaches, pumpkin, and possibly the favorite—dried apples. Blanche Harkins, an expert at making fried apple pies, invited us to watch her make a batch.

To make 4 small pies she uses 1 quart of dried apples. She places them in a saucepan, adds a small amount of water, cooks them until they are tender, and then mashes them up with a fork. She sweetens and add spices to suit her own taste. She makes the pie crusts using the following measurements and instructions:

4 cups self-rising flour   1 cup water
½ cup lard or shortening

Make up crust like any other pie crust; divide the dough into balls about the size of a fist for each tart and roll the dough out into a very thin circle. Mrs. Harkins places the cooked apples on half the circle and folds the other half over the side with apples. She presses the edges together with either her fingers or a fork and makes tiny holes or slits in the tarts, using a fork or knife, to let the air out as the tarts cook and to prevent the edges from turning up. Next, she puts enough cooking shortening in a large iron frying pan to almost cover the pies as they cook. After the shortening is heated, she places the pies in the pan and fries them till brown on both sides. Mrs. Harkins told us that if we preferred to bake them, to spread melted butter on the pies before placing them in the oven. The butter will give it a crispier crust as it bakes. For baking place in a 400°F oven.

COBBLERS AND PIES

With flour came the possibility of cobblers, pies, custards, cookies, cakes, and other desserts.

Ruth Cabe explained about cobblers: "Cobblers were the usual pie—blackberries, huckleberries, rhubarb, fresh apples or dried apples in winter, cherries, sweet potatoes. A deep dish pie, or cobbler, is one that has no crust on the bottom. It has fruit on the bottom. Some people put fruit, a layer of pie dough, a layer of fruit, then their crust on top. They started it cooking on top of the stove because when they put it in the oven, the crust on top would get done before the layer of dough in the middle. By cooking it for a few minutes on top of the stove first, and then finishing it in the oven, it would cook evenly."

Cobblers are a favorite with families in this area. They are simple to make and can be served plain or with ice cream or whipped cream. During the summer, blackberries, blueberries, strawberries, huckleberries, cherries, rhubarb, sweet potatoes, and apples are gathered and preserved for winter use so they can be used for various dishes, preferably cobblers. Bertha Waldroop tells us how she makes a cobbler, which is one of the most popular methods for making them:

"I make cobbler out of peaches or blackberries or cherries—I cut up the cherries and get the seeds out—use any fruit you want to. I use a square aluminum pan now, and make up a biscuit dough. I put the cherries, or whatever fruit I'm using, in the pan, usually a quart of fruit, and put some sugar on them—it takes a lot of sugar. And I use margarine now 'cause we don't have the butter like we used to have. For a quart of berries, I use about two tablespoons of butter, stir it around in the fruit, and cover the fruit with the dough. I do just like I was gonna bake biscuits—roll the dough out right thin, cut it in strips, and put it on top of the fruit. Then I put it in the oven and pour water about halfway up in the pan with the fruit. Bake it at 350 degrees about thirty minutes and when it browns on top, I take it out. If you wish to, it does make it awful good if you put some margarine on top of it. That makes it real good, and it's ready to eat."

Mary Cabe said: "I bake what I call an oven pie. I put fruit in the bottom of the pan. Then I make up my dough and put it on top of my fruit. I cook it on top of the stove till the stuff gets to boiling. Then I set it in the oven and bake it."

APPLE COBBLER

DOROTHY BECK

"I take about five or six apples and cube them up and put them in a sheet cake pan and put a little water over them. I make a pastry using a cup of sugar and a cup of flour and about a half a cup of butter and just mix that up real good and sprinkle it over the top of your apples. Cook that at about 350 degrees for twenty or thirty minutes, or until done."
YIELD: *10-15 servings*

SWEET POTATO COBBLER

2 cups cooked and diced sweet potatoes	½ teaspoon ginger
⅔ cup molasses	Pinch of salt
¼ cup butter	1 recipe biscuit dough
½ cup milk	

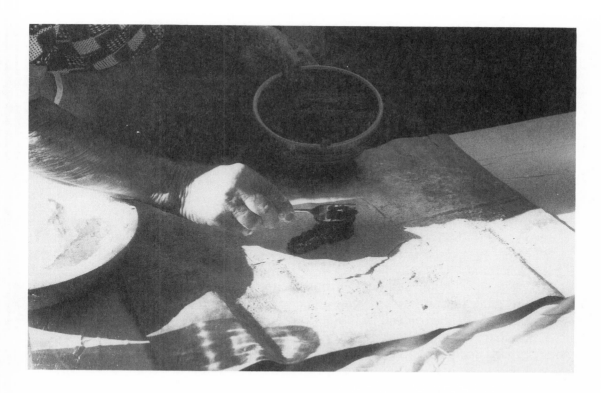

"Half-moon" pies made by Blanche Harkins

Mix together all the ingredients except the dough and bring to a boil. Cut part of rolled dough into cubes and drop into boiling mixture. Cut remaining dough in thin slices and place on top. Put the pan in a oven and bake in 400°F oven until the crust is brown. YIELD: *6 servings*

RHUBARB COBBLER

IONE DICKERSON

"I cooked some rhubarb last week, and I told this woman up on Sylvan Lake, 'You could have heard me smacking my lips if you had been out on the porch [laughter].' That was the best stuff I ever put in my mouth! Oh, that was good!

"To make the cobbler, just cut the rhubarb up in inch pieces and put it in your pan. You have to put a little water and some sugar and butter in it. Slice your crust in lattice strips, put them over the top and bake. Or you can make a rhubarb crisp like apple crisp. Put your rhubarb in your pan, mix your oatmeal, flour, and sugar. You don't put spice in your rhubarb like your apple pie, though. Have it mixed up good, and sprinkle it over the fruit. Or you can make a thin sweet dough like a cake dough and pour it over that and cook it. It's good like that, too."

CUSTARDS AND CUSTARD PIES

"We'd make boiled custards, you know, that's fixed with milk and eggs and sugar and flavoring, and it's delicious; but where you put a lot of eggs in it, it's so rich you can't eat much of it."
— HARRIET ECHOLS

AUNT ARIE'S EGG CUSTARD (COOKED ON A WOOD STOVE)

AUNT ARIE CARPENTER

1 recipe biscuit dough　　　　　*Handful of flour*
1 egg, well beaten　　　　　　*1 teaspoon nutmeg*
1 cup milk　　　　　　　　　*½ cup sugar*

Line a small pie pan with plain biscuit dough rolled thin. In a separate bowl, mix together all remaining ingredients and pour it into the crust, using just a little wood so the fire won't be too hot. Bake it slowly until it "sets." It will "blubber up"—or bubble—and then the bubbles will settle.

EGG CUSTARD

BELLE LEDFORD

3 eggs, slightly beaten
2 cups milk
½ cup sugar
1 teaspoon vanilla

Dash of nutmeg (optional)
¼ teaspoon salt
1 unbaked pie shell

Combine first 6 ingredients in the order listed; pour into pie shell. Bake in a 400°F oven for 50 to 60 minutes.

CUSTARD AND APPLE WHIP

MARY PITTS

2 cups milk
2 egg yolks, beaten
½ cup sugar
1 rounded tablespoon flour

Pinch of salt
1 teaspoon vanilla
1½ cups applesauce
2 egg whites, beaten stiff

Scald milk and set aside to cool. Combine egg yolks, sugar, flour, and salt in a second saucepan. Add cooled milk very gradually to the egg mixture. Put back on the stove and cook slowly until mixture thickens. Flavor with vanilla. Fold applesauce into the stiff egg whites. To serve, put a few spoonfuls of the custard in a saucer, then put a spoonful of the apple whip on top.

PIES

CUSTARD PIE

ANNIE LONG

2 eggs
2 tablespoons sugar
Pinch of salt

1½ cups milk
1 teaspoon nutmeg or cinnamon
1 unbaked pie shell

Mix eggs with sugar and salt. Gradually add milk and nutmeg or cinnamon. Pour into an unbaked pie shell. Bake in a 400°F oven for 10 minutes. Reduce the heat to 325°F and bake an additional 20 to 30 minutes, until done. Pie is best served with a meringue. YIELD: 6-8 *servings*

CHOCOLATE CUSTARD PIE

MARY PITTS

½ cup cocoa
2 cups sugar
¼ cup cornstarch
2½ cups milk

8 egg yolks, well beaten
1 cup butter
1 baked 9-inch pie shell

Mix together cocoa, sugar, cornstarch, and milk and cook over medium heat until thickened. Gradually add ¾ cup of cooked mixture to beaten egg yolks, then slowly pour it back into remaining cooked mixture and cook an additional 5 minutes on medium heat. Take off the heat and add butter, mixing well. Pour into the pie shell. Let stand until set.

"Pies are first put on the bottom rack of the oven and then moved up to a higher rack to brown."
— LUCY YORK

PIE CRUST

ANNIE LONG

1½ cups flour
½ teaspoon salt
2 teaspoons baking powder

5 tablespoons lard
4 to 5 tablespoons ice water

Sift and then measure the flour. Sift flour, salt, and baking powder together. Work in lard with fingers or fork. Stir in ice water. Roll out on a floured board or cloth and make into pie crust. If crust needs baking before pouring in filling, bake in a 425°F oven for 5 to 7 minutes.

VINEGAR PASTRY

ARIZONA DICKERSON: "One teaspoon vinegar added to pie dough makes a flaky pastry."

4 cups unsifted flour
1 tablespoon sugar
1½ cups shortening

1 egg
1 tablespoon vinegar
½ cup cold water

Blend dry ingredients. Cut in shortening. Blend egg, vinegar, and water together and sprinkle over the flour mixture 1 tablespoon at a time, tossing lightly with a fork until all is moistened. Gather into a ball with hands. Chill for several hours or overnight. Keep in a covered bowl. YIELD: *2 crusts*

COLD PIE

DAISY JUSTUS

Use leftover cold homemade biscuits. Slice a layer of biscuits. Cover with applesauce, sprinkle with sugar. Repeat until you get as much as you want fixed. Cinnamon or nutmeg can be sprinkled on applesauce, if desired.

APPLESAUCE PIE

RUTH HOLCOMB

"Slice your biscuits left over from breakfast or last night's supper and lay them in the bottom of a baking dish. Spread applesauce on top of them. You may stir cinnamon into the applesauce, if you wish. Then put another layer of sliced biscuits on top of the applesauce, and another layer of applesauce. Make as many layers as you wish, ending with applesauce on top. Sprinkle brown sugar on the top layer. Put into the oven and warm. The brown sugar will melt and make a crust on top of the applesauce."

BLACKBERRY PIE

MARY PITTS

"To seed a quart of blackberries, put two cups of water in them and let them come to a boil on the stove. Let it cook for fifteen to twenty minutes, and then run it through a sieve and get all that juice and pulp out. And you can make a pie out of that just like you can with the berries. I've got tame blackberries right down here in the garden, and they grow in big bunches, each berry bigger than the end of my thumb. I juice them and make pies.

"To start out [with blackberry pie], I put my berries in a saucepan. I put a cup or a cup and a half of sugar to a quart of blackberries and I put it on the stove till it comes to a boil. Then I use self-rising flour and make up my dough, just like I make my biscuit dough, and roll it out. I put them berries in a deep dish and cover them with dough— solid or in strips—and put it in the stove and brown it. Then I take it out and put in the rest of my berries and put on the top crust. I dot the top crust with butter and sprinkle a little sugar on it and put it in the stove and brown it [at 400°]." YIELD: *10-15 servings*

TAME GOOSEBERRY PIE

2 cups gooseberries
¾ cup sugar

1 tablespoon butter
1 recipe biscuit dough

Mix berries with sugar and butter and cook, stirring to mash the berries, until thick. Pour the berries into a pie plate. Make up biscuit dough, roll it out and cut ½-inch wide strips. Place the strips of dough crosswise on the berries and bake in a 450°F oven until the crust is brown. YIELD: *6-8 servings*

CUSHAW PIE

SANDRA ROBINSON

1 cup brown sugar
¼ cup flour
¼ cup granulated sugar
1 teaspoon salt
1 teaspoon cinnamon
½ teaspoon ginger
½ teaspoon nutmeg
1 cup milk

3 eggs
3 tablespoons butter
2 cups cooked mashed, cushaw, candy
roaster, or pumpkin
1 teaspoon vanilla
1 deep-dish unbaked pie shell
Nuts (optional)
Whipped cream (optional)

Sift together the dry ingredients. Add milk, eggs, and butter and beat well. Add cushaw and vanilla. Pour into deep unbaked pie shell. Bake for 15 minutes at 425°F. Reduce temperature to 350°F and bake for 25 to 30 minutes longer, or until a knife inserted 1 inch from edge comes out clean. If desired, garnish with nuts and whipped cream. YIELD: *6-8 servings*

LEMON CUSHAW PIE

LILLIAN STINSON

1 cup cooked mashed cushaw
2 eggs
6 tablespoons butter

½ teaspoons lemon extract or more to taste
½ cup sugar
1 unbaked pie shell

Blend ingredients. Pour into pie shell and bake for 45 minutes in a 425°F oven. YIELD: *6 servings*

PUMPKIN OR CUSHAW STACK PIE

MONTENE WATTS

This recipe was found by Mrs. Watts in an 1880 newspaper. "I remember Mommy making stack pies like these when we had corn shuckins. You can make as many as you want. This recipe called for using the 'spider' pan [iron griddle] and that's what Mommy would use."

OLD-TIME PIE CRUST
¼ cup water

¼ cup liquid shortening
Sifter full of flour

Mix up until right consistency. Roll out thin and lay bottom of griddle (of pie plate) down on rolled-out dough and cut around. Lift the dough up from underneath and place in the bottom of griddle. Should make 2 to 3 crusts depending on desired thickness. MIX TOGETHER:

3 cups cooked mashed pumpkin or
 cushaw
1 cup sugar
1 egg

2 tablespoons flour
1 heaping teaspoon cinnamon
1 teaspoon ginger
Salt to taste

Pour mixture into pie shells. Can sprinkle more cinnamon and ginger on top. Cook in slow to moderate (250° to 350°F) oven for 15 minutes or until done—time will depend on how thick you are making them. When cooled, flip out of pans carefully stacking one on top of the other.

SWEET POTATO PIE

MARGARET NORTON

3 cups cooked mashed sweet potatoes
1 teaspoon cinnamon
¼ teaspoon nutmeg
1 cup sugar

1 tablespoon butter
¼ cup cream
1 prebaked pie shell

Add spices and sugar to sweet potatoes. Mix together the butter and cream and stir into sweet potato mixture. Pour into baked pie shell and bake the pie in a 325°F oven.

BUTTERY SWEET POTATO PIE

MARY PITTS

"For sweet potato pie, cook two potatoes about the size of your fist—enough to make a cup—till they get done. I just drop mine in a pot of water whole, and then you take them out and take that skin off and put them in a bowl. I use one stick of margarine, a cup of sugar, one teaspoon vanilla, and one-half to three-quarters cup of sweet milk. Then I take my potato masher and just mash and stir that until it's good and thick. If it's thicker than you want it, add a little milk. But let it be pretty thick, and put it in a nine-inch pie crust. Put it in the stove and cook it at 350 degrees for 30 minutes."

SPICY PUMPKIN PIE

ANNIE LONG

¾ cup sugar
½ teaspoon salt
1¼ teaspoons cinnamon
½ teaspoon ginger
½ teaspoon nutmeg
½ teaspoon cloves

1½ cups cooked mashed pumpkin
3 eggs, well beaten
1¼ cups whole milk
⅔ cup evaporated milk
1 unbaked pie shell

Mix dry ingredients together. Blend in pumpkin and then the eggs. Gradually stir in the milk. Pour into unbaked pie shell and bake at 425°F for 15 minutes, then 30 minutes more at 325°F.

DAMSON PIE

1 cup butter
1½ cups sugar
6 eggs

1 cup damson preserves
1 teaspoon vanilla
Dough for a 2-crust pie

Cream butter and sugar. Beat eggs until light; add to first mixture, then add preserves and vanilla. Fill bottom crust, cover with top crust, and bake in a 350°F oven until brown.

DRIED FRUIT STACK PIE WITH GINGERBREAD PASTRY

2 cups flour
1 teaspoon ginger
1 teaspoon cloves
2 teaspoons soda
½ teaspoon salt
¾ cup shortening

1 cup sugar
1 egg
½ cup dark molasses
Any canned fruit in thick sweetened
    syrup

Sift together dry ingredients. Cream together shortening and sugar until fluffy. Add egg and beat well. Mix in the molasses. Slowly mix the flour mixture into egg mixture. Divide dough into 3 or 4 balls; roll out to ¼-inch thick, and bake each circle about 10 minutes in a 350°F oven. Let pastry cool and then spread fruit between each layer of pastry and stack.

BEST-EVER LEMON PIE

BELLE LEDFORD

1¼ cups sugar
6 tablespoons cornstarch
2 cups water
3 eggs, separated
⅓ cup lemon juice

1½ teaspoons lemon extract
3 tablespoons butter
2 teaspoons vinegar
1 prebaked deep-dish 9-inch pie shell

Mix sugar and cornstarch together in top of a double boiler. Gradually add water. Beat egg yolks and lemon juice and then add to sugar mixture. Cook until very thick over boiling water 25 minutes. Add lemon extract, butter, and vinegar and stir very well before pouring into baked pie shell. Cover with meringue. (See meringue recipe on page 235.) Let stand until set.

LEMON SPONGE PIE

MARY PITTS

1 cup sugar
3 tablespoons flour
1 tablespoon butter, softened
3 eggs, separated

1 cup milk
½ teaspoon lemon juice with peel
1 unbaked pie shell

Mix sugar and flour; beat in butter. Mix in egg yolks, one at a time, then milk, and lemon juice and peel. Beat egg whites until they form stiff peaks. Fold into lemon mixture. Bake in the unbaked pie shell for 35 to 45 minutes in a 350°F oven.

NO-CRUST COCONUT PIE

DOROTHY BECK

1¾ cups sugar
¼ cup margarine
½ cup self-rising flour
2 cups milk

2 small cans flaked coconut
4 eggs, well beaten
1 teaspoon vanilla

Cream together sugar and margarine, then add the flour. Add milk and vanilla to eggs. Blend egg mixture into the first mixture; add coconut and pour into a well-greased 9-inch pie plate. Bake in a 350°F oven for 40 minutes.

BUTTERSCOTCH PIE

ANNIE LONG

1 cup brown sugar
Pinch of salt

6 tablespoons flour
1½ cups milk

3 eggs, separated
1 teaspoon vanilla

¼ cup butter
1 baked pie shell

Mix sugar, salt, and flour together in a saucepan. Gradually add the milk and cook in saucepan stirring constantly until slightly thick. Beat egg yolks and gradually mix in a small amount of cooked mixture (approximately ¾ cup), then slowly stir this egg mixture into the remaining cooked mixture. Cook until very thick, about 4 minutes, stirring constantly. Take off the heat and add the vanilla and butter. Mix well and pour into baked pie shell. Make a meringue with the egg whites and spread on top of hot pie. (See the following recipe for meringue.) Bake in a 400°F oven for 10 minutes.

NEVER-FAIL MERINGUE

1 tablespoon cornstarch
2 tablespoons cold water
½ cup boiling water
3 egg whites

6 tablespoons sugar
Pinch of salt
1 teaspoon vanilla

Blend cornstarch and cold water in a saucepan. Add boiling water and cook until clear and thickened. Let cool completely. Beat egg whites with an electric beater at high speed until foamy. Gradually add sugar and beat until stiff but not dry. Add salt and vanilla, then gradually add cornstarch mixture and beat well until stiff peaks form. Spread over cooled pie filling. Bake in a 350°F oven for 10 minutes. This is a beautiful meringue which cuts smoothly and does not leak.

PUDDINGS

PUDDING AND CREAM PIES (TWO PIES)

STELLA BURRELL

"I just memorized this recipe, and I've always used it through the years for puddings and pies. I think it was something that I learned from my mother or grandmother when I was real young, and I still use it.

"You would take four cups of milk, one-half cup flour, one-half cup sugar, four eggs, and your vanilla [1 teaspoon], and you would beat that all the time it was cooking. That will make two pies. If you're making pudding, you'd use the same recipe except you'd add about a tablespoon of milk for each cup to make it a little thinner. To vary the basic pudding recipe, for chocolate pie you just add cocoa [about 3 teaspoons] to it before you start your cooking process. And if you're making coconut pie, you would wait until it's almost finished to put your coconut in. If you were making lemon, you would add your lemon juice and the lemon rind; and you'd add bananas for banana pudding."

ALEXANDER PUDDING

MONTENE WATTS

"Use sweetened fruit which has been spiced with cinnamon or ginger. Thin fruit with small amount of milk. Pour into bottom of dish. Slice leftover biscuits (cold) over fruit, being careful not to get it too thick. Then place another layer of fruit on top of biscuits. If the mixture seems too dry, make a small hole in the middle and pour small amount of milk in it. Set aside for a few hours (Mama would set that in the cupboard to sit awhile) and then eat anytime."

RICE PUDDING

DAISY JUSTUS

3 tablespoons butter
3 cups hot cooked rice (1 cup uncooked
   makes about 3 cups)
4 eggs
3 cups whole milk

¾ cup sugar (use more or less, as desired)
1 tablespoon grated lemon rind
2 teaspoons vanilla
⅛ teaspoon salt
Lemon Sauce (recipe follows)

Stir butter into rice. Beat eggs, then add milk, sugar, lemon rind, vanilla, and salt. Stir together the 2 mixtures. Mix well and pour into a baking dish set in a pan of hot water. Bake in a 350°F oven for about 1 hour, or until a knife comes out clean. Serve warm with lemon sauce. YIELD: 8 servings

LEMON SAUCE

½ cup sugar
1 tablespoon cornstarch or 5 tablespoons
    flour
⅛ teaspoon salt

1 cup boiling water
1 tablespoon butter
1 tablespoon grated lemon rind
3 tablespoons lemon juice

Combine the sugar, cornstarch, and salt. Stir in water gradually. Cook, stirring constantly, about 5 minutes. Blend in remaining ingredients. This sauce is also good on gingerbread.

POOR MAN'S RICE PUDDING

2 level tablespoons rice
3 tablespoons sugar
Pinch of salt

1 tablespoon butter
4 cups milk

Wash the rice well and place it in a baking dish with the sugar, salt, and butter; pour milk over the mixture and bake slowly in a 250°F oven at least 2½ hours, stirring twice during the first hour. YIELD: 8 servings

CLASSIC SWEET POTATO PUDDING

MARY PITTS

4 large sweet potatoes, cooked and
    mashed
2 eggs
1 cup milk
1 cup sugar
½ teaspoon salt

½ cup butter
1 teaspoon nutmeg
1 cup seeded raisins
Meringue (optional; see page 235)
Marshmallows (optional)

Mix all the ingredients except the optional ones well and pour into a hot greased baking dish. Bake in a 350°F oven for 45 minutes, stirring pudding from the bottom occasionally to make sure that it is well cooked. When nearly done, smooth top over and let brown. When done, pudding may be topped with meringue, if desired, or dotted with marshmallows. YIELD: 8 servings

SWEET POTATO PUDDING WITH COCONUT

FLORENCE BROOKS AND MARINDA BROWN

2 cups cooked mashed sweet potatoes
½ cup brown sugar
1 cup sweet milk
2 eggs

1 teaspoon vanilla
½ cup raisins
½ cup grated coconut

Combine ingredients in a casserole dish. Bake in a moderate (350°F) oven for 30 minutes, or until firm. Serve hot or cold. YIELD: *6-8 servings*

BANANA PUDDING

ARIZONA DICKERSON

2 tablespoons flour
¾ cup sugar
¼ teaspoon salt
2 cups milk

3 eggs, separated
1 teaspoon vanilla
Bananas
Sweet crackers, such as vanilla wafers

Mix flour, sugar, and salt in top of a double boiler. Stir in milk. Cook over boiling water until thick. Beat egg yolks and gradually mix into hot mixture. Cook 5 minutes longer. Remove from heat and add vanilla. Let cool. Line a casserole dish with desired amounts of crackers and sliced bananas. Pour cooled sauce over them. Use egg whites for a meringue and put on top. (See meringue recipe on page 235.) Brown the meringue in a 350°F oven for 5 minutes.

CARROT PUDDING OR CAKE

MARGARET NORTON AND MARY PITTS

⅔ cup sifted flour
1 teaspoon baking powder
¾ teaspoon baking soda
¾ teaspoon salt

½ teaspoon cinnamon
¼ teaspoon cloves
¼ teaspoon nutmeg
⅔ cup sugar

⅔ cup currants	1 cup grated raw carrots
⅔ cup raisins	⅓ cup milk
⅔ cup grated raw potatoes	Sauce for Carrot Pudding (recipe follows)

Mix and sift together dry ingredients. Add the fruits; stir until well coated. Stir in the potatoes, carrots, and milk. Pour into a greased pan, cover with a lid, and steam in a large pan of hot water for 2½ hours. Serve with the sauce.

SAUCE FOR CARROT PUDDING

| 1 cup confectioners sugar | 2 egg yolks, beaten |
| 1 generous teaspoon vanilla or wine | 1 cup heavy cream, whipped |

Mix the sugar, vanilla, and egg yolks, and when ready to serve, fold in the whipped cream.

REFRIGERATED DESSERTS

GRAPE JUICE SPONGE DESSERT

MARY PITTS

¼ cup cornstarch	2 cups grape juice
6 tablespoons sugar	1 tablespoon butter or margarine
Dash of salt	2 egg whites
⅛ teaspoon lemon juice	

Combine cornstarch, sugar, and salt in a saucepan. Gradually add lemon and grape juice. Stir until well blended. Cook over medium heat until the mixture boils (stir constantly) and then boil 1 minute. Add butter and stir until melted and blended. Beat egg whites until stiff peaks form. Gradually pour hot grape mixture over beaten egg whites and beat until well blended. Pour into sherbet dishes and chill for 1 hour. YIELD: *eight ½-cup servings*

LEMON MOUSSE

ARIZONA DICKERSON

1 13 ounce can evaporated milk
Juice of 2 lemons
1 tablespoon grated lemon peel

1 cup sugar
Graham cracker crumbs

Freeze milk in bowl long enough for ice to form. Whip. Add lemon juice and peel slowly while beating. As you continue to beat the mixture, add sugar slowly. Line a 9 × 9-inch pan with a thin layer of Graham cracker crumbs. Pour lemon mixture into it. Sprinkle more crumbs on top, if desired. Cover with waxed paper and freeze. YIELD: *20 servings*

GELATIN DESSERTS

Gelatin desserts are thought to be a recent discovery, but while visiting with Arizona Dickerson she showed us a Jell-O recipe booklet she has. The booklet, copyrighted in 1930, contained award-winning recipes presented at the Louisiana Purchase Exposition in St. Louis, Missouri, in 1904; the Lewis and Clark Exposition in Portland, Oregon, in 1905; and others of similar early dates.

RASPBERRY BAVARIAN CREAM

ARIZONA DICKERSON

1 package raspberry gelatin
1 cup boiling water
Raspberry juice plus cold water to equal
    1 cup liquid

¼ cup sugar
1 cup fresh raspberries,* crushed and
    drained (save juice)
½ cup whipped cream

Dissolve gelatin in boiling water. Add raspberry juice and cold water and sugar. Chill. When slightly thickened, beat with a rotary egg beater until the consistency of whipped cream. Fold in berries and cream. Turn into a mold. Chill until firm. Unmold to serve. May be garnished with whipped cream and whole berries.

*Strawberries or blackberries may be substituted for raspberries. Use the correct flavored gelatin for substitution used.

SNOW PUDDING

1 tablespoon plain gelatin
¼ cup cold water
1 cup boiling water
¼ cup lemon juice

¼ cup sugar
¼ teaspoon salt
3 egg whites

Soak gelatin in cold water; dissolve in boiling water. Add lemon juice and sugar. Chill mixture until set. Add salt to egg whites; beat to a stiff froth and combine with lemon mixture. Continue beating until mixture holds its shape. Chill; serve with custard sauce (see page 265). YIELD: *4 servings*

FRUIT WHIP

1 lemon
1 cup sugar
1 tablespoon plain gelatin
¼ cup cold water
¼ cup boiling water

1 cup crushed fruit, such as berries,
    peaches, plums, or apricots
Pinch of salt
4 egg whites

Grate lemon rind into sugar. Set aside. Soak gelatin in cold water, dissolve in boiling water; add lemon-mixture, and when sugar is dissolved, remove gelatin from the fire. Add the juice of the lemon and crushed fruit. Place the saucepan in ice water to cool, then whip until frothy. Add salt to the egg whites and beat until stiff. Fold them into gelatin mixture and whip the sponge until it holds its shape. Chill and serve with cream. YIELD: *6 servings*

COOKIES

Of all the desserts, cookies probably rank number one with children. This is the one dessert children can help make unless they run into the problem Stella Burrell did with her mother: "Mama never let me cook many cookies. She said I always made too big a mess."

Tea cakes seemed to be an old favorite with many of our contacts, and they shared their recipes with us.

OLD-FASHIONED TEA CAKES

MARY ELLEN MEANS

1 cup butter
2 cups sugar
4 eggs

2 teaspoons vanilla
2 teaspoons nutmeg (optional)
8 to 10 cups of self-rising flour

Cream together butter and sugar, then add eggs, one at a time, beating well. Add vanilla and nutmeg. Beat until fluffy. Gradually start stirring in flour until a fairly firm dough is formed. Place dough on a heavily floured surface and knead more flour into dough until it is firm enough to roll out. Working with only a small amount of dough at a time, roll out ½-inch thick, then cut out with a cookie cutter and place on an ungreased cookie sheet. Sprinkle sugar on each before baking. Bake in a 375°F oven for 5 to 8 minutes. YIELD: 6 dozen cakes

HONEY TEA CAKES

BELLE LEDFORD

2 cups flour
½ teaspoon soda
1 teaspoon baking powder
½ teaspoon salt

2 eggs
1 cup strained honey
1 cup sour cream
1 teaspoon lemon juice

Mix and sift together dry ingredients. Beat eggs and honey together until smooth. Add egg mixture alternately with sour cream and lemon juice to the dry mixture until batter is smooth. Pour batter into greased muffin pans and bake in a 350°F oven for 15 to 20 minutes. "This was made during the war when we couldn't get sugar." YIELD: 1½ dozen cakes

MOLASSES WAFERS

1 cup molasses
Butter and shortening to equal ½ cup
1 tablespoon ginger
1½ teaspoons salt

1 tablespoon soda
Milk
3 cups flour

Bring molasses to a boil; add butter and shortening. Add ginger and salt. Dissolve soda in a little milk and add to molasses mixture. Mix well and add flour, stirring in gradually. Turn mixture onto a floured surface and knead well. Roll thin, cut out into 2-inch circles and place on greased cookie sheets. Bake in a moderate (350°F) oven till done. Let cool before removing from pans. YIELD: *5 dozen wafers*

MOLASSES COOKIES

DOROTHY BECK

½ cup butter
½ cup sugar
1 egg
¼ cup molasses
2 cups sifted flour
½ teaspoon cinnamon

½ teaspoon ginger
¼ teaspoon allspice
¼ teaspoon cloves
¼ teaspoon salt
¼ teaspoon baking soda

Cream together butter and sugar; add eggs and molasses. Sift together dry ingredients and blend into the creamed mixture. Roll out and cut or put through a cookie press. Bake in a 375°F oven for 8 minutes, or until done. YIELD: *4 dozen cookies*

VANILLA WAFERS

1 cup sugar
½ cup butter
1½ cups flour
½ cup milk

1 egg, well beaten
2 teaspoons baking powder
½ teaspoon salt
½ teaspoon vanilla

Cream together butter and sugar. Add egg and mix well. Sift together dry ingredients, resift, and stir into egg mixture alternately with milk. Add vanilla and let mixture chill. Turn out onto a floured surface and roll to a ¼-inch thickness; cut into 1½-inch circles and place on a lightly greased cookie sheet. Sprinkle tops with sugar. Bake in a 375°F oven for 7 to 15 minutes. YIELD: *4 dozen wafers*

GINGER SNAPS

½ cup shortening or butter
1 cup brown sugar
1 cup molasses
6 cups sifted flour

1 teaspoon ginger
1 teaspoon soda
1 teaspoon salt
½ cup hot water

Cream together shortening and sugar. Beat in molasses. Resift flour with other dry ingredients and add to molasses mixture alternately with water. Turn out onto a floured surface and knead well; roll thin and cut into 2-inch circles. Bake on a greased cookie sheets in a 350°F oven. Cool before removing from cookie sheets. YIELD: *10 dozen cookies*

CRISP SUGAR COOKIES

IONE DICKERSON

½ cup shortening
1 cup sugar
2 eggs, well beaten

2 cups flour
3 teaspoons baking powder
1 teaspoon vanilla

Cream shortening and sugar. Add eggs. Sift together dry ingredients; add to mixture. Add vanilla and beat well. Knead dough slightly and roll out thin. Cut out and place on a cookie sheet. Bake for 10 minutes in a 350°F oven. YIELD: *4 dozen cookies*

SUGAR COOKIES

ARIZONA DICKERSON

⅔ cup butter or shortening
1½ cups sugar
2 eggs
2 teaspoons vanilla

3⅔ cups sifted flour
2½ teaspoons baking powder
4 teaspoons milk

Cream the butter thoroughly. Slowly add sugar and beat well. Add eggs, one at a time, and beat. Add vanilla. Sift together dry ingredients and add to egg mixture alternately with the milk. Blend well. Chill the dough overnight. When ready to bake, roll out ⅛-inch thick. Cut out, using a floured cookie cutter. Put on greased baking sheets and sprinkle with granulated sugar. Bake in a 400°F oven for about 10 minutes. YIELD: *5 dozen cookies*

OLD-FASHIONED OATMEAL COOKIES

1 cup butter or shortening	1 teaspoon soda
1 cup brown sugar	1 teaspoon salt
½ cup water	2½ cups rolled oats
2½ cups flour	

Cream butter and sugar. Slowly add water. Sift together flour, soda, and salt. Mix this with the first mixture. Stir in oats. Roll the dough out thin and cut with a cookie cutter. Bake in a 350°F oven for 10 to 12 minutes. YIELD: *4 dozen cookies*

VARIATION: Spread jelly between 2 cookies, seal up edges, and bake.

OATMEAL CRISP COOKIES

BELLE LEDFORD

1 cup shortening	1½ cups sifted flour
1 cup dark brown sugar	1 teaspoon salt
1 cup granulated sugar	1 teaspoon soda
2 eggs	3 cups uncooked quick-cooking oatmeal
1 teaspoon vanilla	½ cup chopped nuts (optional)

Cream together shortening and sugar. Add eggs and vanilla and beat well. Sift together dry ingredients and add to creamed shortening and sugar. Add oatmeal and nuts, stirring well. Either shape into a roll and slice or drop from a teaspoon onto a greased cookie sheet. Bake in a 350°F oven for 8 to 10 minutes. YIELD: *4 dozen cookies*

CRY-BABY COOKIES

MARY PITTS

1 cup plus 2 tablespoons shortening	1 teaspoon salt
1 cup plus 2 tablespoons sugar	1½ teaspoons soda
1 cup molasses	2 cups grated coconut
2 eggs, beaten	2 cups chopped walnuts
4¾ cups sifted flour	1½ cups raisins
1 tablespoon baking powder	1 cup milk

Cream shortening, then add sugar, molasses, and eggs. Sift together dry ingredients, then combine with coconut, walnuts, and raisins. Add dry ingredients alternately with milk to creamed mixture. Drop by tablespoonfuls onto a greased baking sheet. Bake in a moderate (350°F) oven for 10 minutes. "It makes a big batch [8 dozen]. We made 'em at Christmas time." YIELD: *8 dozen cookies*

SANDIES

BELLE LEDFORD

1 cup butter or margarine	*2 teaspoons vanilla*
⅓ cup sugar	*2 cups sifted flour*
2 teaspoons water	*1 cup chopped pecans*

Cream together butter and sugar. Add water and vanilla and beat well. Blend in flour and nuts. Beat well with a spoon. Drop from a teaspoon onto an ungreased cookie sheet. Bake in a 325°F oven for 15 minutes, or until lightly browned. Cool before removing from the pan. YIELD: *40 cookies*

CARAMEL COOKIES

JUDY MARCELLINO (HER GRANDMOTHER'S RECIPE)

4 cups dark brown sugar	*1 teaspoon cream of tartar*
1 cup lard, margarine, or butter	*1 cup seedless raisins (optional)*
4 large or 5 small eggs	*1 teaspoon vanilla (optional) or*
6 to 7 cups flour	*1 teaspoon of desired spice for*
1 tablespoon soda	*varied flavoring*

Cream together sugar and lard. Add eggs, one at a time, beating well. Sift together dry ingredients and pour into a large mixing bowl, making a pit in the center. Pour creamed mixture, vanilla, and raisins into the pit and work into the flour. Knead well. Form into 2 large loaves and let stand a few hours, then slice thin and place on a cookie sheet, being sure to leave plenty of room between each cookie for spreading as they cook. Place no more than 12 on a 17 × 13-inch ungreased pan. Bake in a 350°F oven for 10 to 15 minutes. Remove from the pan as soon as you take it from oven. The cookies will stick if left to cool on the pan. YIELD: *8 dozen cookies*

CAKES

In the beginning, ingredients for cakes were very simple, yet sometimes it was a complicated process to bake a cake in a fireplace or wood stove. Several contacts gave us some baking hints for cooking cakes in a fireplace or wood stove.

BERTHA WALDROUP: "Instead of having to grease and flour my cake pans everytime before I pour my cake batter into them, I cut out some circles of waxed paper and have them on hand to line my pans with. Just turn your pan upside down on a piece of waxed paper and mark where the edge of the pan comes on the paper. Then cut it out around the mark. Then just lay it in the pan. I rub some Crisco around the edge of the pan where the paper touches the sides. The cake will come right out without coming apart."

ADDIE NORTON: "I'd get my oven about 350 degrees. Then I'd put my cake in and put in one or two little sticks of wood every once in a while—just enough to keep it the same heat. It'll cook a cake just as pretty as you please. If it does get too hot when you've already got your cake or biscuits in there and you can't cool it off fast, you just have to take them out and let it cool down. You just don't put in too much wood."

LETTIE CHASTAIN: "I put my cakes on the top rack in the oven unless it's a thick cake. Then I put it on the bottom rack. To keep it from burning on the bottom of the cake, I'm careful to not put much wood in the stove, just enough to get it hot."

POUND CAKE

With the availability of new ingredients (especially with what our contacts called "cake flour") through the years, cake recipes have become more sophisticated, but it seems that the "pound cake"—a cake cooked in a tube pan—remains the favorite in this area of the South. The convenience of making a pound cake is that most require only ingredients that are normally stocked in the kitchen—milk, eggs, flour, sugar, and shortening. Other cake recipes are used often in this area, but if the cook doesn't have the necessary ingredients needed to make something different, they can always resort to making the pound cake.

Stella Burrell explained, "I have a plain cake that I've used if I wanted something real quick. It's something I keep the measurements for in my head. If I had a bunch that come in, that cake was something that I could just go ahead and be doing while I was doing other things. You could use most any easy sauce to go over a cake without having to think too much about it."

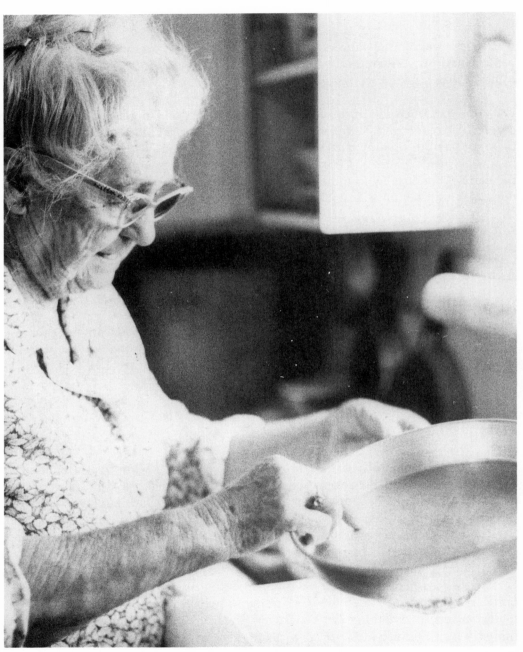

Mrs. Waldroop prepares her cake pan by rubbing shortening around the inside edges.

Belle Ledford showed us an old cookbook she had, and in it she had written down steps for making a pound cake:

STEP 1. Grease and flour cake pan; set aside.
STEP 2. Assemble all ingredients. Let butter, eggs, and milk reach room temperature. Measure dry ingredients.
STEP 3. Combine softened butter and sugar; cream thoroughly until light and fluffy. Beat about 7 minutes with standard mixer, longer with portable mixer.
STEP 4. Add eggs, one at time, beating 1 minute after each addition.
STEP 5. Add dry and liquid ingredients alternately to creamed mixture, beginning and ending with dry ingredients. Beat well after each addition, but only until batter is smooth; do not overbeat—vigorous beating at this point will result in a coarse, tough cake. To ensure that batter is uniformly mixed, scrape bottom and sides of bowl often with a rubber spatula. Stir in flavorings.
STEP 6. Spoon batter evenly into prepared pan. Remove air bubbles by gently cutting through batter with a spatula. Place pan in center of oven; follow specific recipes for oven temperature and baking time.
STEP 7. Cool cake 10 to 15 minutes before turning out on wire rack to cool. If pan has been properly prepared, the cake should slip out easily.

POUND CAKE

MARY PITTS

"Every time I make a pound cake, I pick up a salt shaker and just [makes a shaking motion with hand]. All sweets need a little salt. Not much—I just give a little shake."

1 cup shortening or lard	¼ teaspoon salt
¼ stick margarine or butter	¼ teaspoon baking powder
3 cups sugar	1 cup milk
6 eggs	1 teaspoon vanilla or other flavoring
3 cups flour	

Cream shortening, margarine, and sugar. Add eggs, one at a time, and beat well. Sift together flour, salt, and baking powder twice and add with the milk and vanilla to creamed mixture. Beat well. Bake in a 325°F oven for 1½ hours.

OLD DOMINION POUND CAKE

MARY PITTS

2¼ cups flour
¼ teaspoon baking powder
1¼ cups sugar
1¼ cups butter
2¼ teaspoons vanilla

2 tablespoons lemon juice
6 large eggs, separated
⅛ teaspoon salt
1 cup sugar
1½ teaspoons cream of tartar

Sift together flour, baking powder, and 1¼ cup sugar. Cream butter and blend in vanilla and lemon juice. Add egg yolks, one at a time, beating well after each addition. Gradually blend in flour mixture. Beat egg whites until peaks form and add salt; then gradually add 1 cup sugar with cream of tartar, beating well after each addition. Beat until soft peaks form. Gently fold whites into batter. Turn into a greased and floured tube pan. Cut through batter one or two times, then bake 1 hour 20 minutes in a 325°F oven.

HAM CAKE

MARY ELLEN MEANS

(Ham is a family name, not an ingredient.)

3 cups sugar
1¼ cups shortening or butter
5 eggs
3 cups plain flour

½ teaspoon baking powder
½ teaspoon salt
1 cup milk
1 teaspoon flavoring

Cream together sugar and shortening. Beat in eggs, one at a time. Add sifted dry ingredients and mix in milk, ½ cup at a time. Add flavoring. Pour into greased and floured tube pan. Bake in a 350°F oven for 1 hour 15 minutes.

MILLION-DOLLAR POUND CAKE

BELLE LEDFORD

1 pound butter, softened
3 cups sugar

6 eggs (at room temperature)
4 cups flour

¾ cup milk

1 teaspoon almond extract

1 teaspoon vanilla

Cream butter, add sugar, and beat until light and fluffy. Add eggs, one at a time, beating well after each addition. Add flour to the creamed mixture alternately with milk. Beat well. Stir in flavoring. Pour the batter into a well-greased and floured tube pan. Bake in a 300°F oven for 1 hour 30 minutes.

BUTTERNUT POUND CAKE

MARY PITTS

1 cup shortening

2 cups sugar

4 eggs

2½ cups plain flour

½ cup self-rising flour

1 cup milk

1 tablespoon butternut flavoring

Cream together shortening and sugar. Add eggs, one at a time, and beat well for 1 minute at high speed in an electric mixer. Sift together the plain and self-rising flour. Add 1 cup of flour mixture to creamed mixture, beating for 1 minute, then add remaining flour alternately with milk. Stir in flavoring. Pour into a greased and floured tube pan. Bake at 325°F for 60 minutes, then at 350°F for 15 minutes.

CHOCOLATE POUND CAKE

FAY LONG

3 cups sugar

1 cup butter

½ cup shortening

5 eggs

3 cups flour

½ teaspoon salt

½ teaspoon baking powder

4 heaping tablespoons cocoa

1 cup milk

2 teaspoons vanilla

Cream sugar, butter, and shortening until fluffy. Add eggs, one at a time, beating well after each addition. Sift flour before measuring and then sift with other dry ingredients. Add flour mixture alternately with milk. Beat until well blended. Bake in a well-greased and -floured tube pan in a 350°F oven for 1 hour 15 minutes.

PLAIN CAKES

Plain cakes differ from pound cakes in that they are baked in flat pans, as opposed to tube or Bundt pans, and are iced, or layered and then iced.

ADDIE NORTON: "The easiest cake I bake is the plain ol' cake. I don't know nothing about this fancy cooking cakes. A lot of folks won't eat a pound cake or anything like that. They got to have all this fancy do-dad's in it. I don't know how to cook those, I never have practiced. They're good but too costly for me. I don't have all the ingredients to put in one of that kind. The kind I usually make is just a plain cake."

WHITE LAYER CAKE

½ cup butter
1 cup sugar
2 cups flour
½ teaspoon salt

3 teaspoons baking powder
1 cup milk
1 teaspoon vanilla
2 egg whites, beaten stiff

Cream butter and sugar. Mix dry ingredients and add alternately with milk to creamed mixture. Add vanilla. Fold in egg whites. Pour batter into three 8-inch layer pans. Bake in a 325°F oven for 25 minutes.

VINEGAR CAKE

EXIE DILLS

"The first cake I ever tried to bake by myself was a vinegar cake. You'd be surprised at how it'll taste. I've knowed of women getting a blue ribbon at a fair from using that same cake. It's really good. I hope you all can make it.

"I bake three [plain yellow layers]. And then you make your filling [icing]. You take a cup of good apple vinegar, and you put two cups of sugar in that and boil it until it makes a syrup. It'll be as hard as it can be if you boil it *too* long. When it makes a thick syrup, you take it off the heat, and you put in a little lump of butter about that big [measuring about a tablespoon with her thumb] and melt it. It'll turn kind of white looking. You let the syrup cool till it's not runny; and when your layers cool, you put that between them and then over the top."

QUICK AND EASY PLAIN CAKE

GLADYS NICHOLS

This cake is good covered with chocolate icing and sprinkled with chopped walnuts.

1½ cups sugar
½ cup shortening or butter
2 eggs

3½ cups self-rising flour
1½ cups water
1 tablespoon flavoring of your choice

Cream sugar and butter; add eggs, one at a time, beating well. Sift flour and add alternately with water. Blend in flavoring. Pour batter into greased and floured layer pans—two 9-inch pans, or three 8-inch pans—and bake in a 350°F oven for 30 to 45 minutes for two layers, or 20 to 25 minutes for three.

SYRUP PLAIN CAKE

1 cup butter
2 cups light corn syrup
3 cups flour
1 teaspoon baking powder
Pinch of salt

3 eggs
¾ cup buttermilk
¼ teaspoon soda
2 tablespoons water
1 teaspoon vanilla

Cream butter and syrup. Sift together flour, baking powder, and salt. Alternately add eggs, flour mixture, and buttermilk to the butter mixture. Add soda dissolved in 2 tablespoons water. Add vanilla. Pour batter into two greased and floured 9-inch layer pans or a 13 × 9-inch sheet cake pan. Bake in a 375°F oven for 25 to 30 minutes.

VARIATION: For chocolate cake use ½ cup cocoa, filling remainder of cup with flour and using as 1 cup flour.

GOLD LOAF CAKE

MARY PITTS

"Mother always made this when she was making an angel food cake. She'd use her egg whites in the angel food and the yolks in this one."

½ cup butter
1¼ cups sugar
7 egg yolks
2½ cups flour, sifted

3 teaspoons baking powder
⅔ cup milk
1 teaspoon vanilla

Cream butter and sugar. Beat egg yolks until thick and lemon-colored. Add to butter and sugar. Sift flour and measure; then sift with baking powder three times. Add milk alternately with flour. Add flavoring and beat. Pour into a loaf pan. Bake 40 to 60 minutes in a hot (400°F) oven.

ANGEL FOOD CAKE

1 cup sifted cake flour
¼ teaspoon salt
11 egg whites
1 teaspoon cream of tartar

1¼ cups sifted sugar
1 teaspoon vanilla
½ teaspoon almond extract (optional)

Resift flour three times. Set aside. Add salt to egg whites and beat until foamy, then add cream of tartar and beat until stiff enough to hold a peak but not dry. Fold in sugar, 1 tablespoon at a time. Add flavoring. Fold in flour, 2 tablespoons at a time. Fold as little as possible to blend all ingredients. Pour batter into an ungreased tube pan and bake in a slow (325°F) oven for 45 to 60 minutes. When done, remove from the heat; invert the pan and cool the cake before removing from pan. Dust cake with powdered sugar or ice with a sugar icing.

DEVIL'S FOOD LAYER CAKE

NARCISSE DOTSON

⅔ cup shortening
1½ cups sugar
3 eggs
2½ cups flour

¼ teaspoon salt
3 teaspoons baking powder
1 cup milk
1 teaspoon vanilla
3 squares chocolate, melted

Cream together shortening and sugar. Add eggs, one at a time, beating well after each addition. Sift together dry ingredients and add alternately with milk. Mix in vanilla and melted chocolate. Pour into two 9-inch layer pans and bake in a 350°F oven for 20 to 30 minutes.

FILLING   *½ cup butter*
2 cups sugar   *¾ cup buttermilk*

Mix ingredients together in a saucepan and cook until thick. Take away from the heat and beat until cool.

COCONUT CAKES, SPICE CAKES, FRUIT CAKES, NUT CAKES

As cooking desserts became more sophisticated other products to be used as ingredients in recipes were introduced, such as various nuts, raisins, coconut; rarer fruits such as bananas, pineapple, oranges, and lemons; and an unlimited number of spices and flavorings.

Mary Pitts told us about having raisins as a child: "We got our raisins in the store. They didn't come in boxes; we got them dried and on the stem. I never did see no raisins in a box until I was a big girl." She also remembers having coconut: "I've had coconut all of my life. You could get it at the store for a nickel or a dime apiece. I can just see my daddy taking a little hammer and going around that hard-shell hull, tapping it real good. You know, it's got a little monkey face—two eyes and a mouth—and you bore a hole in one of those soft spots and drain out all of that milk. They'd be a glass of coconut milk in there. That's good to put in your pies, and the kids love to drink it. It's good to drink. And he'd bust that open and the coconut would come out of that hull. It'd come out in great big chunks. You'd take a good sharp knife and peel the brown off the back of it and then you could grate it or grind it. Mother always grated hers and one coconut would always make a big bowl. I can just see them now. Us kids always did like to eat it. We got it at Christmas. Santa Claus always left some on the table."

NO-FAIL COCONUT POUND CAKE

ARIZONA DICKERSON

This cake may be prepared and frozen for a later date. Freezing gives it a moist texture.

3 cups flour
1 teaspoon baking powder
½ teaspoon salt
1½ cups shortening
2½ cups sugar

5 to 6 eggs
1 cup milk
1 cup grated coconut
1 tablespoon coconut flavoring

Sift together dry ingredients twice and set aside. Cream together the shortening and sugar; add eggs, one at a time, beating well after each addition. Add milk and flour mixture alternately to creamed mixture, beating continuously. Mix in coconut and coconut flavoring last. Pour batter into a greased and floured tube pan and bake in a 325°F oven for 1 hour 25 minutes.

SPICE LAYER CAKE

Frost this cake with a white seven-minute icing.

¾ cup butter
2 cups brown sugar
2 egg yolks
2¾ cups flour
1 teaspoon soda

1 teaspoon cinnamon
1 teaspoon cloves
1 teaspoon allspice
1 teaspoon nutmeg
1 cup buttermilk

Cream together butter and sugar. Add egg yolks, one at a time, beating well after each addition. Sift together dry ingredients and add alternately with buttermilk to the creamed mixture. Pour batter into three 8-inch round layer pans. Bake in a 350°F oven for 20 minutes.

SCOTCH CAKE

2 cups flour
2 cups sugar
½ cup butter
½ cup oil
¼ cup cocoa
1 cup water

½ cup buttermilk
2 eggs
1 teaspoon soda
1 teaspoon cinnamon
1 teaspoon vanilla
Icing for Scotch Cake (recipe follows)

Combine flour and sugar. Mix butter, oil, cocoa, and water in a saucepan; bring to a rapid boil and pour into flour and sugar mixture. Mix well. Add buttermilk, eggs (one at a time), soda, cinnamon, and vanilla. Mix well. Pour batter into two greased and floured 9-inch layer pans or a greased and floured 13 × 9-inch sheet cake pan. Bake at 350°F for 30 minutes. When cool, frost.

ICING FOR SCOTCH CAKE
½ cup margarine
¼ cup cocoa
6 tablespoons milk

1 teaspoon vanilla
1 box confectioners sugar
1 cup chopped pecans
1 cup flaked coconut

Cream together margarine and cocoa. Add milk and vanilla. Stir in confectioners sugar and mix thoroughly. Last add pecans and coconut.

PUMPKIN CAKE

MARGARET NORTON

1½ cups butter or corn oil
2 cups sugar
3½ cups flour
2 teaspoons baking powder
2 teaspoons soda
1 teaspoon salt

2 teaspoons pumpkin pie spice
2 cups cooked mashed pumpkin
4 eggs, well beaten
2 teaspoons vanilla
1 cup chopped nuts
1 cup raisins or other dried fruit

Cream together butter and sugar. Sift together dry ingredients, using 1 cup of the flour, and add to creamed mixture along with the pumpkin. Add eggs and vanilla, beating well. Fold in nuts and raisins, which have been mixed with remaining ½ cup flour. Bake in a greased and floured loaf pan in a 400° to 450°F oven for 60 minutes.

APPLE CAKE

CONNIE BURRELL

1 cup oil
2 cups sugar
3 eggs, beaten
3 cups flour

1 teaspoon salt
2 teaspoons vanilla
1 cup chopped nuts
3 cups chopped apples

Mix together oil, sugar, and eggs, beating well. Sift together dry ingredients and mix into the creamed mixture. Fold in nuts and apples. Bake in a 325°F oven for 1 hour in a greased and floured tube pan.

DRIED APPLE CAKE

OLENE GARLAND

"Mrs. Garland [my mother-in-law,] used a similar recipe for making what she called an apple torte, making four or five thin layers and spreading this mixture between and on top of layers."

1 white or yellow layer cake (or pound cake)
1 pint dried apples

1 pint water
½ to 1 cup sugar
1 tablespoon cinnamon

Bake the cake in four 8- or 9-inch round layer pans and adjust baking time stated in recipe so as not to overcook. Mix dried apples with water in a saucepan and cook until thick and the apples are mashed up. Sweeten to taste and add cinnamon. Let cool, then spread between the cake layers and on top of the cake, letting it drip down sides.

VARIATION: Spices—nutmeg, allspice, cloves—¼ teaspoon of each, can be added in addition to cinnamon.

UPSIDE DOWN CAKE

ANNIE LONG

2 cups sifted flour
¼ teaspoon salt
2 teaspoons baking powder
¾ cup sugar

¼ to ½ cup butter or lard
2 eggs, well beaten
½ cup milk

Sift together dry ingredients. Beat in butter and eggs. Gradually add milk. This makes a thick batter.

½ cup butter
1 cup sugar

2 cups fruit, such as berries, apples, or
    peaches

In the bottom of a large casserole dish, melt the butter and stir in the sugar and fruit. Spoon the previously mixed batter on top of the fruit mixture. Bake in a 325°F oven for 40 to 50 minutes. Serve warm. Good topped with whipped cream or vanilla ice cream.

BLACKBERRY CAKE

1½ cups sugar
1⅔ cups butter or margarine
4 eggs, separated
⅔ cup buttermilk
1 teaspoon soda
2 cups sifted flour

1 teaspoon cinnamon
1 teaspoon allspice
1 teaspoon cloves
1 cup blackberry jam
Refrigerated Icing (recipe follows)

Cream sugar and butter until well blended; beat egg yolks and add. Add soda to buttermilk and add to the creamed mixture. Sift flour with spices and sift into batter. Add jam and mix until blended. Beat egg whites until stiff and fold gently into the batter. Bake in three 8-inch pans that have been lined with waxed paper, greased, and floured. Bake in a 350°F oven for 30 minutes. Ice with refrigerated icing.

REFRIGERATED ICING
2 eggs, beaten
1 cup milk

1 tablespoon butter
1 cup sugar
1 tablespoon cornstarch

Mix cornstarch with sugar in a saucepan. Stir in eggs and milk. Cook over medium heat until thick and smooth. Remove from heat; add butter and cool in refrigerator. Spread on cake and refrigerate.

PERSIMMON CAKE

NORA GARLAND

2 cups sugar
¾ cup butter or margarine
3 eggs

3 cups flour, plain or self-rising (if using
    plain flour, add 1 teaspoon soda
    and ½ teaspoon salt)

1 teaspoon vanilla
1 cup persimmons, scalded and mashed
    through a sieve or colander

Cream Cheese Icing (recipe follows)

"Cream your sugar and margarine. I use margarine now since I can't get the country butter. Add your eggs, one at a time. Mix the dry ingredients and add them to the blended ingredients. Add the flavoring. Stir in one cup persimmons. Make sure you cook them, mash them, and run them through a colander first to get all the seeds out. You can cook this in three layers or a Bundt pan, either one, at 350 degrees. You can tell when it gets done." (20 minutes for layers and 45 to 60 minutes for Bundt pan.)

CREAM CHEESE ICING
8 ounces cream cheese, softened
½ stick margarine, softened

1 pound box confectioners sugar
1 cup persimmons, cooked and strained
    (see above)

"Beat all this till it's smooth and add your persimmons last. Be careful about the persimmons. It wouldn't do to have any seeds in your icing."

BELLE'S PRUNE CAKE

BELLE LEDFORD

2 cups sifted flour
1 teaspoon baking soda
¼ teaspoon salt
1 tablespoon cinnamon
1 tablespoon nutmeg
1 tablespoon allspice
1 cup corn oil

1½ cups sugar
3 eggs
1 teaspoon vanilla
1 cup buttermilk
1½ cups pitted prunes, coarsely cut,
    cooked, and drained
1 cup walnuts or pecans, chopped

Sift together dry ingredients. Beat corn oil and sugar; add eggs, one at a time, beating well after each. Add vanilla. Mix in dry ingredients alternately with buttermilk. Blend well after each. Stir in prunes and nuts. Pour batter into an ungreased tube pan. Bake in a 350°F oven for 1 hour. Fifteen minutes before the cake is done, prepare the glaze.

GLAZE
1 cup sugar
½ cup buttermilk
¼ cup butter or margarine
¼ cup light corn syrup
½ teaspoon soda
½ teaspoon vanilla

Mix together all ingredients and boil for 10 minutes. Pour glaze over the cake in the pan while still hot.

CARROT CAKE

MARY PITTS

1 cup corn oil
2 cups finely grated carrots
3 cups self-rising flour
2 cups sugar
1 tablespoon cinnamon

1 teaspoon salt
1 teaspoon baking soda
1 teaspoon vanilla
4 eggs
1 cup chopped nuts

Mix together oil and carrots. Sift together dry ingredients and add to oil and carrot mixture. Mix in vanilla and beat in eggs, one at a time. Stir in nuts. Pour into a greased tube pan. Bake in a 325°F oven for 50 to 55 minutes. This cake is especially good after sitting for a couple of days, becoming more moist.

JAM CAKE

NARCISSE DOTSON

2 cups sugar
1¼ cups butter
6 eggs
2 teaspoons baking powder
1 tablespoon each of cinnamon, cloves,
    allspice, nutmeg

1 teaspoon soda
1 cup buttermilk
4 cups flour
2 cups jam

Cream together butter and sugar. Add eggs, one at a time, beating well after each. Sift together flour, baking powder, and spice. Dissolve soda in buttermilk and add alternately with dry ingredients to the egg mixture. Mix in jam. Bake in four 8-inch or 9-inch layer pans in a 350°F oven.

FRUIT FILLING

1 cup raisins
1 cup chopped nuts
1 cup pear honey or fig preserves
Grated peel and juice of 1 orange

BUTTER FILLING

2 cups sugar
1 cup whole milk
½ cup butter or margarine

Mix together fruit filling and set aside. Mix and cook butter filling until slightly thickened. Spread the two alternately between cooled layers by spreading fruit filling on layer first and pouring butter filling over that.

GEORGIA FRUIT CAKE

MARY PITTS

¼ cup butter
1 cup brown sugar
3 eggs
1 cup blackberry jam
1 cup fig jam
½ cup sorghum syrup
3 cups flour (or more to make a stiff batter)
1 tablespoon mixed spices
½ teaspoon salt
½ teaspoon soda

2 teaspoons baking powder
¼ cup fruit juice
1 cup crystallized citron or watermelon rind preserves
1 cup crystallized orange or grapefruit peel
1 pound raisins or muscadine jelly (see "Pickles, Relishes, Jams and Jellies")
1 cup pecans or other nuts

Cream together butter and sugar. Add eggs, one at a time, beating well after each addition. Add jam and syrup. Beat. Sift all the dry ingredients together and add gradually to first mixture. Add the juice. Chop fruit and nuts, flour well, and add last. Bake in a 350°F oven for 4 hours.

NUT CAKE

MARY PITTS

½ cup butter
1 cup sugar
3 eggs
2 cups flour
2 teaspoons baking powder

1 teaspoon nutmeg
1 cup wine
1 cup nuts
½ pound raisins

Cream together butter and sugar. Add eggs, one at a time, beating well. Sift together dry ingredients and add alternately with wine to creamed mixture. Fold in nuts and raisins. Pour into three 8-inch layer pans and bake in a 325°F oven for 1 hour. Frost with caramel filling.

WALNUT CAKE

2 cups butter	3 teaspoons baking powder
2 cups brown sugar	½ teaspoon salt
3 eggs, separated	⅔ cup milk
1 cup ground walnuts	1 teaspoon vanilla
2 cups flour	

Cream together butter and sugar. Add egg yolks, one at a time. Beat well. Sift together dry ingredients and add to creamed mixture. Stir in milk and vanilla. Fold in egg whites and then gently fold in ground walnuts. Pour into two 8-inch layer pans or a 13 × 9-inch greased and lightly floured pan. Bake for 1 hour 10 minutes in a 250°F oven. Frost with soft chocolate frosting or cocoa frosting (see pp. 269).

MINCEMEAT CAKE

4 cups shortening	2 teaspoons salt
6 cups sugar	4 teaspoons baking soda
1 dozen eggs	8 cups mincemeat
13 cups flour	5 cups chopped apples

Cream together shortening and sugar. Add eggs, a few at a time, beating after each addition. Sift together dry ingredients and add to creamed mixture. Mix in mincemeat and apples. Bake in two 16½ × 26-inch pans in a 350°F oven for 35 to 40 minutes.

"We didn't get much for Christmas. If we got an apple or an orange, some raisins and a little candy that was fine. We got bought candy—stick candy, bucket candy, hard candy, sugar candy. Some of it had coconut in it. It was like it'd been molded in little molds. Back then there wasn't any toys."

ICINGS

In the beginning honey and syrup were used as a topping for plain cake and spice cakes such as gingerbread. Several contacts told us how they made a glaze by boiling white sugar and water together until the sugar was dissolved, then pouring it over the cake while hot. With the addition of other products, more flavorful cake toppings were introduced.

To ice a cake, lay the bottom layer of the cake on a plate. Spoon the icing in the middle of the layer and spread it to the edge with a knife or spatula. Gently place the top layer on; spoon the icing in the middle of the layer and spread to edge and down the sides of the layers, while gradually turning cake around, until cake is completely iced.

To spread coconut, sprinkle on top and gently stick to sides with hand.

PLAIN ICING

MARY PITTS

1 tablespoon butter
1 box confectioners sugar
1 teaspoon extract (any kind)

¼ cup cream
Water (optional)

Soften the butter; add the sugar and extract, then add the cream. If the mixture is stiff, add a drop or two of water.

IONE DICKERSON: "I baked my husband a birthday cake one time that fell as flat as that pound cake did. I covered it over just as thick as I could with white icing and coconut, and that was the best thing [laughter]! He never would forget that birthday cake."

IVORY FROSTING

ARIZONA DICKERSON

2 egg whites
¼ cup brown sugar, firmly packed
1¼ cups granulated sugar

5 tablespoons water
1 teaspoon vanilla

Combine egg whites, sugar, and water in the top of a double boiler. Beat with a rotary egg beater until thoroughly mixed. Place over rapidly boiling water and beat constantly, cooking 7 minutes or until frosting will stand in peaks. Remove from the boiling water; beat in vanilla and spread on cake.

CUSTARD SAUCE

4 egg yolks
¼ cup sugar
⅛ teaspoon salt

2 cups hot milk
½ teaspoon vanilla

Beat egg yolks slightly, add sugar and salt. Stir in hot milk gradually. Place custard over very low heat and stir constantly. See that it does not boil, or cook over hot water in a double boiler until it begins to thicken. Strain the custard if necessary, and cool; add the vanilla and chill thoroughly.

LEMON SAUCE

½ cup sugar
1 tablespoon cornstarch
1 cup boiling water
2 tablespoons butter

1½ tablespoons lemon juice
⅛ teaspoon nutmeg (optional)
⅛ teaspoon salt

Combine sugar and cornstarch in a saucepan and add water slowly, stirring constantly. Boil over low heat until thickened (approximately 5 minutes). Remove from heat and add remaining ingredients.

VARIATION: One egg may be beaten in.

BUTTERMILK FILLING

BELLE LEDFORD

2 cups sugar
1 cup buttermilk

1 teaspoon soda
1 teaspoon vanilla

Mix all ingredients except the vanilla in a saucepan and cook until thick enough to spread. Add vanilla.

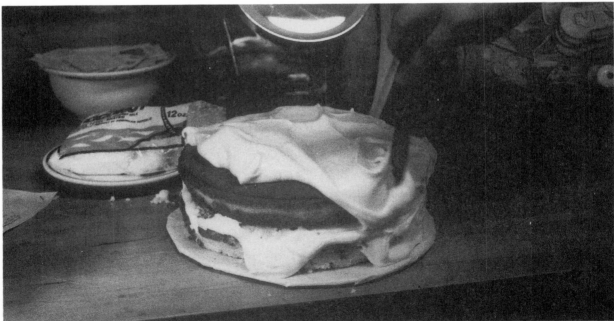

DOUBLE BOILER FROSTING

MARY PITTS

2 egg whites
1½ cups sugar
5 tablespoons cold water

½ teaspoon cream of tartar
1 teaspoon vanilla

In the top of a double boiler, combine egg whites, sugar, cream of tartar, and water. Place over rapidly boiling water and beat constantly with a rotary beater or electric mixer until mixture will stand in peaks. Mix in vanilla. Spread on cake.

CARAMEL FILLING

MARINDA BROWN

"My favorite cake was a white caramel cake I used to make and take out a lot. It always got a good reception. You can use any ordinary batter recipe that you know to make a white layer cake. I used a caramel filling, and it was just about the best cake I've ever made, I think."

1 box brown sugar, light or dark
½ cup milk
¼ cup butter

2 eggs, separated
1 teaspoon vanilla

In a saucepan, combine brown sugar and milk. Boil until mixture will spin a thread when dropped from a spoon. Remove from heat; stir in butter. Beat in egg yolks and vanilla. Beat egg whites stiff, then fold into filling. Spread mixture on white layer cake.

SOFT CHOCOLATE FROSTING

ARIZONA DICKERSON

4 squares unsweetened chocolate, cut in
    pieces
1¼ cups cold milk
¼ cup flour

1 cup sugar
2 tablespoons butter
1 teaspoon vanilla

Put chocolate and milk in the top of a double boiler and heat. When chocolate is melted, beat with a rotary beater until smooth and blended. Remove from the heat. Blend flour and sugar, then stir into the chocolate slowly until smooth. Return to the heat and cook until thickened. Add butter and vanilla and stir until well blended. Cool and spread on cake.

COCOA FROSTING

MARY PITTS

¼ pound softened butter
1 egg, beaten
¼ cup cocoa
1 tablespoon lemon juice

1 tablespoon vanilla
1 box confectioners sugar, sifted
1 cup nuts (optional)

Cream together butter and egg. Add cocoa, lemon juice, and vanilla. Beat well. Mix in sifted sugar and beat until smooth. Fold in nuts.

16

Pickles, Relishes, Jams, and Jellies

*"I like to cook my jellies fast
and my preserves slow."*

PICKLES, RELISHES, CHUTNEYS, AND SAUERKRAUT

Pickles and relishes are sliced, chopped or, whole fruits or vegetables preserved in a brine or a vinegar-sugar mixture. Chutneys are relishes that are made of fruits or vegetables or both. They may be hot, spicy, sweet, and sour all at one time. Ginger, fresh or crystallized, is a common ingredient in chutneys.

The earlier method for pickling involved using wooden tubs. Gladys Nichols remembered using them: "People didn't used to have cans [glass canning jars]. The old-time way they made it back when this world here was settled was to pickle in [crockery] jars and wooden tubs and things like that. My daddy made wooden tubs to pickle beans and make kraut in. He'd cut a big old hickory tree, split it out and then shave them staves about that wide. He put that thing together, put a head on it and fixed it to where it'd hold water. Then we'd chop up cabbage in there and put the salt in. Done pickled beans the same way."

Many of our contacts follow the signs of the zodiac when they perform certain tasks. This is especially true when making pickles and relishes, as explained to us by Addie Norton. "I don't pay so much attention to it in cooking, but I do in pickling beans and putting up things like that. You can make kraut, pickled beans, and things like that, and I go with the signs all the time to do that. I avoid the heart and the head, anywhere from the head down to the waist. After the signs gets down in the legs, it's better, but it's better to wait till they get below the knees to pickle beans. In the new of the moon when the signs are below the knees is the best time you'll ever make pickled beans and anything else that you work in vinegar with [laughter]."

Many of our contacts use canning manuals and pamphlets as aids to perfect canning results. They are of especially good use in helping with the particulars of canning pickles. One of our contacts suggested using the instructions given by the *Blue Book,* published by the Ball Corporation.

Brined pickles, also called fermented pickles, go through a curing process of two to three weeks. The curing process changes cucumber color from a bright green to a yellow green and the white interior becomes uniformly translucent. Pickle-making begins with the brine, and carelessness in making or maintaining the brine is the reason for most of the soft and unfit pickles. Fresh-pack or quick-process pickles are brined for several hours or overnight and then drained before continuing with the recipe. Use only sound, tender, freshly gathered fruits and vegetables. If purchasing fruits and vegetables from the store, use a firm brush or other available object suitable for scraping off wax because the brine solution will not penetrate through the wax. Always use fruits and vegetables as soon as possible after gathering or purchasing.

Soft water makes better brine than hard water. To soften hard water boil it for 15 to 20 minutes. Let it stand for 14 hours and then remove the scum that has accumulated on top. Be very careful when dipping water out from the kettle so the sediment at the bottom is not disturbed. Add 1 tablespoon of vinegar per gallon of boiled water before using.

Using the correct type of vinegar is important. A high-grade cider or white distilled vinegar of 4 to 6 percent acidity (40 to 60 grain) should be used. It is wise not to use vinegars of unknown acidity. Cider vinegar gives a nice blending of flavors but may darken white or light-colored fruits and vegetables. White distilled vinegar is used when a light color is desired. The two vinegars do have different tastes—cider vinegar with its mellow acid taste and the white vinegar with a sharp acid taste. If a less sour product is desired, adding sugar rather than decreasing vinegar is suggested.

Un-iodized table salt may be used for the pickling process but pure granulated salt should be used if it is available. The un-iodized table salt has materials added to prevent caking which may cause the brine to become cloudy. Iodized table salt should never be used because it will darken the pickles.

For the fermenting or brining process a crock, churn, glass jar, or an enamel-lined pan should be used. A heavy plate should be used to fit just inside the container to cover the vegetables in the brine. A heavy board, a rock, or other heavy object is used to hold the cover down and keep vegetables below the surface of the brine. The time for fermentation will vary. It is complete when no bubbles rise to the surface when the side of the crock is pounded with the hand.

Special utensils such as enamelware, stainless steel, aluminum, or glass should always be used for heating pickling liquids. Never use copper, brass, galvanized, or iron utensils because these metals cause color changes in the product as a result of acid or salt reaction. Canned pickle products require processing to prevent spoilage. Our contacts advised us to follow the instructions for processing with each recipe.

Sauerkraut, or "sour kraut" is eaten year round in our part of the country, but because this is a good way to preserve cabbage, it's served often throughout the winter.

Willie and Bessie Underwood demonstrated their method for making kraut. They use a small wooden box for chopping their cabbage. It is about 18 to 20 inches square and 12 inches high, just made of scrap wood. The small chopper is actually a garden hoe that has been straightened and wired to a short handle. The cutting edge is sharpened each year before kraut-making time.

To make kraut, use freshly picked cabbage (3 large cabbages, 10 to 12 inches in diameter, will make 2 gallons of kraut) and noniodized table salt (¾ to 1 cup per gallon of chopped cabbage). Equipment needed: an earthenware churn of 5-gallon (or more) capacity, a wooden box or other container to chop the cabbage in, and a kraut chopper.

Trim off and discard the outer leaves of several heads of cabbage. Wash the cabbage thoroughly, drain off excess water, and cut from the stalk. Discard stalks and chop the cabbage into fine pieces, ¼ inch or smaller.

Measure 1 gallon of chopped cabbage and place in a large churn. Spread ¾ to 1 cup salt over the cabbage and pack the cabbage down firmly. Do *not* add water to the cabbage in the churn. An accumulation of water from the cabbage itself will appear.

Add a second gallon of chopped cabbage, spread ¾ to 1 cup salt over it, and pack it down. After 2 to 3 gallons of cabbage have been packed down in the churn, water will rise above the level of the cabbage. Keep adding a gallon of cabbage and ¾ to 1 cup salt until the level of water is at the mouth of the churn. At this point, put clean cabbage leaves over the chopped cabbage in the churn. Clean and scrub a smooth stone and lay on top of the cabbage leaves. This will prevent the chopped cabbage from floating to the top. Cover the top of the churn with a clean white cloth and tie securely with string.

Let the churn sit 7 to 10 days in the kitchen. The higher the temperature at which the cabbage stays, the faster it will ferment. The kraut may remain in the churn indefinitely, with the amount needed to eat being taken out and the churn re-covered with the cabbage leaves and stone. It will become saltier as it gets older if left in the churn, but it will still be suitable to eat throughout the winter.

The Underwoods pack their kraut in clean canning jars and heat them in a boiling-water bath on the stove to seal. They store the jars of finished kraut in a cool, dark place.

One of our other contacts told us how they prepare kraut.

MARGARET NORTON: "You make your kraut when your cabbage is tender. You wash and trim your cabbage and chop them up. I've got a little chopper that my husband made for me that looks like a little hoe. I've got a small churn jar that's great big around and holds about four gallons. It's good to chop in. I put my cabbage in there and chop it up. Then I pack it in a big jar and put a layer of cabbage and a little salt, more cabbage and more salt. Then you may need to add a little water to cover the cabbage and let it set in there nine days. You taste your kraut along (while it's in the churn) and when it gets just right, like you want it, you put it in canning jars. It gets too sour if you leave it in that big churn jar and don't can it. Then you set the jars in a pan of water on the stove. Let it come to a boil and can the kraut. Then just set them out in the can house."

PICKLED CUCUMBERS

GLADYS NICHOLS: "You can also pickle green tomatoes and bell peppers this way; onions may be added.

"Wash and slice vegetable to desired size. Put in container. For six to eight quarts add a handful of salt, cover with water, and let sit overnight. Pour off salty water and rinse with cold water. Pour boiling water over them; drain and pack into cans."

Prepare vinegar solution by mixing:

3 cups vinegar
1½ cups sugar

1 cup water
1 tablespoon mixed spices

Bring to a boil. Pour over pickles in jars. Seal. Process 15 minutes in boiling water bath.

THIRTEEN-DAY CUCUMBER PICKLES

MARY PITTS

2 gallons fresh, firm pickling cucumbers
10 percent salt solution by mixing ⅔
    cup salt with 1½ gallons water
1 ounce alum
2 quarts vinegar, not too strong

¾ cup water
1 box stick cinnamon
1 tablespoon whole celery seed
2 tablespoons whole mixed spice
8 cups sugar

1st day: Wash cucumbers, drain thoroughly, cover with salt solution strong enough to float an egg.

2nd to 7th days: Let pickles stand, removing scum and stirring about every other day.

8th day: Drain; cover with boiling water; let stand.

9th day: Drain; cover with boiling water to which alum has been added.

10th day: Drain; cover with boiling water; let stand until cold. Drain well, then cover with hot syrup made of the vinegar, ¾ cup water, spices tied in a bag, and 2 cups of the sugar.

11th day: Drain off syrup and add 2 more cups sugar. Heat and pour over pickles.

12th day: Repeat.

13th day: Repeat, adding last 2 cups of sugar, only this time pack pickles in jars, add syrup and seal.

CUCUMBER OR GREEN TOMATO PICKLES

BELLE LEDFORD

7 pounds cucumbers or 7 pounds green
   tomatoes

2 gallons water
9 cups pickling lime

Soak for 24 hours, then rinse by letting cucumbers soak in clean water for 4 hours. Drain well between each change in water, and after final water. Bring to boil the following syrup:

5 pounds (10 cups) sugar
3 pints (6 cups) vinegar

1 teaspoon each of whole cloves, ginger,
   allspice, celery seeds, mace, and
   cinnamon

Once mixture comes to a boil, pour it over the cucumbers or tomatoes and let stand overnight. Next morning, simmer for 1 hour. Pack in sterilized jars and seal. Process 20 minutes in boiling water bath.

SWEET DILL PICKLES

RUTH CABE

30–36 cucumbers
3 cups vinegar
6 tablespoons salt
1 cup sugar

3 cups water
Fresh or dried dill
Clove garlic
Mustard seed

Make a brine of vinegar, salt, sugar, and water. Bring to a boil. Place one large handful dill, ½ to 1 clove garlic, and ½ tablespoon of mustard seed in each jar. Add cucumbers. Pour boiling brine over the cucumbers in each jar and seal. Process 5 minutes in boiling water.

SWEET PICKLES

CLYDE BURRELL

1 bushel green and red bell peppers
8 medium-sized onions
Vinegar to cover

3 cups sugar (reduce to 2 cups for sour
   pickles)
Hot peppers to taste (optional)

Grind or chop into small bits the pepper, onions, and cabbage. Salt the mixture (about 2 tablespoonsful) and let it sit 2 or 3 hours. Pour off juices that accumulate. Put vegetable mixture into a large metal dishpan or saucepan. Add the vinegar and sugar and cook until the mixture changes color; it will have a brownish tint. Bring to a boil. Then pack in canning jars. Process 5 minutes in boiling water bath.

Margaret Norton describes the steps in making icicle pickles: "First thing you do is gather a peck of cucumbers. Try to get some that are small and tender. Don't peel them. Just cut them up longways and put them in a churn jar. Add one-half cup salt and fill the churn to the top with boiling water. Put a plate over the churn, cover with a white cloth, and place a weight over that. Let them set one week. Then pour off the salty water and add a fresh batch of boiling water without salt. This will remove excess salt from the pickles.

"Next day melt a lump of alum the size of a walnut in a small amount of boiling water. Add this to the churn of pickles to crisp them. Leave this on the pickles overnight. Then prepare a mixture of three quarts of vinegar, eight pounds of white sugar, a cinnamon bar, and two tablespoons pickling spices. Bring to a boil and pour over the pickles. Each morning, for four days in all, pour this mixture back into a pan, bring it to a boil, and pour it back over the pickles.

"You see, they're not any trouble. I just pass by and fix mine while I'm doing something else, because I'm always working in the garden or something.

"That will make about twelve or thirteen pints of icicle pickles. The recipe says they're guaranteed to keep in an open jar, but I don't want them setting there in an open jar so I put mine in pint cans and place the cans in some water on the stove and bring them to boiling, and that seals them and then I've got my cucumbers."

ICICLE PICKLES

2 gallons cucumbers
1 gallon boiling water
2 cups coarse salt
2 quarts apple cider vinegar
1 grain (pill) saccharin

2 tablespoons celery seed
1 walnut sized lump of alum
16 cups sugar
1 tablespoon pickling spice
3 tablespoons cinnamon sticks

Split the cucumbers lengthwise, no matter how small. Add salt to the gallon of boiling water. Pour over the cucumbers. Let stand 1 week.

Drain. Cover with boiling water. Let stand 24 hours. Drain, dissolve the alum in boiling water, then pour over pickles. Let stand 24 hours. Drain the pickles. Boil together the vinegar, sugar, and spices; pour over the pickles. Do this for 4 consecutive mornings (boil what liquid was poured off and pour back on mixture again). Then seal in cans—but they *will* keep in an open jar.

CUCUMBER, SWEET BELL PEPPERS, OR GREEN TOMATO ICICLE PICKLES

This is a process that takes 14 days, but is actually much easier than it sounds.

Select and cut up a peck of the above, peeling and all. Cut cucumbers into 6- to 8-inch strips. Leave the tomatoes whole if they are small ones. Put vegetables in a crock and over the top pour boiling water to fill the crock. Add ½ cup salt per peck of vegetables. Let this mixture sit for 9 days.

At the end of 9 days, pour out the liquid, wash the pickles, put them back in the jar, add 3 tablespoons of alum (to make pickles brittle), and fill again with boiling water. Let this mixture sit for 24 hours.

After 24 hours, empty the liquid again, wash the pickles again, and replace them in the jar.

Meanwhile, be cooking together the following mixture:

9 cups sugar	1 tablespoon pickling spice
2 quarts vinegar	4 to 5 pieces ginger
3 sticks cinnamon	1 tablespoon celery seed

Cook this mixture until it boils, then pour it over the pickles and let it sit for 24 hours. Then pour the liquid into a container, reboil it, and pour it over the pickles again. Repeat this procedure for 4 consecutive days.

On the fourth day, the pickles are ready to serve. Keep them in the open jar in a cool place or can them for convenience.

When pickling the above, the old-timers in the area would usually let them sit overnight in a crock in salty water, then remove them the next day, boil them in vinegar, sugar, and spices to suit taste, and can them immediately. Grape leaves were often added while they were sitting overnight in the crock. These had approximately the same effect as the alum.

For spices and added flavor, they used pickling spice, strips of sassafras, and spice-wood. These were called "bread and butter pickles."

BREAD AND BUTTER PICKLES

GLADYS NICHOLS: "I never have knowed of nobody fixing them like I fix them until I give them the recipe. It's not so hard to do, and they *are* good.

"Soak twenty-five cucumbers and twelve onions in salt water one hour and drain off. Add one box mixed pickling spices and one and one-half cups sugar. Cook together until cucumbers are tender, and can."

CANNED PICKLED SWEET PEPPERS

ARIZONA DICKERSON: "Quarter and seed as many peppers as desired. Cover with salt water and let come to a boil. Drain and put the peppers in canning jars. Make a solution of vinegar and sugar, two cups of vinegar to two cups of sugar. Bring to a boil and pour over the peppers and seal."

PICKLED GREEN TOMATOES

Wash and quarter green tomatoes. Pack raw into pint jars, adding to each jar 2 or 3 small whole pods of hot pepper and 1 quartered pod of bell pepper. Make a brine of 2 parts vinegar, 1 part water, and 1 part sugar, and heat it until the sugar melts. Pour into the packed jars, leaving ½ inch at top. Process 15 minutes in a water bath.

FLORENCE BROOKS: "We made tomato pickles—you've got to take them green, when they're good and green, just before they go to turning. I always soaked mine overnight in salt water and then took them out, and made my brine with sugar and vinegar—have to taste to know when you've got them as sour or sweet as you want them, and put it all in a pan and let it get to boiling and just as quick as the tomatoes turn white looking, put them in the can."

RIPE TOMATO PICKLES

3 pints tomatoes (peeled and chopped)   *1 cup celery*
¼ cup chopped red peppers   *¼ cup chopped onions*

2 cups vinegar
¼ cup salt
6 tablespoons sugar
6 tablespoons mustard seed

½ teaspoon cloves
½ teaspoon cinnamon
1 teaspoon nutmeg

Place the vegetable ingredients in order given into a stone jar. Mix together the remaining ingredients and pour over vegetable mixture. Allow this uncooked mixture to stand a week before using.

ICEBERG GREEN TOMATO PICKLE

7 pounds green tomatoes
Pickling lime*
2 pounds sugar

3 pints vinegar
1 teaspoon each of cloves, ginger, allspice,
    celery seed, mace, and cinnamon

Soak the tomatoes in a mixture of 1½ cups lime to 1 gallon water, making enough to cover the tomatoes. Drain and soak for 4 hours in fresh water, changing it hourly. Make a syrup of the sugar, vinegar, and spices, and bring it to a boil. Pour it over the tomatoes (after the last change of water has been drained off) and let stand overnight. Then boil for 1 hour and seal in jars.

LIME PICKLES

7 pounds cucumbers or tomatoes, cut up
3 cups pickling lime*
2 gallons cold water

3 pints vinegar
5 pounds white sugar
2 tablespoons pickling spice

Combine cucumbers in the lime and cold water mixture; let soak 24 hours. Drain and then soak in clear water for 4 hours, changing water every hour.

Bring vinegar, sugar, and spices to a boil. Add the cucumbers and let stand overnight, then boil 1 hour. Pack in glass jars or a large crock. Seal. Process in a boiling water bath for 10 minutes. YIELD: *7 quarts or 14 pints*

*Be sure lime is pure enough for cooking use.

SCHOOL GIRL PICKLES

NANCY SEWELL

Make a brine strong enough to float an egg (1 pint salt to 1 gallon water). Let cucumbers soak whole for 2 to 3 weeks (do not cut up). Drain and soak in fresh water overnight, then cut up the cucumbers. Soak in alum water (7 teaspoons alum to 6 pounds cucumbers) for 6 hours. Then take out of alum water.

Heat enough apple cider vinegar to cover cucumbers. Add pickling spices (about 1 heaping tablespoon in a cheesecloth bag) and let stand 25 hours. Take out of vinegar. In a churn put in a layer of sugar and a layer of cucumbers (using 8 pounds sugar to 12 pounds

of cucumbers). Let stand 3 days after which they are ready to use. May be covered to stand in stone jars for years.

VARIATION: When you bring vinegar to boil put loose pickling spices in vinegar.

BEET PICKLES

GRANNY GIBSON: "I make beet pickles. You have to boil your beets until they're tender, and then you have to peel that skin off of them. Then you just slice them up, put vinegar and sugar in them and boil them a while and can them."

PICKLED CORN

MARGARET NORTON: "Shuck and silk corn that is in roasting ear. Boil on cob. Cool with cold water and pack in clean churn jar, sprinkling a little salt over each layer as you fill jar. Some prefer to line the churn with a white meal sack and tie at the top. When corn is pickled it will keep without canning. You can eat as is off cob or cut it off with a knife and fry in bacon grease.

"Pickled corn is good mixed with pickled beans and fried in bacon grease or in butter. Some people even pickle them together, first slicing the corn off the cob."

WATERMELON PICKLES

4 pounds watermelon rind
3 quarts cold water
1 tablespoon pickling lime
2 tablespoons whole cloves

2 tablespoons whole allspice
1 quart cider vinegar
4 pounds sugar
10 pieces (2 inches each) stick cinnamon

Remove all the pink pulp from the watermelon rind. Peel the outside peeling from the rind. Weigh. Cut in 1-inch circles or cubes. Combine 2 quarts of the cold water and the lime. Pour over rind. Let stand 1 hour. Drain. Cover with fresh cold water. Simmer 1½ hours or until tender. Drain. Tie the spices in cheesecloth. Combine the vinegar, remaining 1 quart water, and sugar. Heat until the sugar dissolves, then add the spice bag and rind. Simmer gently 2 hours. Pack the rind in clean hot sterile jars. Fill the jars with boiling hot syrup. Seal. Process 10 minutes in boiling water bath. YIELD: *about 12 half pints*

PEPPER RELISH

"Grind up twelve pods of [sweet] red pepper, twelve pods of green pepper, and twelve onions together. If you have the vinegar-spice mixture left over from icicle pickles, you can use that. Otherwise, make up a vinegar-sugar mixture to pour over them. Use about a pint of vinegar for that many peppers and onions. I don't add any other spices because you'd be chewing on them when you eat the relish. The vinegar mixture I used on the icicle pickles has been strained, and there's always more than I need to put up those pickles so I save it, and the flavor of the spices is in there but nothing to bite down on."

MR. SHORT'S PEPPER RELISH

BELLE LEDFORD

3 pecks sweet red peppers
1 peck sweet green peppers
1 gallon onions
1 stalk celery

5 pounds sugar
2 quarts vinegar
3 tablespoons pickling salt

Grind peppers, onions, and celery. Let stand 30 minutes and then drain. In a 6-quart kettle combine the sugar, vinegar, and salt; cook, drain. Process 10 minutes in boiling water bath.

PEPPER RELISH

ARIZONA DICKERSON

1 gallon red sweet peppers
1 gallon green sweet peppers
1 cup diced celery
2 cups diced sweet apples

1 cup diced onion
2 cups sugar, 2 cups vinegar, 3
   tablespoons salt, and spices if desired

Dice the peppers. Pour boiling water over the peppers, celery, apples, and onions, and let stand for a few minutes. Drain off. Add sugar, vinegar, and spices and cook until apples, peppers, and celery are tender. Stir often and blend well. Seal in jars. Process 10 minutes in boiling water bath.

GREEN TOMATO PICKLE RELISH

8 pounds green tomatoes, chopped fine
4 pounds brown sugar
1 quart vinegar

1 teaspoon mace
1 teaspoon cinnamon
1 teaspoon cloves

Boil the tomatoes and sugar for 3 hours. Add the other ingredients and boil 15 minutes more. Let cool and seal in jars. Process 10 minutes in boiling water bath.

WHITE HOUSE RELISH

ARIZONA DICKERSON

12 sweet green peppers
12 sweet red peppers
12 onions
1 head cabbage, ground fine

2 cups vinegar
3 tablespoons salt
2 cups sugar

Chop the peppers and onions up into small pieces. Add the cabbage and cover with boiling water. Let stand 5 minutes. Drain. Add vinegar, sugar, and salt. Boil 5 minutes. Seal in canning jars. Process 10 minutes in boiling water bath.

MUSTARD PICKLE RELISH

MARGARET NORTON

1 cup salt
1 gallon water
1 quart cucumbers, chopped fine
1 quart green tomatoes, chopped fine
1 head cabbage, chopped fine

4 sweet peppers, chopped fine
6 tablespoons dry mustard
1 cup flour
1 tablespoon turmeric
2 quarts vinegar

Make a brine of the salt and water, and let the first 4 ingredients stand in brine for 24 hours. Drain. Make a mixture of the last 4 ingredients, add to the first mixture, and cook for 3 minutes. Seal in jars. Process 10 minutes in boiling water bath.

SQUASH RELISH

BELLE LEDFORD

Chop very fine by hand or in blender:

12 cups squash (6 to 8 medium sized squash)
4 cups onion (6 to 8 large onions)

1 sweet green pepper
1 sweet red pepper
5 pounds salt

Mix and let set overnight. In the morning put in colander and run water over it. In a large saucepan mix:

2½ cups vinegar
6 cups sugar
1 tablespoon dry mustard
¾ teaspoon nutmeg

¾ tablespoon flour or cornstarch
¾ teaspoon turmeric
1½ teaspoons celery seed
½ teaspoon black pepper

Let this cook until it begins to thicken, then add the squash mixture and let boil slowly for 30 minutes. Put in jars and seal. Process 10 minutes in boiling water bath. YIELD: *8 pints*

CUCUMBER RELISH

12 cucumbers
4 green peppers
4 onions
½ cup salt
1 cup sugar

1 teaspoon celery seed
1 tablespoon mustard seed
1 cup grated horseradish
Vinegar

Remove the seeds and skin from the cucumbers and chop. Also chop the peppers and onions. Add the salt, mix well, and let stand overnight. Drain, add the sugar, spices, and horseradish and mix with enough vinegar to provide moisture but not make the mixture watery. Seal in jars. Process 10 minutes in boiling water bath.

PEPPER SAUCE

14 large onions
12 green bell peppers
12 red bell peppers

2 to 3 pints vinegar
2 cups sugar
2 tablespoons salt

Chop vegetable ingredients up fine, pour boiling water over them, let stand for 5 minutes, and then drain. Put ingredients back in a kettle and pour on more boiling water to cover. Let boil 2 minutes, drain, and then put back in kettle again. Add vinegar, sugar, and salt. Boil for 15 minutes. Fill jars and seal. Process 20 minutes in boiling water bath.

CHOWCHOW

1 peck green tomatoes
2 large heads of cabbage
2 quarts small white onions
1 peck string beans
2 quarts sweet green peppers
2 quarts sweet red peppers
¼ cup white mustard seed

2 ounces white or black cloves
2 ounces celery seeds
2 ounces allspice
1 1½ ounce box yellow mustard seed
1 ounce turmeric
1 pound brown sugar
Vinegar

Chop the tomatoes. Let them stand overnight in their own juice. Drain well. Chop the cabbage, onions, beans, and peppers, mix together, and add the tomatoes, spices, and sugar. Put in a porcelain kettle, cover with vinegar, and boil 3 hours. When cool, seal in jars. Process 10 minutes in boiling water bath.

ADDIE'S CHOWCHOW

5 pounds apples
5 pounds sweet peppers
2 onions
1 pound hot peppers
2 quarts vinegar

1 cup water
3 tablespoons cinnamon
3 pounds sugar
½ box pickling spices
Salt to taste

Grind in food chopper, or chop up fine with a knife, the apples, onions, and peppers. Let set 10 minutes and drain. Combine remaining ingredients; simmer 10 minutes. Add the apples, peppers, and onions and let mixture simmer 3 hours. Fill immediately and seal. Process 10 minutes in boiling water bath.

MARGARET NORTON'S CHOWCHOW

"My chowchow has green tomatoes, peppers, onion, and cabbage in it. It's made like kraut. It isn't cooked. You just chop up all your vegetables and put them in your jar. It sets in there till it gets as sour as you want it. Then you can it. Some people put hot pepper in it, but I use sweet peppers."

CHUTNEY

6 green tomatoes
4 onions
2 green peppers
1 cup seedless raisins
2 tablespoons mustard seed
Hot pepper (optional)
2 tablespoons salt

2 cups brown sugar
2 cups white sugar
1 quart vinegar
2 tablespoons pickling spices (in bag)
12 very tart apples, cored, peeled if
    desired, diced

Chop all vegetables up finely. Put all ingredients except the apples into a kettle and cook 1 hour. Add the diced apples and cook until they become soft. Pack into jars and seal. Process 10 minutes in boiling water bath.

PEAR RELISH

1 peck pears, peeled and cored
6 large onions
4 red sweet peppers
4 green sweet peppers

3 stalks celery, chopped up finely
5 cups vinegar
1 tablespoon allspice
3½ cups sugar

Grind up the vegetables and pears in a food chopper. Add the vinegar, salt, allspice, and sugar and mix together well. Let stand overnight. Cook for 30 minutes. Pack mixture in jars and process for 20 minutes in boiling water bath. YIELD: 9 pints

SWEET PICKLED PEACHES

3 pounds peaches
4 cups sugar
2 cups vinegar
1 cup water

2 ounces stick cinnamon
1 ounce ground white cloves
¼ to ½ inch piece ginger root

Select uniform peaches and blanch in boiling water for 1 minute, or long enough to loosen skin. Chill by dropping in cold water for just a moment, then drain and peel. Freestone peaches may be cut in halves and the pits removed (a few pits may be boiled with the peaches and then removed). Clingstone peaches may be pickled whole.

Make a syrup by boiling 2 cups of the sugar, the water, vinegar, and spices (in bag) together for 5 minutes. Add the peaches and boil 3 minutes, if whole; 1 minute if cut in halves. Let peaches cool in syrup. Add the remaining 2 cups sugar and cook until tender but not mushy. Cover and let stand overnight. Drain off syrup and reheat. Pack peaches in hot sterile pint jars. Cover with hot syrup. Process in water bath at simmering temperature (180°F) for 20 minutes.

PICKLED PEACHES OR APPLES

Peel apples or peaches, quarter, and put in a pot. Make enough brine of 2 parts vinegar, 2 parts sugar, and 1 part water to cover the fruit. Add ground cinnamon, nutmeg, and allspice to taste. Cook until tender. When done, lift the fruit out and pack into jars. Keep the brine simmering, and pour into jars over fruit the leaving ½ inch at the top. Seal immediately. Process 15 to 20 minutes in boiling water bath.

TOMATO KETCHUP

RUTH HOLCOMB

1 gallon cooked tomatoes (approximately
    1 peck)
½ cup sugar
2 tablespoons dry mustard

1 tablespoon ground allspice
1 pint cider vinegar
3 tablespoons salt
1 tablespoon black pepper
½ tablespoon ground cloves

Select good, ripe tomatoes. Scald and strain through a coarse sieve to remove seed and skin. When the tomatoes become cold add the remaining ingredients. Let simmer slowly for 3 hours. Pour in bottles or jars. Process for 15 minutes in boiling water bath.

JAMS, JELLIES, PRESERVES, AND FRUIT BUTTERS

Nora Garland remembers picking cherries and wild strawberries as a child for canning purposes:

"Law, yeah. That's all we had to can on. We had four big cherry trees and they were hanging just as full as they could be. They wasn't big ones, guess just as high as the ceiling. I was so little—I didn't weigh but about seventy-five pounds—that I was the only one that could get up in them [trees]. They'd put me up in the cherry trees. They'd be hanging just as full and red as they could be. I'd sit up there and pick cherries and eat my part of them. I'd pick a bucket full and then take them down and we'd can, I guess, seventy-five cans of cherries. And wild strawberries, the ground was just full of them, just red with wild strawberries. I've knowed us to have fifty or sixty cans of wild strawberries."

When we asked cooks if there was any difference between canning jams and jellies on the wood stove and the conventional stove, most of them agreed that you don't do anything different except for putting the wood in the stove.

Jams are made of whole crushed berries or fruits cooked with sugar to a soft consistency. Almost no other liquid is added.

Jellies are the juice of berries or fruits boiled with sugar. Some of our contacts like to use Sure-Jell, a commercial pectin. Others refuse to use it, cooking their jelly the "old way"; boiling down with nothing but sugar.

ANNIE LONG: "I can here at home. I usually have pretty good luck with jelly. Lot of people prefer it flavored, but I like it just plain the best. You put your juice and your sugar on —I usually put a cup of each—and let it come to a boil, and then boil it for about fifteen minutes. You can stir it and let it stream to see if it's thickening like thread when it gets done. It's usually jelled by then. I don't like it when you add Sure-Jell. Tastes salty to me, especially if you keep it any time over a year."

GRANNY GIBSON: "I used to make jelly without the Sure-Jell, but I haven't made none in a long time. For apple jelly you'd add a cup of sugar to a cup of apple juice. Then you'd boil it till—you can kind of guess at it. Lift it up and drop off a drop to see if it's done. It don't take long for it to make. Do grape or any kind the same way. I used to just can peaches and pears straight."

MARY PITTS (remembering her mother using crab apples as a thickener): "I've seen my mother cut up crab apples and cook her up a pan full a many a time. She'd mix a little bit of that crab apple juice in with her blackberry juice and her apple butter. And you'd have to use some for peaches and pears and blackberries. It don't change the taste any. It just helps them jell. We had big crab apples, and you could take the core out and cook them."

VIOLET "JAM"

Stella Burrell has never before given her recipe for violet jam to anyone, not even to the girls in her family; but since she is now unable to can because of arthritis in her hands, she decided to share the recipe with us for this cookbook. This is really a jelly, even though it's called a jam.

"Years ago I had a little jelly and jam shop and I made violet jam from an old English recipe. It's the richest food we have in vitamins, and it's still in the drugstores in England. They call it 'vitamin paste' there, and pharmacists use it for the vitamin content. You just take a little bit of it each day, like taking a vitamin tablet. Lemon juice has always been used in violet jam, and it does have the lemony flavor. This is the first time I've given the violet jam recipe out, but now I can't get out and pick the violets to do it with.

"The blue or purple wild violets is what I always used. The purple violets will give the jam a pink cast; the blue violets come out a little clearer. There is a little dark red-purply violet and it will give your jelly or jam more of a reddish-purplish cast. I've had a lot of people to buy it just to sit in the window to look at."

1 package Sure-Jell
2½ cups water
½ cup lemon juice

3 cups sugar
1 cup violet blooms, packed

Mix together the Sure-Jell, water, and lemon juice. Bring to a boil, add the sugar, and boil for 3 minutes. Stir in the violet blooms and remove from the heat. Pour into hot sterilized jars and seal. Stella continued:

People didn't used to have Sure-Jell, and we would take crab apples—they're real sour —and use that as pectin for our juice. There're certain fruits that just don't jell as well as others, and you need this added pectin. Some people used a little vinegar to make their jellies jell. You need something sour for any juice from a sweet fruit. In my jelly recipes I've used Sure-Jell because that's the way I make it now, but years ago you wouldn't have had the Sure-Jell and you would have substituted that sour crab apple juice. [To make plain crab apple jelly] just boil the crab apples and take the juice off like you would for apple jelly. It's maybe not as good as apple jelly, but it's edible and it has its own flavor. It's more of a novelty.

I put wax on everything that I sold in the shop. If you're going to store it for a while, you need to put paraffin on it. If you're going to use it within two or three months, you don't need to put the paraffin on. People used to use beeswax a lot to go around the outside as well as on the inside like paraffin.

CORNCOB JELLY

STELLA BURRELL: "To make a run of corncob jelly, you need twelve red corncobs. You wash these, break them up, and cover them with water in your pot. Let them come to a boil and then boil them for thirty minutes. You strain this broth with a cloth to get the particles from the cob out of it so that it will be clear. The red cob has its own color. Mix three cups of the juice with a box of Sure-Jell, and when that comes to a rolling boil, add three cups of sugar. Let this boil for two minutes. Pour into sterilized jars and seal."

MISCELLANEOUS JELLY RECIPE

BERTHA WALDROOP: "Pick your berries—blackberries, blueberries, huckleberries, whatever kind are available. Wash them and put them in a pan with a small amount of water. You don't want to add more water than just enough to keep them from scorching, because as they cook they will have lots of juice. Cook the berries until they are soft. Then allow to cool. Strain the juice through a good strong cloth that's not too thick. Cheesecloth is good if you double it. Also a cloth flour sack will probably do. Strain the juice and then squeeze the cloth to get all the juice out. Measure the juice and put into a pot to cook. Add one cup of sugar for every cup of juice. Bring to a slow boil, stirring often. Keep boiling until it makes jelly."

CRAB APPLE JELLY

Select sound crab apples. Wash and remove the blossom ends. Slice crab apples without peeling. Barely cover with water and cook until the fruit is tender. Strain through a jelly bag. Measure juice and boil rapidly until the jelly stage is reached. Skim and pour into hot sterilized glasses. Seal with airtight cover.

MAYHAW JELLY

Cook 1 pound mayhaws (part underripe) with 2 cups water until tender enough to mash. Strain the juice and add ¾ cup of sugar for each cup of juice. Cook rapidly to the jelly stage. Pour into jars and seal.

MINT JELLY FROM APPLE JUICE

Pour boiling water over 1 cup clean, finely chopped, tightly packed mint leaves. Cover and allow to steep for 1 hour. Press the juice from the leaves and add 2 tablespoons of this extract to 1 cup apple juice and ¾ cup sugar. Boil until the jelly stage is reached. Add green food coloring. Pour into hot glasses and seal.

MUSCADINE JELLY

BELLE LEDFORD: "I use the recipe that's on the Sure-Jell box for muscadine jelly. I think I just read the recipe for grapes and worked out what I thought would work, and it did. To prepare your muscadines, you punch out the inside. By the time you're through, your hands are black and sore as they can be. You cook the inside and then put it through a strainer or sieve. A colander is hardly fine enough to put it through, because if the seeds are small some of them will go through it. And then you put that and the hull back together and cook the hull and all."

Preserves are made from whole or sliced fruits preserved in a heavy sugar syrup. Nora Garland explained to us, "Well, preserves are made out of fruit cut into slices. The figs are used whole sometimes. I like mine split half in two. [Preserves] stick but jellies won't unless you got a real hot fire. I like to cook my jellies fast and my preserves slow."

PEAR PRESERVES

Peel and cut into quarters, then wash pears. Rinse and place a layer of sugar and a layer of pears until all the fruit has been used. Let this sit overnight. Put over moderate heat and cook until well done and syrup has been made from the mixture. Put into sterile jars and seal.

WATERMELON PRESERVES

Cut off all the red part. Cut in pieces 4 to 5 inches in size. Stand each piece on its side on the cutting board. Cut off the peeling and the soft side using one cut of the knife for each. Put into boiling water and boil 5 minutes. Cut the rinds in any shape desired. Pieces 1½ × ⅞ inches are attractive and pack conveniently. Thirty-six pieces (1 pound or about 3 cups full) and 1 round piece for the top fill one 12-ounce jar, and 16 round pieces fill one 12-ounce jar. Soak in lime water (1 tablespoon air-slaked lime to 1 quart water for 1 pound) for at least 4 hours. Freshen ½ hour. Drain, weigh, place in the preserving kettle, and cover with cold water. Cook 30 minutes, or until tender. Then add ¾ cup sugar for each pound of rind and cook until clear. Cool, plump, pack, cover with syrup, and process for 20 minutes at simmering. Seal. One pound rind yields 1 cup of preserves on an average.

Fruit butters are made by cooking fruit pulp with sugar. After making jelly, butter may be made using leftover pulp. Making apple butter is customary after making a "run" of applesauce.

Because the article on "Making Apple Butter" as it appeared in *Foxfire 3* (pp. 416–23) was so concise, we decided to reproduce it for this section on food preservation.

"It's so good that if you put some on your forehead, your tongue would slap your brains out trying to get to it!" Mr. and Mrs. Pat Brooks still make apple butter the old-time way. Pat told us, "Back years ago, you either made it or you didn't eat it. This day and time everybody has got enough money. They don't have to work like us poor folks. Nobody wants to take the time to make it, but they've all got their hand out for a jar." Pat and his wife showed us how to make apple butter the way the Brooks family has made it for over forty years. Mrs. Brooks and Pat took turns giving us directions.

It takes three bushels of apples to make a stir. You can keep the apples for three or four days before using them in the apple butter. Mrs. Brooks explains, "I wouldn't have nothing but the Winesaps. That's the only kind that makes good butter. The other kind won't cook up good. Sour apples do. An apple that has a sweet taste to it [won't] make good butter.

"So first you peel the apples and cook them on a stove for fifteen or twenty minutes. Then run them through a collander. Clean the kettle with a solution of vinegar and baking soda. Some people use wood ashes. Brass is the only kind [of kettle] I would have. It just makes better butter somehow. I don't like a copper kettle because it makes the butter taste, I think."

1

2

3

The apples must be washed and peeled (1).

The apples are cooked on a stove for 15–20 minutes, then run through a colander (2).

The applesauce is poured into a 20-gallon brass kettle heated by an open fire (3). (Kettle must be cleaned with a solution of vinegar and baking soda prior to use.)

○

*"Brass is the only kind {of kettle} I would have. It just makes better butter somehow. I don't like a copper kettle because it makes the butter taste, I think."—*MRS. BROOKS

○

*"You can use any kind of wood for the fire except pine. {Pine would make the butter taste.} Don't let the wood touch the bottom of the kettle or the butter will burn."—*PAT BROOKS

The applesauce is constantly stirred until it's hot enough to melt sugar. Then, using one five-pound bag at a time at regular intervals, fifty pounds of sugar are poured in. The mixture must cook for about two hours, with constant stirring.

"When you stir, you go once on one side, once on the other side, and once in the middle. You see, the bottom is narrow, and that way it won't stick."—PAT BROOKS

Pat made the butter-stirring stick himself out of cypress. Wood with acid in it can't be used, because it will taste. He likes yellow poplar the best.

Pat Brooks points out that "you can use any kind of wood for the fire except pine, because it would make the butter taste funny. Don't let the wood touch the bottom of the kettle or the butter will burn."

Mrs. Brooks says to "pour applesauce in the twenty-gallon brass kettle heated by an open furnace."

Pat made the butter-stirring stick himself out of cypress. He says you can't use a wood with acid in it because it will taste. He likes the yellow poplar best for it.

Pat explains, "When you stir, you go once on one side, once on the other side, and once in the middle. You see, the bottom is marrow and that way it won't stick."

Constantly stir the applesauce until it's hot enough to melt sugar. Then, using 1 5-pound bag at a time, at regular intervals gradually pour 50 pounds of sugar in. Let it cook for about 2 hours and keep stirring.

After it is taken off the fire, add 4¼ fluid ounces of imitation oil of cinnamon [which the Brooks use] or desired flavor. Then pour into jars. Each stir yields about 75 jars [varied sizes].

There's still the emptying of the peelings and the cleaning up to do, but we considered sampling the first stir with hot homemade biscuits a higher priority.

Mrs. Brooks says, "Sometimes [we sell it], but most of the time we keep it. The family likes it. They must, every time I turn around they're asking for some."

APPLE BUTTER

LUCY YORK: "Use tart apples, such as Nancy June, Horse apples, or transparents, as they cook up more quickly than sweet apples. Peel and core, cook until tender in small amount of water. Mash. Add crushed gingerroot or cinnamon, if available. Sweeten with sorghum syrup. It will be the consistency of thick applesauce.

"The Dickersons called this 'apple marmalade' if it was cooked down to a jelly."

QUINCE HONEY

2 pounds sugar   2 cups water
3 quinces

Grate the quinces. Boil the sugar and water and add grated quinces. Let boil 20 minutes. Seal in jars. (Pear honey is made the same way, substituting 3 small pears for the quinces.)

HUCKLEBERRIES IN MOLASSES

Huckleberries should be picked ripe. When ready to use place the huckleberries in a smooth stone jar. Cover them over the top with molasses (homemade syrup). Cut brown paper, cover it with paste and fasten 6 or 7 layers over the top of the jar, and tie on. Put in a cool place.

CROCK GRAPES

Collect dry, sound fox grapes. Pack them in a churn and pour boiling hot fresh molasses or syrup over them. Then take two clean clothes. Dip the first in hot beeswax and the second in hot tallow and tie each cloth separately around the top of the churn.

Make this in the fall when the grapes are fresh and ripe. Then set the churn in a cool place until winter. They can be eaten during the winter after they get mildly fermented.

SPICED GRAPES

GLADYS NICHOLS: "The old-timers picked grapes and put them in jars. They'd pour cane syrup over them to preserve their grapes."

This relish is good with meat, vegetables, and bread.

7 pounds grapes (Concord or wine)	5 pounds sugar
1 cup fruit vinegar	1 teaspoon cloves
2 teaspoons cinnamon	1 teaspoon allspice

Wash, stem, and pulp the grapes. Put the pulp, with seeds, over the fire and cook until the seeds come free. Remove the seeds. Add skins and cook until thick, then can.

ROOT CELLAR

Chet Welch explained about the root cellar: "This root cellar was found accidentally by Tammy Ledford, who spotted it from a car window. The outside cellar is now rare. Today most people store their food in a basement.

"Since we didn't know who owned this root cellar, Tammy, Allan Ramey, and I decided one day that we should just drive up and ask about it. We were greeted by Albert and Ethel Greenwood who kindly invited us to the cool of their porch. They talked about their root cellar, and Ethel shared with us her favorite recipe for preserving fruits, and then Albert told us about the root cellar":

We built our root cellar about two years after we moved here in 1961. I measured it off up the bank. I wanted it built seven feet into the bank and when I got it dug, I only had six. I lost a foot. The slope of the ground made the difference, but I didn't know that till after it was done. I just dug down and back—kept digging it out. The wood in the ceiling and doors is chestnut out of an old-timey house in Dillard, and the rest is oak. When I first built it, I went down to Franklin to the sawmill and got some sawdust. I put that on the overhead ceiling to insulate it. The tar paper that was on it went bad and went to leaking. I just put a sheet of this black plastic over it and that stopped the leak. I just keep putting off fixing it.

When you have a real cold winter a root cellar's about the only way you can keep anything from freezing. It was so cold last winter so I had an oil lamp that I lit in the night. I've checked the temperature a few times in there, and I don't think it ever got below 38 degrees [Fahrenheit]. I didn't think anything would freeze, but I just wanted to be sure. I had potatoes in there, and they're a mighty easy thing to freeze.

The ground is what gives it more protection than anything. You can take potatoes out of the cellar, pour them out on the ground, cover them with hay and then cover them up with dirt. They won't freeze. Ethel keeps all the canned goods and all the flowers she can get in the root cellar during the winter. We've got so many flowers right now it looks like we might not get them all in there. I put that window in there to let in light on the account she had a whole lot of flowers. When you put them in the dark, why, they'll die. They's no ventilation nowhere in that root cellar. I've seen them fixed with a pipe about four inches wide out the top. The pipe had a little top to it to keep rain from going down through it.

I'll tell you, if I had a place of my own and knowed I was going to stay, I'd fix a canning house or a cellar—whatever you want to call it—that would be convenient. I'd dig it out in the bank like that. You can't hardly dig one on flat ground because it'd be hard to keep water out. If you want a good one, dig it out like that and line it with blocks —eight- or six-inch blocks would be the best.

That's the cooler [springhouse] over there. When you cook corn in the canner, and if you just set it down somewhere you have to wait and wait on it to get cool. But if you just take it and set it in that cooler water and go back every once in a while and stir it, it ain't but a little while that it's cool. Then you can put it in the cups [freezer containers] and put it in the freezer. It's a handy thing.

Now you take this later generation of people that's coming up. They don't know anything much about making a living. If all these old-timers was to drop out, they'd starve to death. They wouldn't know how to plant nothing. I hate to say such a thing, but it's the truth. They've got an education and went to school, but it takes more than that to make a living.

17

Cooking for Crowds

"I usually don't have any choice but to cook for a
big crowd—especially on Sunday."

In the mountains, cooking for large numbers of people was once an accepted part of the
daily regimen. Family members often numbered in the teens, either from the nucleus of
parents and children or because other relatives had been taken in. During the Depression,
it was not unusual for families to harbor Eastern European or other immigrants as well.
In addition, it was customary to invite relatives, friends, and hometown or visiting revival
preachers for Sunday dinner.

Inez Taylor remembers these weekly feasts: "On Sundays sometimes my mother'd
bake a ham or sometimes she'd just boil it. And she always had fried chicken with maybe
rice or creamed potatoes. If we ever had company she'd always have big pans of corn, fried
chicken, and fried ham. I usually don't have any choice but to cook for a big crowd,
especially on Sundays. With us there was always a big family, and on Sunday I've seen
Mama have three or four tablefuls."

Nowadays families are increasingly itinerant and manage to get together only at
annual reunions or holiday occasions such as Christmas and Thanksgiving. Marinda Brown
laments the disintegration of her own family.

The happiest days of my life was when I was cooking for my family. We had three
children, and that's a right much cooking, you know, for a few years. But I liked to cook.

I think some of my happiest memories have been when I cooked meals for the whole family—mine and my husband's. We had gatherings, you know. We were all real close.

Now I don't cook any more than I absolutely have to. I do try to have a balanced meal but I don't have very much eating company. Our families are all so scattered we hardly ever all get together at one time any more. We used to have two family reunions a year. My husband's family would have a reunion and then my family would have a reunion. And we nearly always got together at Christmas, Thanksgiving, and Easter. After the children grew up and got scattered, it just kind of dropped off. I just don't like to cook now because you cook in such small quantities it isn't good. I cook one day and make it do two or three. Then I take out and warm up just what I need for one meal at a time so I won't lose vitamins by warming over food so much.

Nora Garland shared with us memories of her long years of preparing food for crowds:

Mother taught me to cook. I've cooked ever since I was about ten years old. I'm eighty-one now, and we've been married sixty-three years. So you can tell about how long I've been cooking.

Yeah, when I was little we had the same thing all the time, nearly, for dinner and supper. We'd have beans, leather breeches beans, some kind of greens and just things like that. We always had a big crowd. Mother never would throw anything away because she said somebody might come hungry. Daddy'd say, "Have you fed the dog?" She said, "No, I don't feed him till I see whether anybody's coming or not." A lot of people come by, and they was always hungry and ready to eat. And there was a good crowd of *us*—seven of us, nine with Mother and Daddy. But Mother never would throw nothing away because she said somebody might come hungry, and I'm just like her.

There was such a big crowd of us that Mother used to make potato dumplings [to "stretch" a meal]. She'd stew her Irish potatoes, but she wouldn't let them get mushy. Then she'd put cream and butter and black pepper in them. She'd roll out a dough, and she'd drop little pieces in the Irish potatoes. Have them a little soupy like chicken gravy, and they was something good. And I've see'd her put dumplings in soup beans and in dried fruit.

I make dressing to make meals go further. That's what my children always want. Even today when we have a big get-together, it's, "Now, Mama, we don't want you to fix a thing—only the dressing." To make it, I sometimes put a few grits if I've got any left from breakfast. Grits makes it good. I put two eggs, my celery, onions, and stuff like that. And I make it with pure chicken grease so it'll be good, and salt and pepper. I put a little pulverized red pepper in mine, too, and that gives it a good taste.

We'd take food to dinners at church. They call them covered-dish dinners now, but we didn't have no covered dishes. We just put it in anything we had. We'd cook chicken and make chicken pie and dumplings, and we had plenty of meat, so we'd take fried ham and things like that.

My favorite things that my mother used to cook when I was a little girl were apple pies and syrup sweet bread. She'd make the sweet bread in a big [Dutch] oven—she called it her potato oven. She'd set it on some coals in the fireplace and make that sweet bread with syrup and put plenty of ginger in it. Boy, it was something good! I haven't made it in a long time. I can't get enough syrup. If my mother made two or three big pones, she'd use two cups of syrup, a cup of sugar, three eggs, about half a cupful of lard, and plenty of ginger. Make it up just like you would biscuit dough, and put it in your pan. Have it greased and set it on some coals where it won't cook too fast. Put the lid on it and just a few coals on the lid. You could smell that stuff when it'd begin to get done. . . .

The preacher and his wife come to the house one time and I was baking sweet bread on the fireplace. I said, "Lord have mercy, there comes the preacher, and what'll we do with this cake of bread?" So he got in before we could take up the bread. He said, "If it's done, take it up. I want a piece of it, ever what it is." I said, "Syrup sweet bread." I made them some coffee, and him and his wife eat that whole cake.

Mother could make a good blackberry pie with cornmeal. You cook your berries just like you was going to make any other pie, and add plenty of sugar and butter and stuff in it. Have your meal sifted, and put it in there to thicken it. That is really good.

Mother would make apple pies, too. They was called tarts then, and I think they're called half-moon pies now. That's what we had for Christmas. She made it up like biscuit dough. Of course, you have to put grease in your pan to fry them. We didn't have no Crisco nor nothing like that; it was just lard. At Christmas she'd make a *big stack* of them pies and a big stack of pumpkin custards. She didn't use eggs and things like we do now. She'd just use the pumpkin and put some sugar and a little flavoring and spice in it and put it on her crust.

We killed a big, fat hen on Christmas, and we had plenty of meat—backbones and ribs—that we cooked. And we had sweet potato pie and apple tarts. And I soon learned to make doughnuts. I'd make about four or five dozen, and I bake them yet. I baked some last Christmas. I take the flour out and fix it. You can't put much sugar in it, or they'll fall to pieces, you know. Add two eggs and make that all up into doughnut dough. You have to fix it hard [stiff] so they'll not fall all to pieces. I had me two black pans on the stove full of grease to drop the doughnuts in and cook them.

And I've made persimmon bread. We'd go and get the persimmons when they was good and ripe, and we'd take the seeds out of them. Mother'd put on two big pones of bread in the oven on the fireplace. She'd mix about two or three cups of them persimmons in with her dough and put a little shortening in it. It was really good. I wanted to make a persimmon cake for Christmas, but I can't get ahold of no persimmons now. I can't get anybody to get me none.

I've got worlds of children and grandchildren. I've got eighteen grandchildren and ten great-grandchildren and I've taught most of them how to cook.

Despite the gradual decline in the number of the large family meals, church suppers and reunions still afford opportunities for congregating—and for feasting on a great variety of dishes. Women often bring their specialties to church homecomings, all-day singings with "dinner on the grounds" and other community events. Covered-dish dinners in our area have quite a reputation for providing all one can possibly eat.

Schools have also played a part in food consumption. Originally children brought homecooked meals to school in lunch pails, but in-house lunchrooms soon became common. Rabun Gap Nacoochee School, a local boarding school, was one of the first in our area to feature a dining hall on the premises.

Mary Pitts lives with her husband, Esco, just a little way down the Wolffork Valley road in Rabun Gap, Georgia. Unlike some women that we interviewed, she still has not lost her great enthusiasm for cooking. Her recipe collection is a treasure of yellowed, meticulously copied sheets of paper and file cards, many spattered with food stains or scrawled with a preschooler's writing.

Here Mary recalls the part she played in supervising the kitchen staff while she was a student at Rabun Gap Nacoochee:

I've always liked to cook. Just give me the kitchen. I'd rather be in the kitchen than any other part of the house, especially on a rainy day and it cold outside. I think I took after my mother about that. She always loved to cook.

When my mother and father separated, she cooked for other people. And when I came to live with her, well, I wanted to go to school. Then Mother was working in Commerce, staying with a Dr. Hubbard and his wife. She had a friend there whose brother had been up to the school at Rabun Gap, and she was telling Mother about it. She gave us the address, and we wrote. Mrs. Ritchie [the founder's wife] wrote back and said, "Yes, come on." So we came up on that little Tallulah Falls railroad to go to boarding school there.

Well, the last year I was at Rabun Gap Nacoochee School—my senior year, 1923 and '24—I had charge of the cooking. See, I went to school half a day and worked half a day. The morning cooks stayed there and cooked lunch, and there was girls to do the dishwashing. Then when I'd come at twelve-thirty to lunch there was four other girls to do the supper cooking, and I helped do the planning and fixing of all of it. We had eight to ten tables, ten to a table.

We cooked on a wood stove bigger than this table is long. It had the firebox in the center, and we had two big ovens and biscuit pans that held sixty-four biscuits, eight biscuits each way. We made ten pans of biscuits for supper. We'd fry sausage and use that grease to make creamed gravy to pour over that. We'd pour it up in a big old dishpan on the edge of the stove so it'd stay hot. And we'd have homemade apple-sauce, and sorghum syrup made at the school, and butter stayed on the table all the time.

I had to oversee the dairy part, too. I can remember staying over on Christmas and milking eight cows, and there was another girl that milked six. It'd take us half of the morning to milk. But we didn't churn the milk; we just churned the cream. We had a twenty-five gallon wooden churn, and it took two girls—one set over here and one over there on the other side of it and [makes a turning upside down–rightside up motion with her hands]. It didn't do this [makes usual one-churner up-and-down motion]. I don't believe it had a paddle on the inside. You just turned the whole churn over and over. And it'd make a dishpan full of butter at a time. We'd use that butter in cooking and on the tables every morning and every night. There was one dairy maid that would make out the butter for syrup. We had two little butter paddles with little creases in them, and we had our butter in a big bucket setting in a big rock trough that water run through all the time. You'd wash your hands good and clean and reach in there and get out a little piece of butter about [measures with her thumb] so big. And you'd take them two little paddles and rub it around and make a butter ball and put ten butter balls on each plate —one plate to each table. And you had to get in there after supper and make out the butter balls for the next morning. For our dinners we'd have all vegetables, and we always had cobbler of some kind for dessert. We had milk to drink.

And we had big crocks, honey, and big pots and bi-i-ig dishpans, because they had to wash the dishes by hand. We had a big tank behind the stove that kept most of the water hot for when we had to wash the dishes.

We even had possum dinners when I was in school. I cooked one one year. We had possum and sweet potatoes. I don't remember the other vegetables; I just remember them greasy possums. But they were nice. Mr. Farmer, the one that brought the possums up from Toccoa, had put them up in cages and fed them for two weeks.

The year I come up here to the school was the last year that they raised beans without having trouble with bean beetles, and Mrs. Ritchie'd send us to pick beans. We'd go down there below where the post office is now. There used to be a big barn down there, and they kept cattle down there when they tended that land. They had a big crop of corn that year, and the bean vines went to the top of it. We'd take tow sacks, and we'd pick beans half a day. And then the other crowd the next morning would pick beans. We put up pickled beans in fifty-gallon barrels. Kraut, too. We had them setting down there in the washhouse. And, law, we'd can beans on the stove. We just had half-gallon jars. Girls would can every morning and girls would pick up where they left off and can in the afternoon.

Yeah, we went to school in the morning and we worked in the afternoon, but I'm telling you, we got as much schooling then as they get now. We met at seven-thirty and we'd get out at twelve-thirty, and we had fifteen minutes' recess. All the girls, ten of us, was in one [dormitory] room. We looked forward to Saturday night. That's when they played what us students called "Big Ring." It was square-dancing. That was a way they could get us to do all our work and get the chores done up early.

I came in August of '21 and I didn't leave until July of '24, and I just did anything there was to do. It was just like one big home, you know. Mr. and Mrs. Ritchie was just like a daddy and a mother. And we had little boys there then. Some wasn't more than twelve or thirteen years old. We always had a bunch of boys and girls around then that seemed more like brothers and sisters. If I could call back time, I'd love to call back the three years I was in school there at Rabun Gap.

In many cases, local instances of volume food preparation have involved some sort of commercial venture. Connie Burrell participated in one of the more uncommon cooking situations in our collection.

Back in the fifties my husband and I cooked at three different sawmills. We cooked at Tacoma River, at Horse Creek down beside of Highlands, and at Rock Creek. The workers would just build their own camp. They'd build the kitchen and dining room off from the bedrooms. We had our bedroom in back of the kitchen, and they had their bedrooms on the side. All the men paid for their board. I don't remember what they paid us, but it was good pay because it was hard work. And you had to stay away from home. Of course, we'd have the weekends off. Everybody'd go home then.

We had a nice kitchen with windows all around it. It was ventilated good, but in the summertime you sure got hot. And we had a big wood stove in there—big as that quilt. They had a man to cut wood for it all the time practically. It was a good stove, and it would heat good.

But we cooked; that is, I cooked. Lawrence took care of the "lobby"—that's the bedrooms. I'd have to get up at about four o'clock in the morning, and I cooked three meals a day for as many as forty or fifty men by myself. There was plenty of them, and it took a lot of food. It'd take four or five pounds of bacon or sausage and about five dozen eggs for breakfast. You'd have to cook three or four *big* biscuit pans full, and the coffee pot'd hold about three gallons of coffee. We served milk, too.

You'd get through with one meal and have to start another one. You'd have to peel and cook about a half a bushel of potatoes. I'd fry them or stew them or mash them. I guess frying them'd be the easiest, but you still had to peel them. Lawrence would help me right smart when he wasn't working in the lobby. Mashing potatoes was a *job* because we just had a hand thing to mash them with. I didn't fry chicken too much, either. It was too hard to fry that much. I'd make chicken and dumplings sometimes, and chicken pie. We cooked bacon and beef and just different kinds of meat. We didn't have any wild game—didn't nobody have time to hunt. They'd just go out to the store and buy it by the truckload.

We had supper at about six o'clock, and I'd get through washing dishes and all at about eight o'clock. Lawrence helped some with the dishes. Between dinner and supper I'd have a rest spell, but, Lord, I got tired. I never did get sick, though [laughter]. It was hard, but we didn't think nothing about it back then. The only thing was you just had to cook a *lot* of it.

Many of our contacts have been involved in the operation of restaurants. Effie Lord is approaching her silver anniversary of operating her own café. Lord's Café is one of the more interesting restaurants in our part of the country. The thing that makes it different from most restaurants is that when you go in for a meal, you don't sit down and have a menu and a waitress. Instead, you go back into the kitchen, get a plate, and serve yourself with whatever you want from the pots and pans of food on the big stoves. Then you take your food back out into the dining room, sit down and eat, and pay your two dollars and sixty cents on the way out. Restaurants like Lord's will eventually go out of business and be replaced by fast-food chains, of which we already have five in our county. Through the years, however, Effie has hung on, and several students have interviewed her about her unusual café.

My husband and I used to own a restaurant up in Clayton on the corner. I cooked on a regular big café wood stove with a reservoir. There used to be a wood yard in back, and we'd buy our wood. I didn't know anything except a wood stove. My husband cooked the meats, and I made the bread and tea and the desserts and vegetables. He would fill the orders, and I would carry them out [to the customers].

After we came down here to this café, I piddled around and washed dishes and Mr. Lord served the plates. Now Mr. Lord's been dead going on twenty-four years, and I've run this café down here by myself for twenty-four years. Ever since I moved here I've been using a gas stove. It's just the same as cooking on a wood stove, but it takes a little bit longer on the wood stove. Slower cooking probably makes the food better then in an electric or gas stove, but I'd rather cook on gas 'cause I'd have a hard time getting in wood. There's nowhere to put wood in this place.

Here I serve meals every day except Sunday. I have to stay at home then. I'm not open to the tourists for breakfast, but I am to my regular local people who come in every day. I can't cook breakfast for a lot of people because I don't have time. Some want their eggs sunny side up, and everybody wants their eggs different or different meats. So I cook a few breakfasts for my locals, and while I'm cooking that I prepare dinner.

I have my customers come in the back and serve theirselves, and ninety-nine percent of them carry their dishes back to the sink when they're through because I don't have any help. I have had help, but I had to wait on *them.* They just wanted to piddle. They were ashamed to wash dishes, sweep floors, mop or clean bathrooms, and I don't need nobody that can't help do, you know. So I do all that myself.

And I do all the cooking myself. My helpers just couldn't do what I wanted them to do. If a customer come in and I had someone back in the kitchen helping, she'd just go to stirring my beans. I had one woman helping me, and she just had to turn my fish over and pat it and pat it, and when I went to pick it up it was in a mush. I had to dump it all out. Then I had another woman, and when I had soup beans she just kept stirring them beans and stirring them beans, and I went to serve them and *they* was in a mush. You can't stir soup beans. You *can* stir them, but if you just keep stirring them and stirring them [you ruin them]. Stirring string beans is all right, but you go to stirring the others —especially those little white ones—and they just mush.

So for me it's better to run the place this way—unless I had a husband and children to help me—because I'm a diabetic and get nervous anyway. Those women got on my nerves so bad I couldn't stand it, and when I get aggravated I won't say nothing. I just keep my mouth shut and fuss to myself. I bottle it up because I don't want to hurt nobody's feelings, and then they get gone and I let them have it!

Not having to pay help lets me keep the price down, anyway, and the people *like* eating this way. If a new one comes in, I have to tell them what to do, or if I'm back in the kitchen the customers will tell them. And it just tickles them to death to get to serve themselves, especially folks from out of town, and that all saves me a waitress. Besides, I have so many vegetables, two meats, the salad, tea, and dessert to fix, and it just takes all my time to cook. They all like it, especially these summer folks, because they *really* eat. I just charge two dollars and sixty cents—that's tax and all—and the tourists go back a second time. I don't have anything fancy with different names and all like most of them. It's all plain cooking. Mountain cooking. Home cooking. And they like that.

The health inspectors don't like it much, though. You're supposed to have the food out front on a steam table when folks wait on themselves, but I'd rather have it on the stove. Then children can't get up there. I don't let children get around the stove because they can get burned. And when you have it out front they are coughing and sneezing and everything else, and they put their hands in stuff, you know. People cough and smoke, and all that goes right in your food. I won't let them go in the kitchen with a cigarette. They're just not clean, and I think it's more sanitary to get food off the stove where it keeps hot, sometimes boiling, all the time. But the inspectors come and say I *have* to have a steam table, and they bring me a picture of one and all. Sometimes there are two of them who come in. The local man's not bad; it's the other two [from the state] that comes in here. They haven't bothered me lately, but they'll be back after me.

I just learned to cook by myself. I didn't know how to boil water nor nothing about cooking till after I was married. I don't go by a cookbook or anything; it just comes to me. I make up my own recipes. Of course, everything I have is just plain cooking, anyway. I used to come [to the café] at five o'clock, but that makes a long day. Now it's six o'clock in the morning when I come. I wait till folks go to scurrying because it's got too dangerous for me to come out that early in the morning. I cook chicken and meat loaf and salmon patties and beef liver. We have beef liver on Wednesdays, and on Friday I have salmon patties. Used to people wouldn't eat beef liver, but now they do. I salt my chicken and put pepper in my flour. Then I batter it good and deep-fry it in beef fat slow. My customers like meat loaf, too, and I don't put a thing in it but oatmeal and onions and the meat and a can of whole tomatoes.

Most of the people I feed are regular mountain people, and they don't go for things like asparagus. They eat broccoli good now, but there's so many things that they don't like. So I fix enough that if there's things that they don't like, there'll be other things they do. I have seven or eight vegetables a day, and I try to change every day and have a balanced meal—you know, something green, something yellow. And today I had two kinds of potatoes—sweet potato patties and mashed potatoes. Then I had string beans and okra, tomatoes, corn, white turnips, kidney beans, some rutabaga turnips, and a slaw. So, you see, I have enough there.

I make a casserole out of squash, and the Florida people say I'm the only person they know that knows how to cook squash to *eat*. I take real small squash, scrape them, cut them up in thin pieces, put them in a pan, add onions, and then put crumbled-up Ritz crackers on top. Then I put butter, a tiny bit of water, and grated cheese on top of that, put foil over it and put it in the oven to cook. I just put green beans on and let them cook a long time. If I've got a ham bone I put that in them. I use bacon grease or whatever I have to season them with. I make a calico salad you don't ever see much nowhere, too. It's made out of onions, bell peppers, cucumbers, and tomatoes. You cut those up and weaken your vinegar a little bit and put a little sugar and salt in there. For bread, I serve mostly corn bread. I use self-rising meal and flour and always add extra eggs and soda and buttermilk. I bake it till the bottom gets brown, and then I take it out and put it under the grill. Then I take it up. To make apple cobbler, I just put sugar to canned or either fresh apples and then put a cake batter over the top of them.

I have a pretty good business. I've got one that come in for dinner at ten-thirty. Sometimes he don't get dessert because it's not ready, but he eats what is there. He's through eating and gone by eleven, and then the others come in—about twenty-five or thirty of them. I don't have too many regulars now that school's out and they eat at home with the kids. Some eat one day and some eat they next, but I have a few regulars that have been eating with me ever since I've been open. I serve until they quit coming in and I'm give out of food.

My food don't stay there long. After I get it cooked, it stays about two hours, and then it's all gone. I just cook enough to last through the meal, and I put the leftover food in the garbage. Most cafés save it and make soup and just use it over and over, but I won't do it. The man I give it to feeds it to his hogs. I won't eat it, and I'm not going to serve it to my customers.

It takes until about three o'clock to do the dishes, and then I go shopping for the next day. I buy fish and tea and coffee and sugar from City Ice, and I buy some canned stuff from Cleveland by the case. But I go to K-Way every day to get my meats and fresh vegetables. It was thirty-seven dollars and something to buy my food yesterday, and it's always twenty-something dollars—wholesale. I used to shop at Winn Dixie, but it's a big store and you buy too much! You don't have so much to choose from at K-Way. I can't can any foods; I don't have time.

I bring the food back here for the next day and finish washing my pots and pans and empty out what's left from dinner. Then I feed one local customer supper and have to wait for him to get done. He's absent-minded, and he'll leave the refrigerator door open! I get out of here any time from six to seven-thirty at night. I try to get home before it gets dark and the beer drinkers get out. I've nearly been run over. I had one come within an inch of hitting me right at my door, backing out and coming this way. I blowed the horn, but he just did miss me that far. If he hadn't stopped he would have butted right into me. Seems like when you go home at night they're just coming this way by the dozen, especially when it's raining and you can't hardly see. It's dangerous.

I don't like that pots-and-pans washing, but I love to cook. If I didn't, I'd done be gone from here. I'm eighty-one now, but I'm not gonna retire till I have to, till I get to where I can't work. I think I'll just keep on till I kick out. My children are trying to get me to quit, but I don't think it'd be a good idea. I'd just sit at home and get lazy, and people don't live long after they retire. After you go home and sit, you don't want to dress or do anything but watch television. Lots of days I work that I'm not able to work, but you work it off and then you feel all right. I'm just old-fashioned, and I think you are better off just to keep at a little something even if you're not really able. I was sick a few summers ago and closed up. My [blood] sugar got too high, and I got weak and couldn't walk. I just slept all the time. My two daughters come and cleaned up and put everything aside. They thought they was going to close me up for good, you know. We had lost all the customers, but I came back and opened up anyway. And I'm still here. When I do retire, I'm just gonna give this place up. Not many people could come in and run it like I do—just one person.

THE DICKERSON HOUSE

For years members of the Dickerson family managed an even larger business venture than Effie's. We visited them to hear their story. The Dickerson House in Wolffork Valley, Rabun Gap, Georgia, was a resort hotel from the early 1920s until 1973, when the

The Dickerson House today

The Dickerson House dining room; the window through which meals were served is at the right.

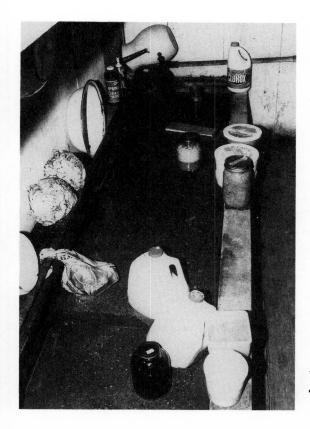

The trough that Terry built still functions as a cooler.

Dickersons retired. Miss Mimi Dickerson, Miss Arizona Dickerson, and their bachelor brother, Terry, still live in the long, rambling house with sixteen bedrooms. Mrs. Lucy York, their other sister—who for many years owned and operated the former Cold Springs Inn—also a resort hotel in the valley—lives with them.

Miss Arizona was responsible for cooking all the meals for the guests at the Dickerson House after her mother's death in 1945 at the age of seventy-nine. She still has many of the recipes and menus she used to serve to the twenty or more guests three times a day from late spring through early September when "cold weather would run them off." Mrs. Lucy also shared some of her Cold Springs Inn favorites with us because she, too, cooked on a wood cookstove until just a few years ago when she gave it up for the convenience of an electric stove.

The Dickerson family lived in a small log cabin near the site of the present Dickerson House when the six children were small. Their father, a carpenter, decided to build a larger house for them, but he had no intention at that time of making their new home into a hotel. The lumber for this house was from trees grown on their land. Mr. Dickerson and his sons, Terry, Melton, and Jim, cut them and had them sawed into boards at the nearby Sylvan

Lake sawmill. Terry told us, "We started with a thirty-foot span," which includes the present kitchen, dining room, pantry, and hallway. Terry added sections on through the years and made it the large place it is now.

He told us:

My father was a carpenter and helped build some of these houses around here in Wolffork Valley. He worked for a dollar a day! He started this house sometime before 1910. He had just got that thirty-foot span in the middle of the house [finished], and he went across the Blue Ridge Gap to haul logs and get lumber off the land to finish the rest of our house. He got sick one evening, so he stopped over at some relative's home and went to bed. He died that night from a ruptured appendix. That was February 11, 1912.

Terry remembered, "When Dad and us boys used to go cut wood, Dad would say, 'Boys, don't you hack on this good timber. If you want to hack, get over there on that old rough stuff.'" Terry soon learned how to make things out of both "good timber" and "rough stuff," including this chair and bench of mountain laurel—a particularly ornery and strong-willed type of wood.

When we first moved in, we didn't have any [indoor] bathrooms. We had no electricity until about 1948. Nobody in this valley did because the power line wasn't run up here till then. We used candles and kerosene oil lamps. We've still got a few of them left.

We operated this house here without a refrigerator for all those years. We had a mountain spring way up on the hill there, and I built a concrete trough in our milk room [a porchlike room behind the kitchen]. That trough's about two feet wide and eight or nine feet long. It's about an inch and a half deep and fifteen inches wide over where they kept the butter, cream pitcher, and little small things in the cold water. That water stayed around forty-three degrees all the time. Then we'd set small jars in a section that's a little deeper, and on down further we had big crocks—two- to three-gallon churns with buttermilk, pickled beans, kraut, and sweet milk. That kept our stuff, and we did without refrigerators.

Finally we got electricity and bought a deep freeze and a refrigerator, but this old boy here is still used to that cold water! It'll keep stuff just as good as a refrigerator. The water comes in here and pours out a little pipe I've got for an overflow. There's never been any ice in that water. All through the wintertime, this water comes in and goes out twenty-four hours a day; so there's never any ice accumulated here. That was cheap refrigeration, wasn't it? I built that trough when I was probably fifteen or sixteen years old.

We were curious to know how the Dickersons got into the hotel business. Terry related the story:

"Mimi's schoolmate at Rabun Gap Industrial School [Rabun Gap–Nacoochee School now], Carrie Kay, started our business. When she was still in school, she and eight or ten of her friends would come up here in a two-horse wagon with tubs and buckets. They'd pick blackberries on that hill up yonder and haul them back to the school.

"Carrie finished school and went to teaching, but her nerves went bad. The doctors said, 'You're gonna have to quit and take a rest,' and Carrie wanted to come back here to rest. We let her come, and before she got her rest period over her father and mother was up here and maybe two or three of the neighbors, and that started our business."

Arizona told us, "Rooms were about twelve dollars and fifty cents a week. I know it wasn't much, but things were cheap back then. We had some people who stayed two weeks, some two months, and a very few would stay three months. We would open about the first of June and close the middle of September—be open about three and a half to four months a year. In October, we'd sometimes let them come back for the weekend to see the leaves turning.

"We cooked and served three meals a day to all the guests staying here—breakfast at seven-thirty, dinner at twelve noon, and supper at six. And we didn't miss them hours by many minutes at any time."

Terry continued: "We raised most of the food we served—vegetables, meat, milk, eggs, and butter. We grew a flock of chickens, and me and two young girls we hired to help us each summer would get out and kill and clean about three fryers every day."

Arizona added: "We milked three or four cows and got a lot of milk. We had to churn every day. I'd get up at the break of day and get out in the garden and hoe until time to start breakfast. Then I'd go after supper and hoe until the gnats run me out of the garden. You know, you can grow a lot of carrots and beets in a little row."

Terry went on: "We just served out through this serving window. The girls in the kitchen would set the big bowls [of food] up there, and they were served on the table family style. When the guests finished their meal we opened up the serving window again, and they put their plates up there to be washed. That helped the girls out in the kitchen. [The guests] didn't mind. They just fell in line—lived like a family."

Many of the rooms have been closed off now. The beds are covered with handmade quilts or spreads and look ready for the next season's guests. As Terry showed us through the house, he said, "I made quite a lot of the furniture in the house. I built shelves and chairs and two single beds. I also designed the bins where we keep all the silver and glasses. J. H. Smith [former principal of Bass High and Tech High in Atlanta] helped me make those five cabinets up there during the thirties.

"When the tornado came through here in '32, it blew down those big trees on the side of the mountain. We hauled those logs down almost to Clayton and sawed them and brought the wood back. That's what those flour bins are made of—that white oak lumber.

"A man who knew one of our guests printed some postcards for us. That's the only advertisement we ever had. We never run a ad, I don't guess, because the people [who stayed here] done that for us. They would advertise our place, and I just kept adding a bedroom or two.

"People would come up here to Rabun County on the Tallulah Falls train and get a taxi from the train station to our place. While they were staying here they didn't go off much. They didn't even go as far as Mountain City to the square dance. They just wanted to eat and talk and walk. One of the ladies—who came for about ten or twelve years until her death—would get up every morning and walk about three or four miles around the loop of this valley down by our brother Jim's place and back by the church and come in here for seven-thirty breakfast. She'd whistle for the dog, get her stick, and go off by herself. She didn't want anyone with her that she'd have to wait on.

"We had an old bachelor from Atlanta who came up here. He was planning to marry a little Scottish lady. They came up here—before they were married—when they had to have a chaperone and stayed for about a month, I guess. Then they were married. That couple came up here for twenty-seven years for July and August on their vacations. He finally died, and I don't know if little Betty went back to Scotland or not.

"We had [as a guest] a Canadian lady who had moved down just below Tampa,

Florida. She had lost her husband real early in life, and she never did marry again. Somebody took her the news down there about this place. She wrote for a reservation one time, and we accepted her. She chose a little single room up here next to the back, right in the corner. So she come up here and stayed about two months every year on that one reservation. She'd get here about six-thirty or seven in the evening. The last time she came, I was in the bed and I heard a car drive up and stop. She got out. She had on hard heel shoes—not high heels—and you could hear her little short steps on that concrete. She pecked on the door. [It was late enough that] I had to have the light to see to get dressed to go out.

"'Aren't you going to let me in?' I said, 'Just a minute, Mrs. Hodge.' When I got to the screen door, she said, 'Where are you going to put me this time?' I said, 'Well, you're early. You can have the same place.' 'Well, that's just good enough.'

"And she stayed in that little room as long as she came here—twelve or fourteen years. She never did write and tell us she was coming. She knew when we opened, and when the first of June come she was right here. She was the nicest person you ever met.

"We had a few little incidents when we had to call down some guests. We had three or four young ladies—I imagine they were teenage girls about eighteen or nineteen years old—one time from South Carolina that were staying in the bedroom above the dining room. They had finished school and they might have come up on their own, or their family may have sent them up. They acted like eight- or ten-year-old girls, jumping from one bed to the other. They were having fun over there, but some of the guests that were staying back there couldn't sleep. So we had to get onto that bunch.

"Then along later on we had a fellow by the name of Coleman and his wife. They were up in their years—about sixty or so. They brought a radio along with them, and they got in the habit of wanting to hear the eleven o'clock news at night. We had our house already trained that ten o'clock was time to pull the light out. I heard the radio down the hallway about eleven, and I got up and went to the switch [fusebox] in there and pulled the switch on them. I left it off maybe just a few seconds; then I pushed it back in, and everything was quiet. I never said a word, and then I heard that man say, 'Something's wrong with that radio. Keep it going. Keep it going.' I pulled the switch again. The next morning they were just about ready to leave. They came for two weeks, and they did finish out their vacation, though. But they were disturbing all of this house by waiting for the eleven o'clock news to come on. When he went to bed after he heard the news, he probably couldn't sleep; so he would be better off to have went to bed at ten.

"I have gone to bed a lot of times [after sitting a while] out there on the front porch. There would be a crowd sitting out there talking and laughing, and they would see me go in there and pull my light out. I would turn in pretty early—as soon as we got the kitchen cleaned up—and I guess I was in bed by about eight-thirty. And when ten would come, they'd say, 'Ten o'clock. Mister Terry wants to sleep.' You would hear them going upstairs like squirrels.''

Miss Arizona said that she also went to bed "quick as [she] got through in the kitchen after supper." She told us, "I had to rest because I did all the cooking. I had two girls to help, but they didn't know much about cooking. I liked the people coming, but I never did visit with them. It took me all my time working and cooking. But I could hear how they were enjoying theirselves, and they would laugh and get along with each other and have such a good time. There wasn't no fussing or contrariness among them. They was all good."

Terry told us they still get requests for reservations. "I had a letter last week from a lady who wanted to come up here for her vacation. She was last here in '55 which would be over twenty-five years ago. She's from some place around central Florida. She said it gets so hot down there and she was by herself, so she wanted to come up and spend some time this summer if she could get a way up here. She says she can't drive she's quite old now but some friends will bring her. We'll have to write and tell her that we quit the business. You can't keep up with the clock when you get your three score and ten, plus some more."

Participants

THE STUDENTS

Eddie Bingham
Scott Bradley
Judy Brown
Laurie Brunson
Andrea Burrell
Harold Burrell
Vivian Burrell
Lynn Butler
Bit Carver
Brenda Carver
Rosanne Chastain
Vicki Chastain
Eddie Connor
Mandy Cox
Ken Cronic

Debbie Crowell
Kenny Crumley
Donna Dickerson
Bill Enloe
Ricky Foster
Shay Foster
Joey Fountain
Marty Franklin
George Freeman
John Garrard
Jeff Giles
Gary Gottchalk
Kim Hamilton
Phil Hamilton
Keith Head

Dana Holcomb
Debbie James
Mickey Justice
Georgeann Lanich
Tammy Ledford
Mike Letson
Gayle Long
Don MacNeil
Pat Marcellino
Bridget McCurry
Michelle McDonald
Karen Moore
Paul Phillips
Allan Ramey
Sheryl Ramey

Aline Richards
Billy Robertson
Tracy Speed
Greg Strickland
Nancy Swenderman
Debbie Thomas

Don Thomas
Mary Thomas
Donna Turpin
Rhonda Turpin
Vance Wall
Chet Welch

Kim Welch
Frenda Wilburn
Lynette Williams
Rhonda Young
Wendy Youngblood

THE CONTACTS

Jennie Arrowood
Jerry Ayers
Lester Baker
Dorothy Beck
Bessie Bolt
Jessie S. Brady
Florence Brooks
Lawton Brooks
Pat Brooks
Harry Brown
Marinda Brown
Clyde Burrell
Connie Burrell
Stella Burrell
Mary Cabe
Ruth Cabe
Lola Cannon
Mike Cannon
Arie Carpenter
Evie Carpenter
Harley Carpenter
"Valley John" Carpenter
Billy Carpenter
Grover Carter
Roy Carter
Buck Carver
Mrs. Buster Carver
Connie Chappell
Lettie Chastain

Clifford Conner
Lassie Conner
Minyard Conner
Ethel Corn
Taylor Crochett
Edith Darnell
Arizona Dickerson
Ione Dickerson
Miriam Dickerson
Terry Dickerson
Exie Dills
Mrs. Carrie Dixon
Narcisse Dotson
Lon Dover
Thelma Earp
Harriet Echols
Ruby Frady
Nora Garland
Olene Garland
O. S. Garland
Carrie Dillard Garrison
Ruth Gibbs
Granny Gibson
Hillard Green
Albert Greenwood
Ethel Greenwood
Blanche Harkins
Ruth Holcomb
Mrs. John Hopper

Mary Hopper
Leonard Jones
Daisy Justus
Betty Keener
Gertrude Keener
Ada Kelly
Bessie Kelly
Lovey Kelso
Bill Lamb
Belle Ledford
James Ledford
Liz Ledford
Margie Ledford
Ruth Ledford
Virgil Ledford
Annie Long
Billy Long
Fay Long
Effie Lord
Garnet Lovell
Lilly Lovell
Verge Lovell
Pearl Martin
Arie Meaders
Lanier Meaders
Bob Means
Mary Ellen Means
Marie Mellinger
Linsey Moore

Lizzie Moore
Gertrude Mull
Mrs. Gatha Nichols
Gladys Nichols
Addie Norton
Mrs. Algie Norton
Clark Norton
Mrs. Mann Norton
Mann Norton
Margaret Norton
Mrs. Edith Parker
Annie Perry
Beulah Perry
Esco Pitts
Mary Pitts
James Phillips

Monroe Reese
Lon Reid
Icie Rickman
Kenny Runion
Lex Sanders
Will Seagle
Nancy Sewell
Lena Shope
Maude Shope
Will Singleton
Lake Stiles
Myrtle Speed
Samantha Speed
Inez Taylor
Melvin Taylor
Nearola Taylor

Will Thomas
Mrs. Dillard Thompson
Bessie Underwood
Willie Underwood
Bertha Waldroop
Jake Waldroop
Hattie Watkins
Ernest Watts
Andy Webb
Mrs. Andy Webb
Rittie Webb
Wade Welch
Adaline Wheeler
Glenn Worley
Sara Worley
Lucy York

THE STAFF
(who accompanied students on interviews and helped in the preparation of this book)

Susy Angier
Margie Bennett
Mike Cook

Dolores Crane
Paul Gillespie
Connie Means

Linda Page
Pat Rogers
Eliot Wigginton

Recipe Index

"My mother used to make loaves of yeast bread, and she'd start with a little cake of yeast. You'd make yeast in cakes then. She'd have a pan about as big as a dishpan, and she'd let her dough rise about three inches. She'd shut it up in the safe, and we'd go to the field and work. When we'd come back to the house that night, it'd be all rose up. Then at dinnertime we'd have that great big old loaf of bread to eat on."

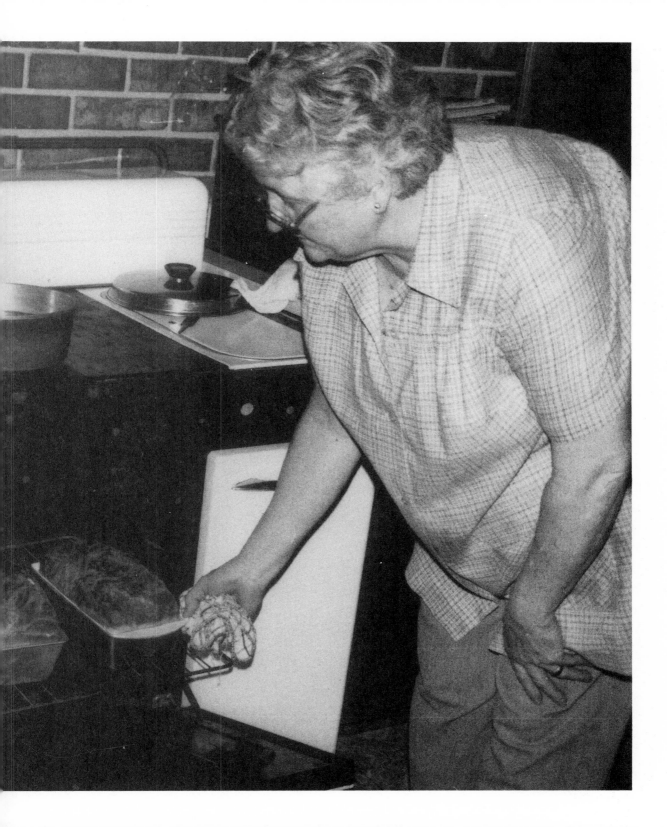

"The easiest one I bake is the plain ol' cake. I don't know nothing about this fancy cooking cakes. A lot of folks won't eat a pound cake or anything like that. They got to have all this fancy do-dad's in it. I don't know how to cook those, I never have practiced. They're good but too costly for me. I don't have all the ingredients to put in one of that kind. But I love pound cake, that's the kind I usually make, not a pound cake, just a plain cake."

—ADDIE NORTON